WITHDRAWN BY THE
UNIVERSITY OF MICHIGAN

People Trees

People Trees

Worship of Trees in Northern India

DAVID L. HABERMAN

Oxford University Press is a department of the University of Oxford.
It furthers the University's objective of excellence in research, scholarship,
and education by publishing worldwide.

Oxford   New York
Auckland   Cape Town   Dar es Salaam   Hong Kong   Karachi
Kuala Lumpur   Madrid   Melbourne   Mexico City   Nairobi
New Delhi   Shanghai   Taipei   Toronto

With offices in
Argentina   Austria   Brazil   Chile   Czech Republic   France   Greece
Guatemala   Hungary   Italy   Japan   Poland   Portugal   Singapore
South Korea   Switzerland   Thailand   Turkey   Ukraine   Vietnam

Oxford is a registered trademark of Oxford University Press in the UK and
certain other countries.

Published in the United States of America by
Oxford University Press
198 Madison Avenue, New York, NY 10016

© Oxford University Press 2013

All rights reserved. No part of this publication may be reproduced, stored in a
retrieval system, or transmitted, in any form or by any means, without the prior
permission in writing of Oxford University Press, or as expressly permitted by law,
by license, or under terms agreed with the appropriate reproduction rights organization.
Inquiries concerning reproduction outside the scope of the above should be sent to the Rights
Department, Oxford University Press, at the address above.

You must not circulate this work in any other form
and you must impose this same condition on any acquirer.

Library of Congress Cataloging-in-Publication Data
Haberman, David L., 1952–
People trees : worship of trees in Northern India/David L. Haberman.
pages cm
Includes bibliographical references and index.
ISBN 978–0–19–992916–0—ISBN 978–0–19–992917–7
1. Tree worship—India, North.   I. Title.
BL2015.T7H33 2013
294.5′212—dc23
2012038598

ISBN 978–0–19–992916–0
ISBN 978–0–19–992917–7

1 3 5 7 9 8 6 4 2
Printed in the United States of America
on acid-free paper

For tree lovers worldwide, especially for Andy Mahler and John Seed

The wonder is that we can see these trees and not wonder more.
—Ralph Waldo Emerson

CONTENTS

List of Figures viii
Acknowledgments ix
Note on Translation and Transliteration xii

Introduction 1

1. Root Issues 7

2. Tree Worship in India 31

3. King of Trees 59

4. Abode of Ghosts and Saturn 106

5. Faces of the Goddess 132

6. Trees of Immortality 160

7. Arboreal Reflections 183

Glossary 205
Notes 209
Bibliography 229
Index 237

LIST OF FIGURES

I.1 Typical neighborhood tree shrine in Banaras   2
3.1 Women performing the Somvati Amavasya Vrat in Banaras   60
3.2 Worshiper applying sindur paste to honor a pipal tree   62
3.3 A Somvati Amavasya Vrat participant kissing a pipal tree   63
3.4 Large pipal tree growing on the outskirts of Banaras   69
3.5 Flower offering left at a simple pipal tree shrine   82
3.6 Stone images of Hanuman smeared with orange sindur paste at a pipal tree shrine   83
3.7 Popular Assi Ghat pipal tree shrine in Banaras   83
3.8 Serpentine naga stones under a pipal tree   86
3.9 Pipal tree shrine at Triveni Ghat in Rishikesh   86
3.10 Maha-Bodhi Temple in Bodh Gaya   96
3.11 Bodhi Tree under which the Buddha achieved enlightenment   97
3.12 Early Buddhist sculpture of Bodhi Tree worship   102
4.1 Black stone images of *nava graha* planetary deities   109
4.2 *Nava graha* deities under the Hanuman Ghat pipal tree   111
4.3 Worship of a pipal tree associated with Shani   113
4.4 Worshiper offering a sesame oil lamp to Shani at a pipal tree shrine   117
4.5 Clay pots of water hanging from a pipal tree in Banaras to care for the dead   124
4.6 Cover of a comic book titled *The Pipal Tree*   126
5.1 Twin neem tree shrine featuring cloth ornamentation and facemasks   133
5.2 Neem tree shrine in the Chetganj district of Banaras   141
5.3 Inside view of neem tree shrine   142

5.4	Inside of Durga temple in Banaras featuring the face of Shitala on a neem tree	143
5.5	Intimate interaction with bare neem tree	145
5.6	Dressed neem tree standing before the author's house in Banaras	148
5.7	Worshipers making an offering to the face of a neem tree	149
5.8	Bhadaini Ghat neem tree shrine	150
5.9	Bhadaini Ghat neem tree	151
5.10	Neem tree shrine in middle of shop selling sweets and snacks	156
6.1	The Akshaya Vata banyan tree at Gaya	163
6.2	Large banyan tree at the Rishi Valley School	166
6.3	Banyan tree shrine in the center of the Sankata Devi temple courtyard in Banaras	171
6.4	Worshiper wrapping the Dharma Kup banyan tree	175
6.5	Group of women worshiping the Dharma Kup banyan tree on the occasion of the Vata Savitri Vrat	177
6.6	Women worshiping a banyan tree for the Vata Savitri Vrat	178

All photographs that appear in this book were taken by the author.

ACKNOWLEDGMENTS

This work on sacred trees in India was nurtured by the assistance of many people and institutions, without which it would have never germinated. I received an ACLS/SSRC National Endowment for the Humanities International Research Fellowship in 2006, which supported a full year of research in India. This kind of federal support is essential to current scholarship and greatly appreciated. I am grateful to Indiana University for giving me time off for the research of this book and for providing additional funding with a supplemental grant. Indiana University supplied financial support for three more visits to India, including a College Arts and Humanities Travel Research Grant that allowed me to return for a two-month stay during the fall of 2008.

Nagendra Mishra not only provided me with transportation in and around Banaras in his auto rickshaw but also became a good friend and productive conversation partner throughout this project. I am grateful for his companionship, enthusiastic interest in my research, useful comments, and willingness share his knowledge of the religious culture of Banaras. I thank Pandit H. D. Upadhyaya for allowing my family to live in his house while I conducted my research in Banaras, and Balbir Jootla for use of his charming cottage to write most of the first draft of this book on a lovely hillside above Dalhousie covered with brown oak and deodar pine trees. I am grateful to Navneet Raman, owner of Kriti Art Gallery in Banaras, and Rana P. B. Singh, professor of geography at Banaras Hindu University, for many fruitful discussions about the sacred trees of Banaras. The artistic animator Prashant Miranda shared with me many stimulating conversations about animism and animation while we sipped tasty chai on the steps of Assi Ghat. I offer a special thanks to Shrivatsa Goswami of the Shri Chaitanya Prema Sansthana in Vrindaban for his keen insights and encouraging support of yet another one of my academic projects.

I am very grateful for those who took the time to read earlier drafts of this book and offer suggestions and critical comments: Christopher Chapple, Sandy Ducey, John Hawley, Laurie Patton, and Sarah Pike. My wife Sandy and son Nathan accompanied me during my full year of research in India and put up with my absences during return visits and long periods of writing. I appreciate their adventurous spirits, continual support, and sustained interest in my research on tree worship.

Finally I wish to thank the tree worshipers of northern India, especially those in Banaras, who took the time to talk with me about their practice. Without their words, views, and actions this book would not exist.

David L. Haberman
Bloomington, Indiana
Spring Equinox 2012

NOTE ON TRANSLATION AND TRANSLITERATION

The translations that appear in this volume are mine unless otherwise attributed. In an effort to make this book more accessible to a wider readership, I have eliminated the use of diacritical marks. Combining transliterations of Sanskrit and Hindi leads to a certain amount of inconsistency. I have transliterated words from these languages in a manner that attempts to represent actual pronunciation, following the standard system as closely as possible without making use of diacritics (thus "*puja*" instead of "*pooja*," although in this case the long *u* will not be differentiated from the short *u* of "Purana"). Consonants have been selected and medial and final vowels have been dropped when such practice more closely reflects local pronunciation (thus "pipal" instead of "pipala," *sharir* instead of *sharira*). The final vowel, however, has been retained in a few words that have become familiar to English-speaking readers in such spellings (e.g., Rama, Purana). Medial and final vowels have also been retained in Sanskrit technical terms (e.g., *svarupa*). A glossary of frequently used names and terms, designed as a quick reference for the general reader, can be found at the end of this book.

People Trees

Introduction

A medium-sized neem tree grows in front of the house in which I lived for most of a year in Banaras, India. I spent many mornings appreciating its light green foliage of slender opposite-branching leaves from the veranda of my second-storey flat. In the spring I enjoyed its lovely small white flowers. I was often greeted at dawn by a red-whiskered bulbul singing its charming songs while perched high atop this elegant tree. For me the tree was a wonderful expression of nature's beauty; but for a family that lived nearby it was much more. They had wrapped the trunk of this tree with bright red cloth trimmed with a shiny golden border. Three dark, round river stones had been placed on an old red brick at its base. Every morning a member of the household would bring a blue plastic wicker basket full of offerings and instruments for worship, sit before the tree facing east, and proceed to honor the tree as a life-blessing goddess by offering her water, flowers, incense, red sindur powder, and prayers. Clearly, this family had a different perception and experience of this tree than had I, coming from the United States.

If I have learned anything as a lifelong student of the world's multitude of religious traditions, it is that there is nothing that is essentially anything in human experience. Reality for humans is malleable and quite varied. Almost everything gets filtered through and shaped by a particular cultural lens. Something as simple as a tree is not so simple after all. From a biological perspective trees have much in common worldwide, but from a cultural perspective there exists an immense difference between them. Human perception and understanding of any aspect of the world seems to be determined largely by the particular interpretive lens through which it is viewed. Importantly, different cultural perspectives result in very different experiences of and behavior in the world. What might a tree be when seen from another cultural viewpoint? What range of interactive experiences is possible with it?

This is a book about religious conceptions of trees within the cultural world of tree worship at the tree shrines of northern India. Sacred trees have been worshiped for millennia in India, and today tree worship continues there with abundance among all segments of society (figure I.1). In the past, tree worship was frequently regarded by many Western anthropologists and scholars of religion as a prime example of childish animism or decadent "popular religion," while more recently this aspect of world religious cultures is almost completely ignored in the theoretical concerns of the day. Yet I hope to demonstrate that by avoiding both of these dismissive attitudes and seriously investigating the world of Indian tree worship, we can learn much about not only this prominent feature of the landscape of South Asian religion but also something generally about the cultural construction of nature, as well as religion overall.

Toward the end of the nineteenth century, the scholar J. H. Philpot published a book entitled *The Sacred Tree* in which she wrote, "Now of all primitive customs and beliefs there is none which has a greater claim upon our interest than the worship of the tree, for there is none which has had a wider distribution throughout the world, or has left a deeper impress on the traditions and

Figure I.1 Typical neighborhood tree shrine in Banaras

observances of mankind."¹ Philpot moves beyond this more or less descriptive statement to the pejorative claim that there is no study of any other "pagan ritual" that is "better calculated to throw light on the dark ways of primitive thought" than "the worship of the spirit-inhabited tree."² For Philpot, tree worship is a central, pervasive, and exemplary feature of what she calls the "primitive religion" of the "uncivilized races."³ Consideration of tree worship was fundamental to many scholarly theories about religion near the beginning of the twentieth century, and yet today sacred trees and tree worship have practically disappeared from the academic terrain of religious theory. Why is this so? In part, there is a simple answer to this question: the theories of religion so commonly accepted by most scholars at the dawn of the twentieth century have long been discarded by those interested in this endeavor today.⁴ Nonetheless, after abandoning theories about religion routinely worked out toward the end of the nineteenth century, might there still be something worth pondering about human possibilities in the case of tree worship?

Three scholars greatly influenced Philpot's understanding of the place of tree worship in religion: Edward B. Tylor, W. Robertson Smith, and James G. Frazer, who in turn were influenced by Max Muller, David Hume, and Auguste Comte. Together these scholars had a tremendous impact on how religion was viewed in the academic world of Western Europe and North America at the close of the nineteenth century. Although there were significant differences among them, they shared an important idea: they all agreed that religion evolved from the personification of nature and that tree worship was clear evidence of this. They also shared a developmental view of history that regarded such practices as tree worship as involving a primitive and ultimately mistaken stage of thought in which nonhuman life was viewed as being sentient, an idea that had to be expunged from modern civilized thought if true progress were to occur. Tylor, the first Professor of Anthropology at Oxford and the one who coined the word "animism," was enormously influential in characterizing the most primitive thought as that which ascribes spirit not only to humans but also animals, plants, and natural entities; in short, the belief that holds "everything to be animate in the universe."⁵

My interest in scholars such as Tylor, Frazer, and Smith is threefold. First, I am drawn to them because they take tree worship seriously in their theorizing about religion. Second, I am concerned with understanding how their particular approach effectively shut down consideration of tree worship in a postmodern age of scholarship that is highly critical of the politics of domination in colonial period scholarship. And third, I am interested in some of the ethnographic data that they collected, for I think that with great caution it can be used to rethink the place of tree worship in human experience.⁶ I aim specifically to return tree worship to our consideration of religion and productively revisit such related concepts as animism and anthropomorphism after liberating them from the evolutionary viewpoint and hierarchical judgments so prevalent in past scholarship.

The title *People Trees* relates to the content of this book in at least six ways. First, although other sacred trees are examined, the pipal tree—arguably the most sacred tree in India—receives the greatest attention in this study. The Hindi word "pipal" is pronounced similarly to the English word "people." In this sense, this is a study of "people trees." Second, the "personhood" of trees is a commonly accepted notion in India. Many people there told me, "This tree is a person just like you and me." The trees introduced in this book, then, are "people trees." Third, this is not a study of isolated trees in some remote wilderness area but rather a study of trees in densely populated urban environments. This is a study of trees who live with people and people who live with trees; thus, it is a study of "people trees." Fourth, the trees examined in this book have been planted and nurtured by people for many centuries. They seem to have benefited from human cultivation and flourished in environments managed by humans. In this sense too they are "people trees." Fifth, this book involves an examination of the human experience of trees, of the relationship between people and trees. I am interested in people's sense of trees, and there is no human experience of trees without people. In other words, I am interested in "people trees." And finally, the trees located in the neighborhood tree shrines of northern India are not controlled by a professional or elite class of priests. Common people have direct access to them and are free to worship them in their own way. They are part of the people's religion; consequently, they are "people trees."

This study differs from studies of sacred groves in India[7] in that it focuses on worshipful relationships with individual trees. I conducted most of my investigations of sacred trees in northern India during a year of research in 2006/7 with follow-up visits in October and November 2008 and December and January 2009/10 and 2011/12, concentrating most of my time and energy exploring the tree shrines of the holy city of Banaras (Varanasi) located on the western bank of the Ganges River in the eastern part of the state of Uttar Pradesh. To acquire a sense of how widespread tree worship is in northern India, I also included visits to Rishikesh, Haridvar, Mathura, Vrindaban, Jaipur, Bombay (Mumbai), Delhi, Allahabad, Gaya, Bodh Gaya, and the Himalayan districts of Chamba and Kangra, exploring tree worship wherever I went. Additionally, I had occasion to visit the state of Karnataka in and around the city of Bangalore and a region in southwest Andhra Pradesh, briefly examining the remarkable tree shrines of these parts of southern India.

The worship of trees and the tree shrines of Banaras, however, serve as the primary subject of this study. Banaras is now a city with a population of over a million people. Although the area it occupies is currently covered with many buildings and roads, this was once a heavily forested region; now, however, most of that forest is gone. But there are still many large trees to be found within the city limits of the holy city of Banaras. Several mature trees typically stand on almost every block, and most of these are the sites of shrines wherein the tree is worshiped in a variety of ways. When one turns east into the Assi Ghat area off the Sonarpur Road that runs near and parallel to the Ganges River in Banaras, one passes between three trees. Two of them—a pipal and a neem—are so intertwined that they appear to be a single tree; the other is a banyan tree.[8] Beneath these trees are a few small temples that have been painted bright red with silver trim and house several gods and goddesses. These three trees were the ones that first "called" me to this study in the winter of 2004 while I was visiting India thinking about my next book project. I had always felt attracted to the Assi crossing during previous stays, and on this particular visit I suddenly became aware that this fascination was because of the atmosphere created by the large trees that grew here and the colorful shrines beneath them. This realization opened my eyes to the numerous tree shrines situated in the religious landscape of India; after this I began to see them everywhere I traveled. Interestingly, among all the trees I encountered in Banaras and elsewhere, I was told again and again that the most sacred were the pipal, neem, and banyan. My study, therefore, concentrates on these three species of trees.

This book grew out of a sustained reflection on the worship of sacred trees in India, and its structure is fashioned after the form of a tree. Chapter 1, "Root Issues," reaches deep into the academic soil that determines the questions and feeds the issues that shaped this particular study. Within the overall framework of a consideration of the cultural construction of nature, I reexamine such concepts as personhood, animism, anthropomorphism, idolatry, popular religion, and other related notions associated with tree worship and frequently demonized in the "modern" world, asking anew what possibilities lurk within these much-maligned concepts. I then move out of this fertile ground into chapter 2, "Tree Worship in India." After considering tree worship as a worldwide phenomenon, I examine the massive trunk that is the history of tree worship in India and explore the religious worldviews that make tree worship so common and persistent on the subcontinent. From here, I investigate in the next four chapters the major branches that sprout from the shared trunk of Indian tree worship. Although this tree has many more branches, I concentrate on the pipal, neem, and banyan trees—the three consistently identified as the most important and sacred, and by far the species found most frequently at the tree shrines of India. Since the pipal tree is the most revered tree in India, and since two fairly distinctive attitudes are associated with it—a religion of appreciation and a religion of fear—I devote two chapters to it. Chapter 3, "King of the Trees," explores the more positive life-blessing attitudes associated with the pipal tree within Hinduism, as well as some of the Buddhist views connected with it; whereas chapter 4, "Abode of Ghosts and Saturn," looks at the world of potentially harmful planets, ghosts, and misfortunes associated with the pipal.

The other two trees that are of great religious significance in northern India are the neem and banyan. The neem tree is known to have powerful medicinal qualities that help identify it as a supportive goddess. In the context of an investigation of this tree, which is often adorned with ornate clothing and a metal facemask, I explore in chapter 5, "Faces of the Goddess," some of the culturally specific ideas linked with personhood, anthropomorphism, and relationship. Chapter 6, "Trees of Immortality," takes the reader into the religious world associated with banyan trees, known among other things for their connection with longevity and immortality. The conceptual crown of the tree that configures this book is chapter 7, "Arboreal Reflections." After ascending the limbs comprised of a consideration of Indian tree worship, I reflect in this final chapter on the common elements of tree worship in India, ponder the lessons learned from a study of them, and explore the practical consequences and perceptual possibilities of South Asian notions about sacred trees. It is my hope that this book will help readers expand their sense of the possible relationships that exist between humans and trees. By broadening our understanding of this relationship, we may begin to think differently of the value of trees and the impact of deforestation and other human threats to trees.

1

Root Issues

> The spirits of the tree and grove no less deserve our study for their illustrations of man's primitive animistic theory of nature. This is remarkably displayed in that stage of thought where the individual tree is regarded as a conscious personal being, and as such receives adoration and sacrifice.
> —E. B. Tylor, *Religion in Primitive Culture*

> Yet a man-nature dualism is deep-rooted in us.... Until it is eradicated not only from our minds but also from our emotions, we shall doubtless be unable to make fundamental changes in our attitudes and actions affecting ecology. The religious problem is to find a viable equivalent to animism.
> —Lynn White, "Continuing the Conversation"

What is a tree? Or perhaps we could ask: Who is a tree? The difference between these two interrogatives is significant and—one might add—culturally determined. The first typically signifies an inanimate object or a "thing," whereas the latter signifies an animate being or a "person."[1] The difference between these two, therefore, involves a boundary issue: how or if to demarcate the animate and inanimate, sentient and nonsentient, human and nonhuman, or person and nonperson. Much is at stake in thinking about the nature of these distinctions.

The correct exercise of proper boundary maintenance that sharply divides these categories is the mark of the "civilized." According to Sir Edward Burnett Tylor, one of the most important and influential anthropologists of the latter nineteenth century, "The sense of absolute *psychical distinction* between man and beast, so prevalent in the *civilized world*, is hardly to be found among the lower races."[2] Animism—the belief that spirit (including sentience and personality) is present in nonhuman life forms—is the very basis of "primitive religion" according to Tylor. This distinction, then, is related to another boundary issue: the demarcation of the civilized and primitive. "Animism," he claims, "characterizes tribes very low in the scale of humanity."[3] The question "Who is a tree?" would signal the presence of confused, primitive thought for Tylor, who has written: "In discussing the origin of myth some account has been already given of the primitive stage of thought in which personality and life are ascribed not to man and beast only, but to things. It has been shown how what we call inanimate objects—rivers, stones, *trees*, and so forth—are treated as living intelligent beings."[4] Greatly influenced by Tylor, Sir James Frazer later wrote:

> When man began seriously to reflect on the nature of things, it was almost inevitable that he should explain them on the analogy of what he knew best, that is, by his own thoughts, feelings, and emotions. Accordingly he tended to attribute to everything, not only to animals, but to plants and inanimate objects, a principle of life like that of which he was himself conscious, and which, for want of a better name, we accustomed to call a soul. This primitive philosophy is commonly known as animism. It is a childlike interpretation of the universe in terms of man.[5]

Although much of Tylor's evolutionary theory about religion and culture is no longer accepted, many of his ideas are yet assumed in the Western cultures he labeled "civilized"; there are many today who agree completely with the sentiments expressed in these judgments of so-called primitive cultures. The notion that a tree is a sentient, animate being with whom one can have a meaningful relationship is quite alien to most people in the West.

Whereas Tylor celebrates the establishment and maintenance of a sharp boundary between the human and nonhuman worlds, others more recently have questioned this very boundary and explored its negative consequences. Among them is Lynn White, the late medieval historian who is often credited with founding the emerging field of Religion and Ecology.[6] White viewed the demise of animism and the resulting historical developments that placed a wedge between the human and nonhuman largely in terms of religious competition between pagan animism and a form of Christianity that became dominant in Western Europe and by extension North America. In his now famous article, "The Historical Roots of Our Ecologic Crisis," he writes:

> In Antiquity every tree, every spring, every stream, every hill had its own *genius loci*, its guardian spirit.... By destroying pagan animism, Christianity made it possible to exploit nature in a mood of indifference to the feelings of natural objects.... The spirit *in* natural objects, which formerly had protected nature from man, evaporated. Man's effective monopoly on spirit in this world was confirmed, and the old inhibitions to the exploitation of nature crumbled.... To a Christian a tree can be no more than a physical fact. The whole concept of the sacred grove is alien to Christianity and the ethos of the West. For nearly 2 millennia

Christian missionaries have been chopping down sacred groves, which are idolatrous because they assume spirit in nature.[7]

The result according to White is that we now live in a dead world that is truly animated only by human beings. This opens up the possibility for an excessive abuse of the nonhuman world with gravely negative environmental results. Whether White's account of the role of Christianity in cultural moves away from animism is accurate or not,[8] he contends—a full century after Tylor's celebration of our entrance into the non-animistic "civilized" world—that much of the current ecological crisis is due to the destruction of animistic worldviews, and as the epigram at the beginning of this chapter demonstrates, he calls for a return to some form of animism that will open us to a wider world of being and a greater sense of ethical responsibility.

Obviously, White takes a very different stance than Tylor with regard to the issue of animism—with its concomitant sense of some manner of continuity between the human and nonhuman—and the mental condition of those who embrace it. Interestingly, White's call is even shared by many Christian theologians today who promote a religious worldview in which all living beings are seen as "a community of subjects rather than a collection of objects."[9] The theologian Sallie McFague, for example, puts it this way, "The world as God's body is also, then, a radicalization of divine immanence, for God is not present to us in just one place (Jesus of Nazareth, although also and especially, paradigmatically there), but in and through all bodies, the bodies of the sun and moon, *trees and rivers, animals, and people.*"[10] The continuing conversation concerning animism relates to several other issues, a consideration of which can teach us much about the cultural construction of nature. These include assumptions about the human-nature dualism, prudence with regard to anthropomorphism, and concerns about idolatry, "true religion," and the concomitant division of the "primitive" and the "civilized."

One of the chief lessons learned from a study of the many different cultures of the world is that reality is not a given for human beings, but rather is socially constructed within a specific historical period of a particular culture. One has only to survey the multitude of cultures to see that the ways of being human are highly variable and remarkably different. This facet of human experience, sometimes called "world-openness," has been well noted by many working in the human sciences.[11] The anthropological implications of this are enormous. The world-openness of human beings means that very little regarding worlds of meaning is the same for all human beings; thus we should expect to find great variety and difference with regard to our sense of the world in which we live. The malleable nature of human beings enables us to experience a wide range of possible realities; however, the range of possibilities is limited and reality is defined in a specific way as an individual undergoes the process of socialization into a particular culture. In short, our perception of, experience in, and behavior toward the world are largely determined by the specific culture and historical moment into which we are born.

Significantly, this includes conceptions of and affiliated experiences in the so-called natural world.[12] As the environmental historian Neil Evernden states in his insightful book, *The Social Creation of Nature*, nature "is nowhere near as independent or as 'given' as we like to suppose."[13] That is, like everything else, nature and all ostensible natural phenomena are always viewed through a very particular lens that is determined by the distinct culture and within the precise historical period in which a person is raised. Other scholars concur with this point. William Cronen, for example, writes:

> The work of literary scholars, anthropologists, cultural historians, and critical theorists over the past several decades has yielded abundant evidence that "nature" is not nearly so natural as it seems. Instead, it is a profoundly human construction. This is not to say that the nonhuman world is somehow unreal or a mere figment of our imaginations—far from it. But the way we describe and understand that world is so entangled with our own values and assumptions that the two can never be fully separated. What we mean when we use the word "nature" says as much about ourselves as about the things we label with that word.[14]

A tree, then, is never simply a tree; it is not comprehended in some unmediated fashion, but rather is perceived in accord with the socialization process through which a person has been trained. Since the world one experiences is the world one sees, perception determines one's experience of a tree. What experiential possibilities might be available to human beings through different cultural lenses?

If we accept that nature is culturally constructed, then we must also accept that our own theories about nature are shaped by and reflect very specific cultural understandings about nature, though this is often obscured by an unexamined assumption that our viewpoint is given and universal. In an article entitled "Constructing Natures: Symbolic Ecology and Social Practice,"[15] the anthropologist Philippe Descola not only affirms that nature is culturally constructed but goes on to sound a note of caution about the way our own views of nature affect the study of other cultures. "Many anthropologists and historians now agree that conceptions of nature are socially constructed, that they vary according to cultural and historical determinations, and that therefore, our own dualistic view of the universe should not be projected as an ontological paradigm onto the many cultures where it does not apply."[16] What is the dualistic viewpoint that Descola refers to, and how has it come into being?

One of the foundational tenets of modern Western thought has been the central dichotomy that divides the human and the nonhuman—or society and nature—and maintains a firm boundary between them. This means that spirit, soul, emotions, feelings, sentience, consciousness, and meaningful relationships are all predominantly restricted to the realm of the human. There are many academic accounts that attempt to explain the roots of this cardinal separation. Lynn White placed the culpability for this squarely on the shoulders of Western Christianity: "Christianity, in contrast to ancient paganism and Asia's religions, not only established a dualism of man and nature but also insisted that it is God's will that man exploit nature for his proper ends."[17] Thomas Berry identified the deadly time of the Black Plague in the fourteenth century as the moment when Europeans began to distance themselves from nature, increasingly distrusting it and desiring to control it.[18] Through a discussion of the "purification of nature," Evernden provides another account of this development by contrasting a medieval worldview with a modern Western worldview; the latter he understands to be largely the product of the humanistic revolution of the Renaissance that strongly influenced modern scientific ways of knowing. He maintains that the medieval world was characterized by an empathetic approach to knowing nature, "which is of course only possible if the subject and the object, the knower and the known, are of the same nature; they must be members and parts of one and the same vital complex."[19] That is, empathy hinges on a sense of continuity or unity of being between the knower and known. Empathic knowledge, Evernden explains, implies an underlying similarity or kinship between the human and natural world: "For nature to be knowable through empathy, subject and object must be fundamentally akin."[20]

But this is precisely what gets rejected in the humanistic revolution of the Renaissance in which man becomes the measure of all things. In this context, Evernden demonstrates, the perception of nature must be cleansed of all human projections. "The expulsion of qualities from nature, although radical in the extreme, was justified through the assertion that only when the distorting effects of human projection are removed can we achieve an understanding of the 'primary' or real properties of nature."[21] Much of the objective sciences of today entail the attempt to observe things directly without projectionism. "Given our contemporary acceptance of the necessity of objectivity in the study of nature, we are apt to be easily sympathetic with those who first sought to achieve an uncontaminated vision of the world."[22] This development makes good sense, but did it go too far? Does a metaphysics that assumes a radical division between the human and nonhuman necessarily have to accompany the scientific method? Evernden explains that the resulting picture of nature that emerged from the

Renaissance created a world that was void of animation. Nature by definition is now what is nonhuman: "Indeed, that is what Nature is: a world devoid of properties we associate with humans—in short, devoid of subjectivity."[23] In such a world, meaningful communication and significant relationships between humans and nonhumans become highly suspect, if not impossible.

Consequently, any attempt to see meaning, purpose, emotions, sentience, or consciousness in nature was regarded as a conceptual pollution of reality. A lasting effect of this has been that "in our understanding, in our 'system' called Nature, human characteristics are out of place and constitute a serious contamination."[24] With this development, a thorough separation between human and nature was accomplished. The resulting dualism caused a de-animation of the nonhuman world, while identifying the root of all true animation—the soul—with humanity alone. This claim found additional support within certain developments in Christian theology that favored radically transcendent views of sacrality. It was within this conceptual framework that René Descartes would argue that animals were in principle machines. Any notion of "personhood" or any other human quality in nonhumans was thus dismissed as misguided "projectionism" by many after the Renaissance. Consequently, personhood came to be identified solely with the human. Hence, we enter the modern world with a view of nature that is both devoid of sentience and subject to indifferent exploitation. Importantly, Evernden links all of this to another relevant concept: "And the sin we commit in attempting to attribute such [human] properties to Nature is 'anthropomorphism.'"[25]

This conceptual perspective is beginning to change, however, as we enter a postmodern period now influenced by such disciplines as quantum physics, paleontology, ecology, and especially evolutionary biology that teaches the interconnectedness of all life; the firm boundary that divides the human and nonhuman is starting to crumble. Evernden reminds us that we not only need to treat things differently but also see them differently: "The so-called environmental crisis demands not inventing of solutions, but the re-creation of *the things themselves.*"[26] Evolutionary biology insists that all plants and animals share a common biological ancestry. Contemporary science returns us to a pre-dualistic world in which plants and animals—including trees and humans—share characteristics and in a sense can even be considered kin.[27] If this is true, then meaningful relationships between human and nonhumans may be possible. Evernden highlights one consequence of this development: "Once we accept, through the study of Nature, that all life is organically related, organically the same through the linkage of evolution, then humanity is literally part of Nature."[28] He then raises the significant questions: "If humanity is 'just' a part of nature, then what sense does it make to suppose that nature may not have properties similar to our own? What is the justification for the ban on anthropomorphism?"[29] I will return shortly to further ponder anthropomorphism, but first take up consideration of how the human-nature dualism has affected the study of other cultures.

The scientific developments discussed by Evernden that aim to maintain a sharp boundary between the human and nonhuman are mirrored in nineteenth-century anthropological writings on religion. As noted earlier, the recognition of sentience in nonhuman life was the very mark of primitive mentality for Tylor and others who defined the civilized state as one that reserved sentience for only the human. Many anthropological studies regarding religion, nature, and culture conducted during the colonial period of the nineteenth century were informed by a meta-narrative about progress that assumed an evolutionary view of cultural development. There is perhaps no better representative of the late nineteenth-century meta-narrative I have in mind than Tylor's theory of animism that characterizes primitive thought as that which ascribes spirit or sentience not only to humans but also animals, plants, and natural entities. Tylor is highly representative of a very common nineteenth-century theory of cultural evolution with its concomitant understanding of various hierarchical stages of human development, an idea of the place and role of the worship of natural phenomena or nonhuman life forms in this development, and clear assumptions about the meaning of progress.

Tylor lays out his agenda explicitly in the opening pages of *The Origins of Culture*, the first volume of *Primitive Culture* published in 1871. Herein he makes it clear that he is primarily interested in tracing the development of what he calls the progressive stages of cultures. He writes, "The main tendency of culture from primaeval up to modern times has been from savagery towards civilization."[30] Tylor maintains that modern, educated Westerners establish the norm for the "civilized" state, and—continuing in line with the colonial thinking of his time—he asserts that the primitive stage of culture is still seen among "modern savages." "The educated world of Europe and America practically settles a standard by simply placing its own notions at one end of the social series and savage tribes at the other, arranging the rest of mankind between these limits according as they correspond more closely to savage or to cultured life."[31] In sum, progress for Tylor is the movement from the earlier conditions of mankind to the higher culture of modern Europe; he calls this the "progressive-theory of civilization."[32] And what, we might ask, are the earlier, primitive conditions of humankind? To answer this question we best turn to *Religion in Primitive Culture*, the second volume of *Primitive Culture*, since Tylor employs an analysis of different types of religion to determine whether a particular society is primitive or civilized.

The chief subject of *Religion in Primitive Culture* is animism, which Tylor defines most simply as "the belief in Spiritual Beings."[33] Although one could argue that animism is the root of all religion for Tylor, it is primarily the indicator of "the primitive religion of the savage." A fundamental difference between the "civilized" and "savage" mind is that whereas the civilized person believes that only human beings have spirit or souls, primitive people believe that nonhuman beings also have these. Thus, for the latter, everything in the world is animate. This is due to the fact that according to Tylor the savage, who is deeply invested in animistic thinking, is unable to distinguish between the imaginative and the real: "Even in healthy waking life, the savage or barbarian has never learnt to make that rigid distinction between subjective and objective, between imagination and reality, to enforce which is one of the main results of scientific education."[34] A key element in Tylor's progressive agenda becomes clear: the move toward a rational, scientific way of thinking which is able to correctly discern that spirit is not present in nonhuman life forms. This civilized move, he insists, is mostly absent from "the lower races." This judgment allows Tylor to establish a hierarchically progressive typology of religions.

The very lowest form of primitive, animistic religion for Tylor involves the recognition of sentience in nonanimal forms; that is, in that "primitive stage of thought in which personality and life are ascribed not to men and beasts only, but to things."[35] Importantly, Tylor includes trees in his list of "things." There are degrees to the childish mistake of animism for Tylor, and the belief that all things have spirit or soul is at the very bottom of the hierarchical scale of primitive animism. Speaking pejoratively about our primitive past, Tylor writes, "There was a period of human thought when the whole universe seemed actuated by spiritual life." Significantly, tree worship is a prime example of this: "The spirits of the tree and grove no less deserve our study for their illustrations of man's primitive animistic theory of nature. This is remarkably displayed in that stage of thought where the individual tree is regarded as a conscious personal being, and as such receives adoration and sacrifice."[36] In short, the wider the circle of sacrality, the more primitive is the religion. A step up from the most primitive form of religious animism, which assumes spirit in even objects, is the belief that only life forms of trees or higher have souls, and another step up from this is the belief that only animals and humans have souls. The highest view, of course, is that only humans have souls. "The souls of animals is recognized by a natural extension from the theory of human souls; the souls of trees and plants follow in some vague partial way; and the souls of inanimate objects expand the general category to its extremest boundary."[37] In brief, then, the path of progress increasingly follows the movement away from the belief that spirit or soul is invested in the great multiplicity of life forms. In the case of trees, this means that any society that has effectively silenced the voices of the trees is moving along in the right direction of the progressive scale of cultures. The narrower a culture's conception of sacrality, the more civilized is that culture.

Tylor identifies the crudest form of primitive animism with idolatry, which he associates with immanent conceptions of the divine and notions of "embodiment."

For him idolatry is the result of a childishly ignorant propensity to confuse a symbol (an object) with the symbolized (the deity). He claims that it is rooted in "the tendency to identify the symbol and the symbolized, a tendency so strong in children and the ignorant everywhere, led to the idol being treated as a living powerful being, and thence even to explicit doctrines as to the manner of its energy or animation."[38] Relying unwittingly on Christian conceptions, Tylor reads notions of divine embodiment as idolatry and assumes that it is symbolic representation gone awry wherein an embodied form (the symbol) is confused with the transcendent deity (the symbolized). But what if there is no hardened boundary between the embodied form of a deity and the deity, as in traditions that regard the world as an actual expression or manifestation of divinity? Tylor underscores the religious roots of thinking about symbolic representation—in contrast to metonymic representation, in which the sacred object is assumed to be an actual part of a larger sacred whole and not merely a symbol of it.

In placing idolatrous animism on the very bottom of the hierarchical scale of religions, Tylor evokes the authoritative theories of David Hume and Auguste Comte, citing their respective texts, *The Natural History of Religion* and *The Positive Philosophy*.[39] Hume and Comte shared a developmental view of human culture that held that the lowest stage of religion is that in which all life is regarded as invested with spirit. Hume's primary concern in *The Natural History of Religion* is articulating the origin of religion and tracing an evolutionary development toward perfection that assumes a clear notion of progress. He identifies the lowest and most primitive form of religion to be what he calls vulgar, polytheistic, idolatry. "It appears to me," he writes, "that if we consider the improvement of human society, from rude beginnings to a state of perfection, polytheism or idolatry was, and necessarily must have been, the first and most ancient religion of mankind."[40] More specifically, ancient idolatrous polytheism is that type of religion in which everything is regarded as sacred: "The vulgar polytheist, so far from admitting that idea [namely, the supreme transcendence of monotheism], deifies every part of the universe, and conceives all the conspicuous productions of nature, to be themselves so many real divinities. The sun, moon, and stars, are all gods according to his system: Fountains are inhabited by nymphs, and trees by hamadryads."[41] In addition to this kind of religion Hume posited another, leading him to develop a two-tiered notion of religion: besides the "vulgar religion" of the "raw and ignorant multitude," which involves notions of idolatrous embodiment, there is the "rational religion" of the educated elite, which is invested in abstract, transcendent notions of divinity. Whereas ancient religion springs from nature worship according to Hume, or rather from the belief that "all nature was full of invisible powers,"[42] the "high religion" of the educated elite is based on a "doctrine of one supreme deity, the author [not expression or manifestation] of nature."[43] As "supreme author" of the visible world, God is *not* a part of it.

Tylor's interest in Comte focuses on the latter's understanding of the developmental stages of humankind, especially on the earliest stage, which involves "pure fetishism." Tylor quotes a passage from Comte's *Positive Philosophy* that characterizes "the primary mental condition of mankind" as "a state of pure fetishism" which is "constantly characterized by the free and direct exercise of our primitive tendency to conceive all external bodies soever, natural or artificial, as animated by a life essentially analogous to our own, with mere differences of intensity."[44] Comte maintained that humanity passes through three stages of development in its progressive advance toward perfection: the theological or fictitious stage, the metaphysical or abstract stage, and finally the scientific or positive stage.[45] The earliest stage of development, the theological, involves explanation of unknown phenomena in terms of personified deities. This stage itself has three hierarchical stages. Beginning with the lowest, they are (1) fetishism, in which other beings and natural phenomena are regarded as sacred; (2) polytheism, which involves the worship of many gods; and (3) monotheism, the worship of a single supreme god. Here again, any religious philosophy that conceives of divinity as being pervasive throughout the natural world and embodied in the multitude of natural phenomena is relegated to the very bottom of the progressive scale of human development.

Another key nineteenth-century scholarly figure who shared a similar evaluation of embodiment was W. Robertson Smith, an influential friend to James Frazer. In his book *The Religion of the Semites: The Fundamental Institution*, Smith distinguishes two types of religion: (1) The "positive religions" of Judaism, Christianity, and Islam that are the result of great religious innovators, who were the organs of "divine revelation," and who "deliberately departed from the traditions of the past"; and (2) "ancient heathenism," the unconscious, natural religious traditions of the past.[46] Hinduism, of course, is included in the second category. The central feature of ancient heathenism for Smith is the notion of embodiment. "All acts of ancient worship have a material embodiment."[47] Put another way, Smith maintained that ancient heathenism was based on the understanding of pervasive relationship. "Primitive thought," he writes, "treats all nature as a kindred unity.... The worshipped and the worshippers are parts of one physical unity of life."[48] For this reason ancient peoples erroneously related to natural things, such as trees, as they would people. But again it was the notion of embodiment that most significantly signaled for Smith the presence of ancient heathenism:

> In ritual the sacred object [such as a tree] was spoken of and treated as the god himself; it was not merely his symbol but his embodiment, the permanent centre of his activity in the same sense in which the human body is the permanent centre of man's activity. In short, the whole conception belongs in its origin to a stage of thought in which there was

no more difficulty in ascribing living powers and personality to a stone, tree or animal, than to a being of human or superhuman build.[49]

Moreover, the god was not "wholly outside nature, but was himself linked to the physical world by a series of affinities connecting him not merely with man but with beasts, trees and inanimate things."[50] Tree worship is particularly exemplary of ancient heathenism for Smith, and he asserts that the most ancient form of tree worship is that in which the tree is regarded as "a particle of divine life," or that "the tree…is the visible embodiment of the divine presence."[51] In sum, the mark of the primitive was the belief that all of nature is animated or the understanding that the sacred was pervasive throughout nature, whereas civilized people following the positive religions were able to make a distinction between God and nature and understand the sacred as transcendently removed from the world of physical embodiment.

Frazer—another intellectually leading figure—concurs in many ways with Smith and Tylor. In his book *The Worship of Nature*, he distinguishes the "natural religion" of the "simple folk" from the "great historical religions…created each at a blow by the genius of a single founder, who was raised far above his fellows."[52] Frazer follows the two-tiered classification of religion established by Hume and continued by Tylor and Smith; for him, the revealed historical traditions were far superior to natural religion, which includes the religion of the "savages," "simple folk," and the ancient religions of India and the Mediterranean. The most characteristic feature of natural religion is the worship of nature, defined as: "the worship of natural phenomena conceived as animated, conscious, and endowed with both the power and the will to benefit or injure mankind.… Thus what we may call the worship of nature is based on the personification of natural phenomenon."[53] Consideration of tree worship was central to Frazer's widely read book, *The Golden Bough*. Therein, Frazer maintained, "In the religious history of the Aryan race in Europe the worship of trees has played an important part."[54] While discussing tree worship, he declared: "It is necessary to examine in some detail the notions on which the worship of trees and plants is based. To the *savage the world in general is animate*, and trees and plants are no exception to the rule. He thinks that they have souls like his own, and he treats them accordingly."[55]

The combined weight of these late nineteenth-century theoreticians was enormous; their shared assumption was that the notion that divinity was present and pervasive in the natural world was the mark of a childish, primitive, and mistaken mode of thought. One might add that European Christian theologians—the intellectuals who defended and propagated the religion identified as the "higher religion of the civilized" by many of the anthropologists and sociologists just discussed—agreed for very different reasons with the hierarchical assessment of religion worked out by Tylor and others. Christian missionaries worked together with and built on the sense of cultural superiority shared by European anthropologists in order to advance their religion as paramount.[56] Nineteenth-century British Christian missionaries based in Calcutta, such as William Ward, attacked Hindu nature worship as idolatrous and viewed the worship of trees as an informative illustration of the "popular superstition" that characterizes depraved Hinduism. Most troubling for him was the fact that various sacred trees were regarded "as the embodied forms of particular gods."[57] Both Christian theologians (mostly working in the missionary context of colonialism) and scholars (mostly anthropologists also working in the context of colonialism) shared an understanding that the progressive mind moves steadily toward a perfection that increasingly shifts divinity away from the natural world to ever more transcendent realms. Tree worship was often singled out by both groups as a primary example of idolatrous, savage religion past and present. In this context, modern progress entailed a movement away from the belief that trees were divine, or that they were even sentient or animated in any significant way. In short, progress meant silencing the voices of the trees; relegated to the status of mere physical matter, no longer were trees to be regarded as sentient beings capable of any significant interaction with humans.

Many anthropologists maintain that such views have had a lasting effect on the field of anthropology. Representing a collection of anthropologists who contributed chapters to the volume *Nature and Society*, Philippe Descola and Gisli Palsson contend that "for over forty years the nature-culture dichotomy has been a central dogma in anthropology," which has for the most part taken this "dichotomy for granted and shared an identical, universalistic conception of nature."[58] These authors insist that there are at least two problems with the assumption that this dualism is universal. First, the nonhuman nature/human society dichotomy hinders ecological understanding. "The dualist paradigm thus prevents a genuine ecological approach to human-environmental relatedness."[59] These anthropologists suggest that non-Western cultures have alternative models to offer for rethinking our ethical attitudes and behavior toward the nonhuman world, but lament that "little attention was paid to how non-western cultures conceptualized their environment and their relation to it."[60] The cultural anthropology that arose during the colonial period was often executed to demonstrate the superiority of Western culture and to discern how to be more effective rulers of the colonized other. If we are to abandon this colonial agenda, but wish to continue the study of other cultures, we need to articulate why we do so. What lessons might non-Western cultures have to teach with regard to the natural world?

The second major problem with the nature-society dichotomy for Descola and Palsson is that it does not always fit the ethnographic case. The anthropologists who contributed to this volume found something quite different in the field. "For many anthropologists...the shift from a dualistic to a monist perspective appears to have been triggered by fieldwork among people for whom the nature-society dichotomy was utterly meaningless."[61] Specifically, what is completely obscured by this dichotomy, and therefore most challenging to it when acknowledged, is the notion of "personhood" among nonhuman life forms. "This is the case, for instance, of the Achuar Jivaro of the Upper Amazon who, according to Descola, consider most plants and animals as *persons*." Also, "the Chewong of the Malay rainforest do not set humans apart from other beings; plants, animals and spirits are said to be endowed with *consciousness*."[62] Taking seriously the more extensive concept of personhood found among other cultures is a key to rethinking animism.

In an article titled "'Animism' Revisited," the Israeli anthropologist Nurit Bird-David holds up the ethnography of Irving Hallowell on the Ojibwa of the Lake Winnipeg area of northern Canada during the 1930s as a productive way of reassessing animism.[63]

> Hallowell observed that the Ojibwa sense of personhood, which they attribute to some natural entities, animals, winds, stones, etc., is fundamentally different from the modernist one. The latter takes the axiomatic split between "human" and "nonhuman" as essential, with "person" being a subcategory of "human." The Ojibwa conceives of "person" as an overarching category within which "human person," "animal person," "wind person," etc., are subcategories.... Hallowell's contribution is to free the study of animistic beliefs and practices first from modernistic person-concepts and second from the presumption that these notions and practices are erroneous.[64]

For the Ojibwa the world is populated with many people, only some of whom are human. The result of this exceptionally inclusive sense of personhood for Hallowell is that empathetic relationships with nonhumans become possible: "Thus the world of personal relations in which the Ojibwa live is a world in which vital social relations transcend those which are maintained with human beings.... Speaking as an Ojibwa, one might say: all other 'persons'—human or other than human—are structured the same as I am.... All other 'persons,' too, have attributes as self-awareness and understanding. I can talk with them. Like myself, they have personal identity, autonomy, and volition."[65] The personhood of nonhuman beings is thus clearly recognized in a variety of other cultures. We will see in later chapters that this is also true for those worshiping trees at the tree shrines of northern India. If animals and trees are considered "persons" in other cultures, and if we acknowledge the potential validity of their viewpoint, then what becomes of the firm boundary between the human and nonhuman, between society and nature?

As these anthropologists demonstrate, any earnest consideration of the personhood and consciousness of nonhuman beings leads to a reconsideration of animism, once rejected as illusory primitivism. Without the judgmental and cultural evolutionary perspective of Tylor, which disparages (embodied) animism with the pejorative label "primitive," Descola explores some positive possibilities within animism: "Among other things, animism is the belief that natural beings possess their own spiritual principles and that it is therefore possible for humans to establish with these entities *personal relations* of a certain kind."[66] Again, for Descola, it is the very notion found among other cultures of "personhood" in nonhumans that most challenges the human-nature dichotomy. And this is precisely what he finds in many of the surviving animistic cultures of the world: "Animic systems do not treat plants and animals as mere signs or as privileged operators of taxonomic thought; they treat them as *proper persons*, as irreducible categories."[67] If this is true, if we find many cultures that treat natural phenomena as "proper persons," then the sharp divide between human and nonhuman beings cannot be taken for granted. It also cannot be assumed as universal; other possibilities clearly exist. Nor can it be regarded as part of superior civilized culture, unless we wish to maintain the colonial cultural evolutionary perspective of Tylor. There is little place for such absolute judgments in a perspective that acknowledges the cultural construction of reality. Like all cultural constructs, the fundamental separation of the human and nonhuman must be regarded as a major feature of a particular cultural construction of nature that took place during a specific historical period. Once this is accepted, the door is open for other cultures to teach us something about other possible ways of thinking about human relationships with the nonhuman world.

The crumbling boundary between human and nonhuman, and a reconsideration of such issues as animism and the notion of personhood among nonhuman beings, raises another contentious issue: anthropomorphism. A review of some assessments of anthropomorphism in the study of religion and in ethology—the study of animal behavior—will be useful in considering the larger application of this concept. Anthropomorphism is typically defined as the attribution of human characteristics to nonhuman phenomena. Anthropomorphism has long been recognized as having much to do with religion, but like animism, it too has usually been disparaged as "confused," "childish," or "primitive." One of the early and most influential writers on the subject of anthropomorphism was David Hume. In the mid-eighteenth century he asserted with great authority: "There is an universal tendency among mankind to conceive all beings like themselves, and to transfer to every object, those qualities with which they are familiarly acquainted, and of which they are intimately conscious.... trees, mountains and streams are personified, and the inanimate parts of nature acquire sentiment and passion."[68] For Hume, anthropomorphism is a cognitive strategy for coping with the insecurity of living in a world of unknown causes; it is an application of what is familiar to what is unfamiliar. He relates anthropomorphism in his writings particularly with the popular or "vulgar religion" of the "ignorant multitude."[69] Although Hume is not without sympathy for those who utilize anthropomorphic strategies, ultimately for him their approach is judged to be a mistake that is to be replaced with objective science.

Hume's understanding of anthropomorphism as a cognitive strategy has been taken up more recently by Stewart Guthrie, who has produced a noteworthy and thorough examination of anthropomorphism in his book *Faces in the Clouds*. Guthrie reviews several theories of early figures who influenced the way anthropomorphism came to be viewed within the study of religion; these include Giambattista Vico, Auguste Comte, and Ludwig Feuerbach.[70] What all three of them share is the contention that anthropomorphism represents a very confused approach to the knowledge of things and nonhuman beings. Vico maintained that religion originated in a befuddled anthropomorphized response to a world that lay beyond comprehension. Comte saw anthropomorphism as part of an infantile experience in which humans regard external bodies as animated by a life similar to their own. Feuerbach developed one of the most sustained theories of religion and anthropomorphism, which was to have a great impact on later psychologists who took up the consideration of religion, particularly Sigmund Freud and Jean Piaget. For Feuerbach, gods are projections of human beings; a god represents the "inner nature of man as an objective external being." Although Feuerbach regarded religious anthropomorphism as the first workings of a crude means of attaining self-consciousness, he agreed with Vico and Comte that it is "childish" and "primitive" and is finally to be rejected as illusory. Guthrie also examines the work of the anthropologist Leslie White, illustrating that these attitudes are alive and well in the anthropology of the latter half of the twentieth century. White not only agrees with the rather derogatory views of Vico, Comte, and Feuerbach on anthropomorphism, he takes them one step further. For him the absolutely illusory nature of anthropomorphism makes it "worse than worthless, for false knowledge is often worse than none at all."[71] In sum, although a few of these writers might recognize some value in anthropomorphism, all of them reject it as a childish or confused primitive stage of human thought that has no place in the modern world.

Guthrie reviews still others who have wrestled with the persistence of anthropomorphism in human thought and action, noting "both secular rationalists and theologians find anthropomorphism embarrassing. Secular thinkers, especially scientists, see it as an unfortunate and persistent flaw in human thought. Theologians see it as a discomforting sign that conceptions of God may be limited by, or even founded on, conceptions of ourselves."[72] I will return shortly to the "embarrassment" of scientists who study animal behavior, but first consider briefly with Guthrie the views of Western theologians on anthropomorphism. Western theologians are not only embarrassed by anthropomorphism, which they typically link to the "old man in the sky," but more importantly regard it a source of much anxiety. Besides acknowledging that Western theologians may dislike anthropomorphism because it raises "the possibility that God consists *only* in anthropomorphizing," Guthrie attributes additional resistance to anthropomorphism among these theologians to "the historic transcendence and otherness of the Abrahamic God.... Such a transcendent God could share no important properties with the created world."[73] Although Guthrie does not make the connection explicit, the resistance to anthropomorphism in the Western religious traditions of Judaism, Christianity, and Islam is closely tied to another boundary maintenance issue, namely idolatry. Any instance wherein the transcendent creator becomes confused with a created being or thing is regarded as idolatry and condemned as a grave sin. Only humans were created in the image of God, and the firm boundary between God and nature is to be guarded with zealous vigilance. Anthropomorphism undoubtedly threatens this theological enterprise. Guthrie reminds us, however, that theologians have never been successful in rooting out anthropomorphism; in fact, if they were to do so they would have effectively killed religion, for Guthrie contends that "the *personalism* of religion is no mere idiom. Rather it is fundamental and characteristic."[74] Guthrie's central assertion is that religion essentially *is* anthropomorphism.

Guthrie maintains that the resistance to anthropomorphic images is an anomaly. Surveying a wide range of the world's religious cultures he concludes, "the Western chasm between human and gods is atypical."[75] Furthermore, he finds much continuity between the human and nonhuman worlds in many cultures that do not draw sharp lines of distinction between plants, animals, and humans—a view that is increasingly confirmed by the contemporary biological sciences: "Although modern Western culture, shaped by Judeo-Christian tradition, draws a sharp line between the human and the nonhuman worlds, neither evolutionary biology nor many other cultures do so."[76] Biologists today even have difficulty deciding where to place a boundary between the living and the nonliving.[77] In this sense they are in agreement with Aristotle, who wrote long ago that "nature proceeds little by little from inanimate things to living creatures in such a way that we are unable, in the continuous sequence, to determine the boundary line."[78]

Questioning the Cartesian dualism that regards only humans as animated and living in an otherwise dead world, Guthrie writes, "Ambiguities in the notion of life, and practical difficulties in identifying animals and plants as such, make distinguishing the living from the nonliving perpetually problematic."[79] He cites the scientist Thomas Sebeok, who writes that there "may not be an absolutely rigorous distinction between inanimate matter and matter in a living state," and concludes, "Small wonder, then, that children and laymen are not sure what is alive and what is not."[80] This is particularly true with regard to the distinction between humans and other nonhuman life forms. After a consideration of Darwin's questioning of the radical distinctiveness of the human, Guthrie remarks, "When we see there is no certain line between the human and the nonhuman, we can better see that it is not unreasonable to look for features we are acquainted with in humans elsewhere as well."[81] Recognizing the affinity between all life forms, such tendencies as animism and anthropomorphism do not appear so irrational: "We are able to find, with no sense of incongruity, all manner of humanity in the nonhuman world."[82] Understood as an approach that acknowledges shared characteristics between humans and nonhumans, anthropomorphism appears quite reasonable.

Guthrie's own views on anthropomorphism, however, go far beyond recognizing the persistence of it in many modes of human activity. For him, both animism and anthropomorphism are effective and universal perceptual strategies that are not only at the root of all religion, but are fundamental to all forms of human perception. Guthrie claims that what is most significant in the world are other human beings, and when faced with an uncertain situation, we make a "good bet" by assuming a humanlike being is involved in that situation. Assuming that a shadow is a human being makes more sense than assuming that it is not, for if it turns out to be a human we are prepared for a significant encounter and if it does not we lose nothing imperative. "Uncertain of what we face, we bet on the most important possibility because if we are wrong we lose little and if we are right we gain much. Religion, asserting that the world is significantly humanlike, brings this strategy to its highest pitch."[83] Gods, the most supreme beings, are almost always imaged in human form, since "the highest organization we know is that of human thought and action."[84] When in doubt we typically assume something is alive, and even better, that it is humanlike. This strategy, according to Guthrie, has served us well throughout our development as human beings. Anthropomorphism, according to Guthrie, then, is a reasonable interpretation of the world and "is normal, not aberrant, because it results from a strategy universal in human perception."[85] He goes so far as to claim: "Indeed, anthropomorphism offers the greatest intellectual coherence possible."[86]

In sum, while Guthrie agrees with Hume and others who view anthropomorphism as a cognitive strategy, he differs from them in regarding it as an inevitable and effective strategy in all forms of human activity, rather than one to be abandoned on the march toward civilized modernity. But although it is reasonable and inevitable, anthropomorphism for Guthrie too is still a "mistake" of over-interpretation that must be corrected: "We can label it anthropomorphism only after seeing it as an error. Anthropomorphizing animals, then, only shows once more that we tend to see human features where they do not exist."[87] In short, "Anthropomorphism by definition is a mistake."[88] He concludes: "Choosing among interpretations of the world, we remain condemned to meaning, and the greatest meaning has a human face. Occasionally our interpretations assign too little meaning and we fail to see some real face confronting us. More often our interpretations assign too much and we see a face where none is. Pursuing an uncertain course between too little meaning and too much, we chronically veer, mistaken but safe, toward too much."[89]

While there is much to be appreciated in many of Guthrie's notions about anthropomorphism, some of them beg questioning, particularly in the context of the worship of trees in India. First, his concluding definition of anthropomorphism as a "mistake" seems to contradict his prior work demonstrating the problematic nature of any attempt to draw a clear line of distinction between human and nonhuman life forms, and his insistence that there is often much in common between humans and nonhumans. Moreover, it complicates his earlier and more straightforward general definition of anthropomorphism as "the attribution of human characteristics to the nonhuman."[90] It could be the case that humans and animals, for example, actually do share many characteristics. As Evernden asked, "if humanity is 'just' a part of nature, then what sense does it make to suppose that nature may not have properties similar to our own? What is the justification for the ban on anthropomorphism?" Guthrie labors hard in his book to challenge the human-nonhuman divide that characterizes so many disparaging views of anthropomorphism and to demonstrate that so-called human characteristics are not necessarily limited to the human. Thus, attributing human characteristics to the nonhuman world—i.e., anthropomorphism—may sometimes be correct. Why then limit the nomenclature "anthropomorphism" to refer only to mistaken forms of such attribution?

Second, while I acknowledge the insights Guthrie offers to an understanding of anthropomorphism as a "perceptual strategy" in uncertain situations, I think that something quite different is often involved in anthropomorphic activities. For Guthrie, anthropomorphism is "largely unconscious."[91] But is this always the case? We often find anthropomorphic acts that are planned and performed consciously. After correctly perceiving a tree as a tree, for example, we will see that some tree worshipers in northern India then proceed to apply a human-like facemask to that tree. That is, beyond initial perception, we find cultural instances of consciously cultivated and deliberate acts of anthropomorphism. Why? What is going on in these instances? Acts of anthropomorphism, especially intentional acts of anthropomorphism, strike me as involving something other than mistaken perception, and in the case of Indian tree worship, I think that this something other takes us from a consideration of over-interpretation in perception or cognition to the realm of emotions. Tree worshipers in northern

India report that they add faces to trees to better *relate* to them. Perhaps, then, anthropomorphism can be a consciously constructed and intentional means of connecting with the nonhuman world. Consideration of this issue in the specific case of Indian tree worship will be taken up in chapter 5.

Before leaving an examination of anthropomorphism in the context of the study of religion, there is one more related issue that should be addressed. At least since the time of Hume religion has been divided into two types: popular (and thus low) religion, and philosophical (and thus high) religion. The popular religion of the folk was regarded as being "contaminated" by such "crude" or "vulgar" beliefs as animism, polytheism, anthropomorphism, and idolatry, and therefore was frequently deemed unworthy of the attention of scholars who were much more interested in the "higher," "philosophical," "essential" forms of religion that matched their own interests. In his study of the cult of Christian saints, Peter Brown observes that serious academic consideration of this subject had previously been avoided since "our curiosity has been blunted by a particular model of the nature of religious sentiment and a consequent definition of the nature of 'popular religion.'"[92] Brown notes the influential role that Hume's essay *The Natural History of Religion* played in establishing a two-tiered understanding of religion. The religion of the elite intellectuals was to be distinguished from the common people, who were driven by fears and anxieties and led "to personalize yet further the workings of causes beyond their control, and so slip even deeper into polytheistic ways of thought."[93] As a result, popular religion, Brown argues, is assumed to be a contaminated form of the real philosophical religion of the educated elite, and therefore unworthy of scholarly attention. In his essay, Hume makes the connection between the popular religion of "vulgar" common people and anthropomorphic tendencies clear. This led to the big mistake of identifying "invisible power" with "visible objects"; thus, the popular religion of the "ignorant multitude" is branded as "vulgar idolatry and polytheism." Within this "primitive" form of thought "each grove or field is represented as possessed of a particular genius or invisible power, which inhabits and protects it."[94] Hume contends in his essay that one of the major centers of vulgar idolatry and polytheism is Asia.[95]

Early Oriental scholars settled in Calcutta took up Hume's notions of religion and applied them to the forms of Hinduism they encountered in India. William Ward, a scholar associated with the Fort William College, is exemplary of this attitude. Between 1817 and 1820 he published four volumes of a study of Hindu beliefs and practices entitled *History, Literature, and Mythology of the Hindoos*. He follows Hume in dividing religion into two levels: "The opinions embraced by the more philosophical part of the Hindoo nation, are quite distinct from the popular superstition."[96] Ward sought to understand the popular forms of Hinduism, because he saw them as degraded forms of a truer and purer

Hinduism that needed to be recovered. The popular forms of degraded Hinduism not only negatively affected the great majority of the Hindu population of India, according to Ward, but since he included Buddhism within Hinduism, reached out to affect virtually all of Asia: "A more correct knowledge of this people appears to be necessary when we consider, that their philosophy and religion still prevails over the greater portion of the globe, and that it is Hindooism which regulates the forms of worship and the modes of thinking, feeling, and acting, throughout China, Japan, Tartary, Hindoosthan, the Burman empire, Siam, Ceylon. &c., that is, amongst more than 400,000,000 of the human race."[97] The danger of Hinduism according to Ward lay not only in its influence on so many people but also because of the extreme perniciousness of popular Hinduism: "Impurity and cruelty have been, in all ages, the prominent features of every form of pagan superstition. But nowhere have these features presented a more disgusting and horrible appearance than among the Hindoos."[98] Ward includes the worship of trees under the category of the "popular superstition" that characterizes depraved idolatrous Hinduism. In his brief chapter on tree worship he discusses the worship of the ashvatha (pipal), vata (banyan), and neem trees, which he observes with concern are worshiped "as the forms of particular gods."[99] For Ward and other colonial scholars in India in the nineteenth century, tree worship was a sure sign that Hindus were decadent idolaters. Abbe Dubois, for example, included a chapter in his book *Hindu Manners, Customs and Ceremonies* entitled "Inanimate Objects of Worship." Therein he writes: "What I have already said and what I am now about to say respecting the Hindus will show incontestably that there are absolutely no limits to the follies of idolatry.... Amongst the inanimate substances which they worship, there are four which they consider especially sacred, namely the *salagram* stone, *darbha* grass, the plant *tulasi*, and the *aswatta* [pipal] or sacred fig-tree."[100] Inheriting such ideas, it is little wonder that later scholars—who tended only to be interested in the more abstract philosophical systems of religious thought—paid scant attention to tree worship in India, although it is a very prominent feature of the religious landscape there. Animistic and anthropomorphic religious tendencies were simply dismissed as both popular religion and the uninteresting products of a mistaken mind.

Another significant area in which the human-nonhuman boundary is being reconsidered and the contentious value of anthropomorphism is given serious consideration is ethology, the study of animals. One of the strongest defenses in recent times of the resistance to anthropomorphism in the study of nonhuman animals is John Kennedy's *The New Anthropomorphism*. As an ethologist Kennedy defines anthropomorphism as "the ascription of human mental experiences to animals."[101] Acknowledging the persistence of anthropomorphism in the study of animals today, he writes: "Yet there has never been any direct evidence for this ancient anthropomorphic belief, and some three centuries ago René Descartes broke with tradition by arguing that animals were, in principle, machines.... If the study of animal behaviour is to mature as a science, the process of liberation from the delusions of anthropomorphism must go on."[102] Importantly, Kennedy connects anthropomorphism with animism. He claims that any attempt to see feelings or thoughts in animals is "effectively a throw-back to primitive animism."[103] Here again, the term "primitive" is used in a highly pejorative manner. Attitudes that are sympathetic toward animism and anthropomorphism clearly have no place in the study of animals or any reasonable human thought for scientists like Kennedy.

In sharp contrast to Kennedy, Jeffrey Masson and Susan McCarthy, authors of *When Elephants Weep: The Emotional Lives of Animals*, argue that the very fear of being accused of anthropomorphizing has limited true investigation of the mental and emotional lives of nonhuman animals: "The greatest obstacle in science to investigating the emotions of other animals has been an inordinate desire to avoid anthropomorphism. Anthropomorphism means the ascription of human characteristics—thought, feeling, consciousness, and motivation—to the nonhuman."[104] With ethologists such as Kennedy in mind, the authors report: "Science considers anthropomorphism towards animals a grave mistake, even a sin. It is common in science to speak of 'committing' anthropomorphism."[105] In the introduction to this book, Masson explains that he wrote the book in part to expose this as a false accusation: "Many scientists have avoided thinking about the feelings of animals because they have been frightened—and realistically so—of being accused of anthropomorphism. That is why I have looked carefully at the issue of anthropomorphism. If it can be disposed of as a false criticism, then the study of animal emotions can proceed on a scientific basis, freed from a bogus fear."[106] The remainder of *When Elephants Weep* is an investigation of animals in which their emotional lives are taken seriously.

Today a whole host of ethologists explicitly challenge the views expressed by Kennedy, and in agreement with Masson and McCarthy, openly discuss animal emotions, thoughts, and even culture. These include most importantly the pioneer Jane Goodall, whose studies of chimpanzees changed our understanding of fellow primates and opened our eyes to their intelligence, tool making, and social relationships often marked by close and enduring attachments.[107] Years of research with nonhuman animals have led her to conclude: "Clearly, then, there is no sharp line dividing humans from the rest of the animal kingdom. It is a very blurred line, and differences are of degree rather than kind. This leads to a new respect for the other amazing animal beings with whom we share Planet Earth.... Many theologians and philosophers argue that only humans have 'souls.' My years in the forest with the chimpanzees have led me to question this assumption."[108] In his book *Minding Animals,* Goodall's associate Marc Bekoff celebrates the work of Konrad Lorenz, who "freely used anecdote and anthropomorphism, stressed that it was important to empathize with nonhumans, and believed that animals had the capacity to love, be jealous, experience envy, and be angry."[109] For this reason Bekoff argues that "anthropomorphism can help to make accessible to us the behavior and thoughts and feelings of the animals with whom we are sharing a particular experience."[110] Significantly, both Goodall and Bekoff affirm that the most intimate form of connection between humans and other animals takes place through the eyes.[111] This latter group of scientists obviously draws into question the maintenance of any absolute boundary that sharply divides the human and nonhuman.

It is becoming increasingly acceptable these days to talk about the sentience of animals. This is particularly true among those scientists who work with primates, but as Bekoff's work demonstrates this also includes such animals as dogs, coyotes, and even birds. But do we stop with animals and maintain a boundary here? What about other life forms, such as trees?[112]

The author Louis de Bernieres has written a beautiful novel entitled *Birds Without Wings* about the blended Greek-Turkish culture of the west coast of Anatolia at the beginning of the twentieth century. Interestingly, it is a novel that includes the seeking of blessings from trees: cloth is tied in red pines to secure a healthy life for babies. One day a powerful landowner happens upon the town's imam talking to his beloved horse. Embarrassed, the imam apologizes, but the landowner confesses that he too talks to animals, specifically his pet partridge and cat. The imam replies: "Fortunately it is quite reasonable to confide in an animal. It's when you do it to trees and stones that people call you mad."[113] Indeed. To claim that animals have sentience is today increasingly acceptable, but to suggest that trees too have sentience pushes hard on cultural boundaries and opens one to the accusation of being "childish," "primitive," or even as the imam says, "mad"—all terms formerly applied to animistic or anthropomorphic beliefs.[114] Yet this is precisely what anthropologists who explore different cultural notions of trees sometimes discover.

After studying the indigenous cultures of the American northwest, for example, the anthropologist Marie Mauze reports: "Indeed, on the Northwest Coast, trees are endowed with many human characteristics. Trees have a sentient life, they have a 'soul,' and are capable of feelings and thoughts *just like people*."[115] Further cultural examples of viewing trees as sentient beings will be explored in the following chapter. Additionally, although they tend to be on the edge of current North American culture, one increasingly finds published examples of even contemporary European-Americans referring to trees as sentient beings. The Buddhist scholar Stephanie Kaza, for example, has written a sensitive book about her encounters and relationships with trees in which she refers to them as "persons" and addresses them as "friends."[116] One might also think of Julia Butterfly Hill, the young woman who sat in a

California redwood tree for over two years to save it from being logged, who speaks of redwood trees as sentient beings with whom humans can communicate and relate. In her book, *The Legacy of Luna*, Hill reports how the redwood tree she refers to as Luna and calls "the best friend I've ever had" spoke with her, experienced loving emotions, and offered wise spiritual advice.[117] The nature writer Scott Russell Sanders has written an illustrated book in which he talks about his father's friendship and love of trees as "powerful and mysterious neighbors."[118] He describes the manner in which his father introduced him to trees as a young boy:

> Today in the woods, my father smiled at me with his shiny eyes and said, "I've got somebody I'd like you to meet."
> He led me to a great tree that rose up taller than a barn. Even holding hands, we could not reach around the fat trunk. I ran my fingers in the deep grooves of the bark....
> After I discovered everything I could about the tree, I asked my father,
> "Who is this?"
> "This is Black Walnut," he told me. Putting his arm across my shoulder, he said to the tree, "And this is my son, Scott."

Since positive relationships with trees in the modern West have for the most part been relegated to a childhood (analogous to the "primitive") that is to be left behind as one moves into adulthood (analogous to the "civilized"), one might also mention in this context children's literature, such as Shel Silverstein's *The Giving Tree* and those wonderful Ents in J. R. R. Tolkien's *Lord of the Rings*.[119] Although views that regard trees as sentient beings tend to be on the periphery of American society today, we will soon learn that they are central to the religious activity that takes place at tree shrines in India.

We have seen in this chapter that the related concepts of the primitive, animism, the human-nature dichotomy, anthropomorphism, idolatry, and popular religion are all highly contentious issues that have greatly affected the study of religion and the consideration of human attitudes and behavior toward the nonhuman world. The position one takes with regard to these issues is to a large extent culturally determined and tells us much about a person's *a priori* views of nature. In a very general way, two options emerge from a consideration of these issues. One alternative maintains a sharp boundary between the human and nonhuman and, therefore, rejects animistic and anthropomorphic views of the nonhuman as childish or primitive, and in the realm of religion, as idolatrous popular religion. The other does not recognize an absolute boundary between the human and nonhuman and, consequently, embraces animistic and anthropomorphic views of the nonhuman as being the inherent result of acknowledging a continuity between the human and nonhuman and as being vital to abundance in human experience. Clearly different possibilities for human experience of the world and in the world result from the different worldviews associated with each option. With one a meaningful *relationship* with the nonhuman world is much more possible than with the other. Moreover, I have reviewed these issues as a way of cultivating a more productive consideration of the worship of sacred trees in India, for we now enter a world in which the question "Who is a tree?" makes complete sense.

2

Tree Worship in India

> My dear son, from this finest essence that you can't even see has come this huge banyan tree … and this finest essence constitutes the Self of this whole world.
> —Chandogya Upanishad 6:12

> Trees in India have always been treated like human beings, endowed with a soul, a heart that weeps with grief and laughs with joy. They have feelings like ordinary mortals.
> (Gupta 2001: 69)

> The great wonder is that gods assume the form of trees.
> —Skanda Purana 152:1

The conception of trees as powerful sentient beings is readily found in many cultures past and present, and one response to this has been a widespread variety of attitudes and acts of worship. Although examination of tree worship in India provides an excellent and focused opportunity for reconsideration of the issues raised in the previous chapter, worship of sacred trees has certainly been practiced far beyond the borders of India. Some scholars have even claimed that tree worship was everywhere the very first form of religious ritual.[1] Edward Hopkins writes, "The cult of trees is one of the oldest, as it is one of the most widely extended forms of worship."[2] Before taking up an examination of tree worship in India, a brief overview of the religious conceptions of trees and tree worship worldwide would be instructive so as to avoid any mistaken notion that tree worship is unique to the religious cultures of India. Such a review will also provide further resources for exploring the relational possibilities between humans and trees, as well as adding a comparative frame for considering the particular case of Indian tree worship.

Tree Worship as a Worldwide Phenomenon

Human beings have revered trees on every inhabited continent, at least certain trees during certain historical periods. Not only has our very survival depended upon trees—they have offered protection and shelter throughout the history of our species, as well as being a constant source of oxygen, soil, water, food, tools, fuel, and medicines—they have also often been at the center of our religious life. Max Muller, often called the "father of comparative religion," gives his own explanation for why trees have been venerated worldwide:

> Trees, mountains, rivers and the earth seem all very tangible and completely perceptible objects, but are they so? We may stand beneath a tree, touch it, look up to it, but our senses can never take in the whole of it. Its deepest roots are beyond our reach, its highest branches tower high over our head. Besides, there is something in the tree which, for want of a better name, we call its life, and which to an unscientific, and possibly to a scientific generation likewise, is something mysterious, something beyond the reach of our senses, and it may be, of our understanding also. A tree, therefore, has something intangible, something unknowable, something infinite in it. It combines, as I said, the finite and the infinite, or it presents to us something infinite under a finite appearance.[3]

The extensive range of tree worship has certainly been noted by previous scholars. The nineteenth-century scholar of tree worship, J. H. Philpot, wrote, "There is, indeed, scarcely a country in the world where the tree has not at one time or another been approached with reverence or with fear, as being closely connected with some spiritual potency."[4] In a much more recent book, Nathaniel Altman concurs, "The concept of sacred trees has been one of the most important aspects of nearly every world culture since the dawn of civilization."[5] Trees worldwide have played a great variety of roles in the religious life of human beings; they engage a diversity of meanings and have been used for a multitude of religious purposes.

A World Tree or Tree of Life that is regarded as the vital source of all existence is found in the mythology of many religious traditions. All life sprang from a central sacred tree in several Mesoamerican myths: "According to Tzutujil mythology there existed a god in the form of a tree before the creation began. This tree stood in the center of chaos. This tree-god became pregnant with potential life as the creation of the universe approached. It began to flower and grew, in the form of fruit, one of everything that was to exist in the created world."[6] Yggdrasil, the sacred ash tree in Scandinavian mythology, stands at the center of the world with it roots stretching into the underworld of the dead, its trunk in the middle world of the humans, and its branches reaching into the upper world of the gods, thus forming an essential link between all worlds.[7] Likewise, the Mayan Cosmic Tree, which also located at the center of the world, "is rooted in the underworld, has its trunk in the middleworld, and its high branches or top ascending into heaven or the upperworld."[8] The Tree of Life is a common symbol in Near Eastern mythology that shows up in the center of the Garden of Eden of the Hebrew Bible. An early Accadian myth gives expression to what is perhaps the oldest version of the Near Eastern world tree; this account relates that in a garden at the center of earth grows a huge tree whose roots reach down into the watery abyss, whose foliage supports the primordial heavens, and whose trunk is home to the mother Earth goddess.[9] The vitality of the entire Sioux nation was represented by the sacred cottonwood tree for many from this North American tribe, such as Black Elk, who sought throughout his life to revive this essential tree of life at the center of his threatened nation.[10] The Tree of Life is also commonly found in the mythologies of Africa and Asia. The fact that the World Tree—whether simply mythological or identified with an actual tree—is omnipresent tells us something about a common human experience with trees. According to Mircea Eliade, the cosmic tree that stands at the center of the world in a wide range of religious mythology typically represents "the living cosmos, endlessly renewing itself."[11] Furthermore, trees are physical presences that both express and embody forces vital to life.

Trees have also been used in many different ritual contexts. Laura Rival observes, "All over the world, rituals marking the life cycle make extensive use of trees."[12] Black Elk and others in his tribe, for example, carried a branch from the sacred cottonwood tree in most of their ceremonies that aimed to empower the Sioux people.[13] Leaves from sacred trees often find a place in ritual performances. People dressed in sacred leaves, for example, would represent the emerging powers of spring and renewed life in European rituals designed to celebrate or even assist the return of green vegetation.[14] Since it provides a link with the divine realm, climbing into the sky with the aid of a sacred tree has been a common technique used in various rituals to assist an initiate or shaman in journeying to heaven.[15] The story of Jack and the Bean Stalk may be a remnant of such a notion. Also, since trees connect the earth and the sky, many people have believed that they originated from a tree. The Nuer of Africa, for example, relate that they came down from a sky-reaching tamarind tree "one by one."[16] Trees have also been associated with care of the dead; bodies of the deceased have been placed in trees and the souls of ancestors are sometimes believed to dwell within the branches or trunks of trees.[17] Yet in addition to these diverse views and multiple uses, many people throughout history have felt a powerful kinship with trees, whom they consider fellow sentient beings, and have established mutually beneficial relationships with them.

The worship of trees as the location of divine personalities is a worldwide phenomenon; trees have commonly been regarded as either the abodes or embodied forms of divinities. Although he ultimately disparages tree worship as "idolatrous," James Fergusson articulates his notion of why the conception of trees as the home of the gods is so prevalent in his rather complicated nineteenth-century book, *Tree and Serpent Worship*. "Although the actual worship of Trees is nearly as far removed from our ordinary forms of faith as Serpent Worship, still it can hardly be considered as more than an exaggerated perversion of many of the ideas now current; and we can hardly wonder that in an early stage of human civilization, it may have assumed considerable importance. There is such wondrous beauty in the external form of trees, and so welcome a shelter beneath their over-arching boughs, that we should not feel surprise that in early ages groves were considered as the fittest temples for the gods."[18] The sacred groves of pre-Christian Europe and elsewhere in the world are good examples of this. Not only are groves of trees considered to be fit sanctuaries for divinities, but individual trees are also worshiped as the actual bodies of gods and goddesses. For the purposes of this study, I concentrate on an understanding of a single tree as either the abode or body of a divinity, focusing particular attention on the personhood of individual trees as sacred animate beings.

After its conversion to Christianity, Europe increasingly became a major source of derogatory views about tree worship;[19] but it was once an active center of tree worship. Hopkins writes: "Our forefathers in Europe only a few centuries ago were worshipping trees.... It was not till long after the advent of Christianity that the reverence paid to trees diminished."[20] Philpot emphasizes the fact that "the worship of the tree has prevailed at one time or another in every country of Europe."[21] While there is much to be questioned in Sir James Frazer's general theory of religion in his magnum opus, *The Golden Bough*—a work that hinges on an understanding of tree worship—his book remains a treasure house of information about tree worship in Europe. Herein Frazer declares, "In the religious history of the Aryan race in Europe the worship of trees has played an important part."[22] The seriousness with which Europeans took the sentience of trees may be gleaned from the following quotation.

> From an examination of the Teutonic words for "temple" Grimm has made it probable that amongst the Germans the oldest sanctuaries were natural woods. However that may be, tree-worship is well attested for in all the great European families of the Aryan stock. Amongst the Celts the oak-worship of the Druids is familiar to everyone, and their old word for a sanctuary seems to be identical in origin and meaning with the Latin *nemus*, a grove or woodland glade, which still survives in the name Nemi. Sacred groves were common among the ancient Germans, and tree-worship is hardly extinct among their descendants at the present day. How serious that worship was in former times may be gathered from the ferocious penalty appointed by old German laws for such as dared peel the bark of a standing tree. The culprit's navel was to be cut

out and nailed to the part of the tree which he had peeled, and he was to be driven round and round the tree till all his guts were wound about its trunk. The intention of the punishment clearly was to replace the dead bark by a living substitute taken from the culprit; it was a life for a life, the life of a man for the life of the tree.[23]

It would be difficult to determine whether this law was ever enforced, but its existence certainly gives expression to vital beliefs associated with trees in an earlier historical period. Trees were often considered in Europe to be animate beings with feelings and consciousness. Frazer reports that early Austrians, for whom forest trees were considered to be sentient beings with souls like their own, "heard from their fathers that the tree feels the cut not less than a wounded man his hurt."[24] Beyond prohibitions based on general animistic notions about trees, Frazer emphasizes the positive manners in which trees were regarded in pre-Christian Europe. "The conception of trees and plants as animated beings naturally results in treating them as male and female, who can be married to each other in a real, and not merely a figurative or poetical, sense of the word."[25] European tree worship was believed to result in beneficial effects such as general life-blessings and the fertility and well-being of crops, domestic animals, and humans. May-pole celebrations represent a remnant form of such tree worship according to Frazer. "In Europe the May-tree of May-pole is apparently supposed to possess similar powers over both women and cattle."[26]

Individual species of trees were often singled out in Europe for special attention. Among all trees the oak was considered to be the most sacred and was frequently regarded as an embodied form of divinity; it was referred to in Finland as "God's tree."[27] The oak was considered to be the "king of trees" in much of Europe, and therefore became associated with the most powerful gods. "The oak, excelling all others in majestic strength and inherent vigour, became the emblem and embodiment of Zeus."[28] Frazer writes: "The worship of the oak tree or the oak god appears to have been shared by all branches of the Aryan stock in Europe. Both Greeks and Italians associated the tree with their highest god, Zeus or Jupiter, the divinity of the sky, the rain, and the thunder.... of all European trees none has such claims as the oak to be considered as pre-eminently the sacred tree of the Aryans."[29] In the Germanic regions of Europe, the oak was associated with the eminent god Thor, and the Celts worshiped the oak tree as their supreme divinity. In fact, it is likely that the word for the Celtic priests, "Druids," was a Greek appellation that means "oak men," since included among other duties they attended the divinity of the oak tree.[30] The gender of a particular tree is not always set. In addition to being worshiped as a male deity, Frazer informs us that the oak was sometimes considered to be a form of the goddess Diana, with whom the attending priest might develop an intimate relationship.

"If the sacred [oak] tree which he [the priest, or 'King of the Woods'] guarded with his life was supposed, as seems probable, to be her [the Goddess Diana] special embodiment, her priest may not only have worshipped it as his goddess but embraced it as his wife. There is at least nothing absurd in the supposition, since even in the time of Pliny a noble Roman used thus to treat a beautiful beech-tree in another sacred grove of Diana on the Alban hills. He embraced it, he kissed it, he lay under its shadow, he poured wine on its trunk. Apparently he took the tree for the goddess."[31] In Greece, trees were on special occasions even dressed as Dionysus; the second-century historian Maximus Tyrius reports that "at the festival of Dionysus every peasant selected the most beautiful tree in his garden to convert it into an image of the god and to worship it."[32] Tree worship and intimate relationships with individual trees as sentient divine beings, then, seem to have been plentiful in pre-Christian Europe; Frazer reported that in his day much of this survived, though in a greatly diminished condition.

Historically the Near East has also been a major center for tree worship. Philpot observes, "In regard to the number of trees which they held sacred the Semitic nations rivalled the Greeks."[33] Altars in this region were commonly located under living sacred trees. Not only were the trees considered the natural dwelling of gods, but in many cases the tree itself was regarded as an embodied form of the divinity. In his study of the early religions of the Near East, Robertson Smith maintained that "there is also abundant evidence that in all parts of the Semitic area trees were adored as divine" and that evidence suggests that widespread in the Near East was "tree worship pure and simple, where the tree is in all respects treated as a god."[34] He observes that no Canaanite altar was complete without a sacred tree standing next to it that was deemed to be the embodied form of a deity. Prayers were addressed to the sacred tree to help in sickness and aid fertility; trees were also identified as sources of oracles, divination, and divine revelation. Sacred trees in the Near East were treated "as if they had been *real persons*,"[35] and thus there was a prohibition from plucking even a bough from such a tree. Smith focuses particular attention on the fact that in much of early Near Eastern tree worship it is assumed "that trees are animate, and have perceptions, passions and a reasonable soul."[36] He also notes that where rural populations continue to practice the "primitive rites" even into the nineteenth century, "the worship of 'solitary trees' survived the fall of the great gods of Semitic heathenism."[37] The ancient practice of tree worship continues in the Near East today, even in Israel. The anthropologist Amots Dafni testifies that trees are still worshiped in Israel in the twenty-first century as "wishing trees" for those who seek the help of the sacred trees in matters concerning health, children, good marriages, and long life. "In spite of a monotheistic ban against these ancient pagan manners of tree veneration, trees are still actively worshipped in Israel by Moslem, Druze, and Jewish people."[38]

Throughout Africa individual trees have commonly been considered the body or residence of a divine being. Sycamores, for example, were regarded in this way in ancient Egypt; Philpot notes that the sycamore was considered to be "the living body of [the goddess] Hathor upon earth."[39] In addition to being identified as the body of the tree-goddess Hathor, sycamores were also associated with other deities: "Thus the sacred sycamores of Egypt were believed to be actually inhabited by Hathor, Nuit, Selkit, Nit or some other deity, and were worshipped and presented with offerings as such."[40] Sub-Saharan Africa has also been a site of much tree worship. Frazer cites anthropological literature that suggests that certain Bantu deities in Kenya were associated with sacred fig trees and received worship in this form.[41] He also refers to the Ugandan god Jok, who takes up residence in a tree, usually a sacred fig tree. Jok was said to instruct the headman of a village in such a manner: "Do not you or any of your people cut such and such a tree, for I am present in it, and it is sacred to me."[42] Jok then instructed the headman to arrange for a shrine to be built at the base of the tree for the deity to receive offerings. Altman reports, "As late as 1917, in what was then known as the Belgian Congo, one could see a holy tree planted in front of each village house, with jars of wine under it as an offering to the tree spirits."[43] The Nuer consider certain trees to be divinities and make special offerings to them; they bring their children and sick to these sacred trees for blessings, and even receive advice from the trees about their business dealings.[44] I saw evidence of tree worship on a visit to the northern part of South Africa; here certain old trees are believed to house the souls of significant ancestors.

Peoples of Asia—besides India—have also fostered close relationships with trees. Because of their association with the Buddha, Bodhi trees have been cultivated and revered throughout much of Southeast Asia, and in some cases they have been regarded as a living presence of the Buddha. The Chewong people of Malaysia view trees as self-conscious beings capable of thoughts and feelings and approach them for benefit with great reverence.[45] Trees have been considered sacred for centuries in Thailand and have long been looked upon as the bodies of divine spirits known as *kami*s in the Shinto religion of Japan.[46] Recently trees have been saved from the chainsaw in Thailand by ordaining them as monks and wrapping them in saffron robes,[47] and in Japan by announcing publicly that they are sentient beings imbued with Buddha-nature.[48] Such acts and attitudes reveal that the relationship between trees and people is two-sided: trees nurture people as people nurture trees.

North America too has long been a site of tree worship in which a variety of mutually beneficial relationships have been pursued with particular kinds of trees believed to be powerful animate beings. Northwest Coast Indians worshiped cedar trees to insure favorable health, long life, and good luck. The anthropologist Marie Mauze reports: "Trees, especially cedar trees, were considered to be animate beings imbued with both material and spiritual value. They were believed to possess a spirit or a living force that humans should respect when interacting with trees. Conversely, this living force or vital energy could be communicated to humans, and help them throughout their lives."[49] The redwoods of the west coast have been regarded as embodied divinities worthy of great respect: "The Chilula people, who have lived for centuries in the dense pine and redwood forests near the northern California coast, believe that the sacred redwoods are not only inhabited by spirit beings, but that the trees are spirits incarnate."[50] Native Americans who inhabited the plains worshiped the cottonwood as a sacred presence. The Lakota Sioux, for example, regarded the cottonwood as "the sacred tree, that one which is standing at the center of the tree nation."[51] Although this tree was considered to be very powerful, it is also at times vulnerable and in need of human care. The Cherokee of the eastern woodlands venerated the white oak, but here too the generosity of the oaks required reciprocal care. A story is told in *The Education of Little Tree* about a time when the white oaks and the Cherokee conspired to save the white oaks from being cut down by European commercial lumbermen. The trees communicated their need to members of the Cherokee tribe, who helped destroy the logging roads. A large oak sacrificed itself by falling on a lumber wagon, and chasing away the loggers. In celebration, the Cherokee and the white oaks danced a victory dance together.[52]

The European-American experience of trees has been an ambiguous one that has involved both demonizing and divinizing them. The famous seventeenth-century Puritan minister Cotton Mather, for example, described the vast unbroken forest of New England as the "Devil's Land" or "the empire of the Antichrist," and claimed that it was filled with ominous and powerful dangers, demons, and monsters that could overcome one's soul.[53] The first order of business for many of the early Puritans was to subjugate the frightening wilderness by felling the trees and carving a garden out of its remnants. More positive relationships with trees, however, can also be found. New England Transcendentalists such as Ralph Waldo Emerson and Henry David Thoreau expressed an understanding of trees different from the dominant view of their time, as both referred to trees as "friends." Emerson penned in a poem, "Who leaves the pine-tree, leaves his friend; unnerves his strength, invites his end."[54] And Thoreau wrote, "I frequently tramped eight or ten miles through the deepest snow to keep an appointment with a beech-tree, or a yellow birch, or an old acquaintance among the pines."[55] Although neither of these statements indicates tree worship, they do imply a personal relationship with a tree. Thoreau went so far as to declare that trees possess immortal spirits. "It is the living spirit of the tree, not its spirit of turpentine, with which I sympathize, and which heals my cuts. It is as immortal as I am, and perchance will go to as high a heaven."[56] In more recent times, the iconic American nature lover John Muir expressed his devotion to redwood trees in more religious terms: "Do behold the King in his glory, King Sequoia! Behold! Behold! seems all I can say. Some time ago I left all for Sequoia and have been and am at his feet; fasting and praying for light, for is he not the greatest light in the woods, in the world? ... I'm in the woods, woods, woods, and they are in *me-ee-ee*. The King tree and I have sworn eternal love."[57]

The human impulse to venerate trees appears hard to wipe out. Today we not only witness a resurgence of it and efforts to revive earlier forms of tree worship in the contemporary Wiccan and Neo-Pagan movements of Europe and North America,[58] but also an attempt to reclaim sacred views of trees amongst those who work to preserve trees and forests.[59] Sometimes these two meet; Nathaniel Altman, for example, recently published a book titled *Sacred Trees*. He provides his reason for writing this book in the preface. "In writing this book, my hope is that more of us can become genuinely close to trees. As we get to know trees better by learning about their essential attributes, their beauty, and their roles in human culture, we can develop intimate associations with them. This deepened connection will lead us to devote ourselves more to the protection, preservation, and propagation of both individual trees and larger forest communities."[60] Altman begins with an appreciation of trees rooted in contemporary biology: "We human beings owe our lives to trees. They existed on this planet millions of years before our species came into being, and through their ability to draw carbonic acid gas from the atmosphere and assimilate carbon dioxide to make oxygen, the animal kingdom was able to evolve." From here, however, he moves quickly to a more intimate perspective, noting with encouragement that "many people feel a powerful *kinship* to trees."[61] The remainder of his book is an examination of the sacredness of trees in human history, for he believes that the real key to restoring a healthy relationship with trees comes from augmenting a biological understanding of them with a reawakening to their sacredness:

> Respect, reverence, and communion with the rest of Nature are essential for the healing process of Earth to take place. And coming toward an understanding and appreciation of sacred trees is an important (and exciting) part of this healing process. By familiarizing ourselves with ongoing discoveries of modern science related to the ecological importance of trees, and achieving and expanding an appreciation of the metaphysical aspects of trees through folklore and anthropology, we can gradually achieve new wonder, appreciation, respect, and gratitude towards the vast community of trees in our front yards, streets, parks, and forests.[62]

Trees, according to Altman, have played a very important role in the religious history of human beings. "Since the dawn of human society, trees have been viewed as having souls or spirits, the soul being the 'vital principal'[*sic*] or the 'breath of life' that is found in every living being.... Many people have considered them gods and goddesses.... The belief that trees were the homes of the gods can be found in nearly every culture where trees have played a vital role in community life. It led to both a respect and reverence for the tree itself, which was often protected from cutting or dismemberment."[63] As it was in the past, Altman advocates, so it shall be once again.

Altman is not alone in linking a more reverential attitude toward trees with an effort to better protect them. I had occasion to speak with Andy Mahler, a forest protection activist based in southern Indiana and founder of Heartwood, a national organization dedicated to protecting the hardwood forests of the American heartland. I asked him why he works so hard to protect forests. "I love trees," he said. "I work to protect forests, but trees are the most important presence in the forest. At some point in my life I imprinted on trees. I see them as family. I have developed strong emotional relationships with them and appreciate the role they play in my life." I then asked about his view of individual trees:

> There are times I walk among trees and each one speaks to me with its own personality. I have had close relationships with individual trees. There is a different kind of relationship possible with young saplings and ancient beings who have been here before white people came to these forests. Trees develop a lot of personality and character as they get older. They become very wise, and have a presence that younger trees do not have. When we cut the big mature trees we remove wise elders from the forest.

When asked if a tree is an animate sentient being with feelings and consciousness, he responded: "Of course, that's a no-brainer!" Are trees persons? "Absolutely! My experience with them tells me it's so." Do trees speak to humans? If so, what can they teach us?

> Trees can communicate with sensitive humans, but they don't use language like we do. Trees express something about the elegance of life, about becoming that which is most truly and fundamentally you. Their way of being teaches patience and the benefits of being rooted in a specific place. And they have a sense of humor; they like to be touched, hugged, and have their backs scratched. They return affection when affection is given. They provide guidance—not via specific language, but they convey a deep wisdom as to how you should conduct yourself in the world. I have known some amazing trees in my life, and they have been great teachers for me. Seen in this light we certainly should not be cutting the big old trees in the forest.

Although such views of trees remain for the most part on the periphery of American society, much is expressed within them, including the sentience, personhood, and wisdom of trees.

In sum, the worship of trees has been widespread and has played a vital role in the religious life of humans worldwide. Trees were believed to be at the very center of divine creation and manifestation in much world mythology. Groves of trees or simply the shelter of large shade trees formed temples where divinities could be encountered. Trees sometimes functioned as ladders or connectors between heaven and earth, and were used for a variety of reasons in a number of different rituals. Most importantly, however, individual trees have been regarded as the embodied forms of gods and goddesses in many different cultures, and therefore treated as animated divine persons. Absence of a firm boundary between humans and trees has led to intimate bonds between them. Trees have been approached for a multitude of purposes, and have been appreciated in religious expressions of gratitude for the vital gifts they provide. Mutually beneficial relationships have been pursued with trees, which were worshiped in quest of life blessings, such as fertility, growth, good health, companionship, protection, long life, and material abundance. Trees are also the site of divine revelation and insight, as well as great spiritual achievement, as the Buddha demonstrated long ago by attaining enlightenment under the Bodhi Tree. Regardless how they have been conceived, the mutually beneficial relationship with trees has involved reciprocal care on the part of humans. Besides a whole host of worshipful acts, this has often also lead to a resistance to cutting or harming sacred trees, driven by the understanding that trees are sentient beings with feelings and consciousness somewhat analogous to our own.

Worldviews that Inform Tree Worship in India

Although tree worship is a worldwide phenomenon, each culture views and experiences it in its own particular way. To better understand the specific nature of the worship of trees in India it is useful to be familiar with a general worldview that informs much of it. Trees are certainly approached in India with an understanding of them as sentient beings with whom humans can have intimate relationships. The Indian botanical folklorist K. D. Upadhyaya informs us, "What I want to emphasize here is the fact that trees and plants have always been treated as living human beings."[64] Similarly, the botanist Shakti Gupta reports, "In India trees and plants have been adored not only with devotion but have been affectionately fondled and almost treated as members of a family."[65] Such statements might lead one to assume that India has escaped large-scale deforestation. To be clear, this is certainly not the case. Environmental historians Madhav Gadgil and Ramachandra Guha argue that under British colonialism the forests became increasingly commoditized and were timbered heavily to serve the needs of the empire.[66] Indian teak trees, for example, were highly valued for building ships during maritime expansion, and sal, deodar, and teak were cut in large numbers for the railroad ties needed to construct a huge railway system. This led to new forest policies that caused radical changes for certain segments of Indian society in their relationships with forests and trees; the new commercial value of trees more and more determined attitudes toward them as it replaced social institutions and cultural traditions that formerly regulated forest use. The result of such changes, now augmented by the increasing resource demands and the expanding needs for more urban and agriculture land for a rapidly growing population, has led to rampant deforestation in India. Although the present government, which nationalized most of the forests after independence, has passed many laws to regulate forest use, it is not difficult to find the lasting effects of the changes that began during the colonial period: today many areas of India are denuded. Nonetheless, something of the general attitudes toward trees referred to in the statements made by Upadhyaya and Gupta has survived. This is especially true in the case of relationships with individual trees. The primary focus of this book is the specific conception of trees identified as sacred (*pavitra*) in the context of Indian tree worship. Here trees have faired much better. Moving beyond familial intimacy evident in the two statements quoted above, however, it is important to recognize that sacred trees are approached as beings rather different from ordinary humans, and this recognition takes us into the realm of religion. Sankar Sen Gupta suggests, "The nature of relation between man and tree was founded on the solid rock of religion."[67] Leaving aside the question of the solidity of religion, to better understand tree worship in India we certainly need to be familiar with the religious worldview out of which it grew.

Although there are significant differences among the specific views of individuals, a general religious worldview is assumed by most tree worshipers in India. This general worldview, however, is often expressed with a few words or by gestures rather than lengthy discourse. As Descola remarks, "Except in the western scientific tradition, representations of non-humans are not usually based on a coherent and systematic corpus of ideas. They are expressed contextually in daily actions and interactions, in lived-in knowledge and body techniques, in practical choices and hasty rituals, in all those little things that 'go without saying.'"[68] Although India does possess a long history of religious texts and sophisticated philosophical traditions, and tree worshipers in India actually have access to a systematic corpus of general ideas that inform much tree worship, I nonetheless found that tree worshipers rarely articulate this with great detail and there are virtually no texts that provide lengthy explanation of the philosophical ideas behind tree worship. Perhaps this is due to the fact that being a religion of the people, tree worship never received the royal patronage or led to the establishment of the kind of social institutions that encouraged the production of the more elaborate theological treatises created for temple worship. What Descola says applies to tree worship in India; much of the worldview that serves as a foundation for the worship of trees there is expressed with "hasty rituals, in all those little things that 'go without saying.'" Therefore, the ideas that inform this practice do require some exposition for those attempting to understand it from another culture.

In his informative book, *Trees in Indian Art, Mythology, and Folklore*, the art historian Bansi Lal Malla aptly articulates an important key to understanding a general worldview that is shared by most tree worshipers in India. "The Indian philosophy, thought, values and ethics have always had reverence for all that exists in nature, so much so that it evolved the concept that all that is alive, from plants to human species, belongs to a single family. They have originated from a common source and are interdependent. This cultural dictum was accepted by almost all religions (i.e. Hindus, Buddhists, Jains) which existed in India since ancient times. Even religions like Christianity and Islam have been influenced by these values in India."[69] The ideas expressed in Malla's statement reflect an extensive history of Indian thought; the interconnectedness and sacred nature of all life is a major tenet of Indian religious philosophy that can be traced through a long string of texts.

A good place to start tracking the thread of ideas introduced by Malla is with the earliest recorded text, the Rig Veda. Contained within this text that dates back more than three millennia is an important hymn that has had a weighty impact on the development of religious thought in India. The famous Rig Vedic hymn to Purusha is a creation myth that gives expression to a simultaneously transcendent and immanent view of ultimate reality.[70] In this influential hymn that is referenced repeatedly in later literature, the infinite and all pervasive Purusha—a term that becomes identified with the non-dual reality (Brahman) and the essence of all beings (Atman)—gets divided into two parts: one portion "rose upwards" representing the unmanifest, transcendent dimension of reality; the other portion, representing the manifest and immanent dimension of reality, "spread out in all directions" becoming all animate and inanimate things and beings. Together, these two dimensions of reality comprise the totality of all reality and give voice to the unity (as well as diversity) of all being. Everything and all beings in the world, then, are radically interconnected, for they all sprang from the very same source: the one unified Purusha. This means that all life forms share the same essence. The ideas initially expressed in the Purusha hymn were continued in subsequent texts. The oldest, longest, and philosophically perhaps most important of the Upanishads, the Brihadaranyaka Upanishad, confirms the unified nature of reality: "This very self (*atman*) is the lord and king of all beings. As all the spokes are fastened to the hub and the rim of a wheel, so to one's self (*atman*) are fastened all beings, all the gods, all the worlds, all the breaths, and all these bodies."[71] In short, everything is part of a single (or non-dual [*advaita*]) unified reality. This text explains that there are two aspects of the unified ultimate reality (Brahman or Atman): one is without form (*amurta*) and is unchanging; the other assumes forms (*murta*) and is ever-changing.[72] Thus, the unified sacred reality manifests itself as the multitude of embodied forms. The well-known Bhagavad Gita concurs, stating that there are two forms of Purusha: one is the immutable identified with the sublime; the other is the mutable identified with all contingent beings.[73] Both of these texts confirm the notion that ultimate reality is simultaneously undifferentiated and unmanifest (or transcendent), and differentiated and manifest (or immanent), and that all entities in the world are interrelated.

An account of creation that appears in the Brihadaranyaka Upanishad makes a similar point.[74] In the beginning there was only Atman, the essence of all, in the form of Purusha. This single reality, however, was lonely and bored, and therefore desired another. Motivated by this desire the one Purusha split into a male and female and proceeded to mate with itself in the form of this primordial couple to produce all beings. The Brihadaranyaka Upanishad calls this manifestation of all life forms from the one essence "Brahman's supreme-creation" (*brahmano ati-srishti*) and identifies the entire world with vital divinity ("the whole world is Brahman"). This text explains that the unified reality assumes through the process of creation many different names (*nama*) and forms (*rupa*). The notion that all entities of the world are created from the differentiation of a single divine essence is expressed repeatedly in early Hindu scripture. In short, ultimate divinity is unified and all living beings partake in the same sacred reality. This is an idea that is pervasive among most contemporary Hindus. Regardless of their direct knowledge of texts such as the Upanishads, some reference to this fundamental idea came up again and again in my conversations with tree worshipers in India.

The identification of the world with manifest divinity is further developed in the Puranas. The second chapter of the Bhagavata Purana, for example, delineates the cosmic, manifest body of God. In this description, the oceans are identified as his abdomen, the mountains his bones, the wind his breath, the rivers his veins and arteries, and the trees the hair on his body.[75] Similarly, the Devi-Bhagavata Purana identifies the world with the various parts of the body of the Great Goddess, and following the Bhagavata Purana, this text identifies trees as an important feature of the body of the Goddess.[76] Thus, in a variety of ways and in text after text the idea is expressed that all life is sacred and animated with the essential spirit of the same supreme reality; trees are certainly included as a vital part of the sacred manifest reality.

The unity of all being is an idea that continues to be expressed in India today, and is easily encountered in the teachings of many contemporary religious leaders. It is also present in the teachings of Indian environmentalists with deep roots in Gandhian thought. Gandhi himself had asserted, "All embodied life is in reality an incarnation of God."[77] For Gandhi this not only had direct consequences for the issues of human social justice he struggled to promote in the inequitable arenas of colonialism and caste but also had significant relevancy for the treatment of all life forms. "My religion embraces all life," wrote Gandhi. "I want to realize brotherhood or identity not merely with the beings called human, but I want to realize identity with all life, even with such things as crawl upon earth. I want, if I don't give you a shock, to realize identity with even the crawling things upon earth, because we claim descent from the same God, and that being so, all life in whatever form it appears must be essentially one."[78] Accordingly, Gandhi forbade the killing of snakes and the cutting of trees in his ashrams. One of Gandhi's most famous disciples, Sunderlal Bahuguna, is a founding pioneer of the modern Indian environmental movement and major spokesperson for the Chipko Movement, a group of Himalayan forest protection activists who saved trees from the lumberman's axe by "hugging" them. Bahuguna's activism is rooted in religious thought; he frequently declares, "God is in all nature."[79] Bahuguna is fond of extolling the virtues of what he calls India's "forest culture," from which he claims much of Hindu religious thought arose. Speaking of the ancient sages he explains: "The close association with nature became the basis of a philosophy of life in which they realized ... life in all creation—human beings and animals; trees and plants; rivers and mountains. They saw oneness in life.... They also developed a feeling of respect for all life and thus a worshipful attitude towards nature."[80]

The simultaneously unified and diverse (formless and formed) conception of ultimate reality also informs much Hindu religious practice. *Murti-puja*, or "worship of embodied forms of divinity," comprises the heart of a great deal of the activities that take place in a Hindu temple or home shrine. As already mentioned, early texts assert that the ultimate reality of Brahman is unmanifest and formless (*amurta*), as well as manifest as a multitude of embodied forms (*murta*). Although the majority of Hindus recognize the unmanifest dimension of Brahman, they tend to approach embodied forms of divinity for the purpose of worshipful interaction. Divinity can be more readily known and contacted in its manifest forms. As one text proclaims: "Nameless and Formless Thou art, O Thou Unknowable. All forms of the universe are Thine: thus Thou art known."[81] Therefore, while the unmanifest dimension of ultimate reality or God is clearly acknowledged within Hinduism, most rituals involve the worship (*puja*) of embodied forms of divinity, commonly called *murtis*. Understood correctly, the *murti* is not regarded as a "symbolic representation" of the divine, but rather as a body of the divine, which is simultaneously beyond all form and able to manifest as a great multitude of forms. Diana Eck maintains, "The murti is more than a likeness; it is the deity itself taken 'form.'"[82] If the *murti is* an embodied deity, not merely a symbol of the deity, then as James Preston asserts, the implications are that "*murtis* are treated as persons."[83] These are ideas that are applied to trees in India.

Whereas most Hindus acknowledge that there are a seemingly infinite number of multiple forms of divinity, they usually relate closely to a few or even a single form to which they feel particularly drawn in intimate relationship. This is in line with the relational nature of human beings. Love of humanity, for example, is certainly recognized as an important kind of love, but it is not known to be a particularly powerful or intimate kind of love. Love of a particular person, on the other hand, with whom one feels a strong attraction and develops a close bond is typically recognized as being the most robust kind of loving connection. Likewise it is with a special form of embodied divinity that an individual worshiper develops an intimate relationship; this is frequently called a *svarupa* ("own-form") in northern Indian languages. Expressed theologically, it is often said that as an act of grace God self-manifests in specific concrete accessible forms with which embodied human beings can connect and relate.

In theory, any form will do, since everything is interconnected in the unity of all Being. Some forms, however, are more attractive than others; aesthetics and affectivity are important factors in determining which forms are worshiped. This was all made clear to me in a conversation with an acquaintance in Banaras. We had just come out of a Shaivite temple where a large stone had been installed and decorated as a *linga*, the most common embodied form of Shiva, and were standing next to a pile of stones to be used in the construction of a road. My friend explained that since God is everything, any of the stones in the pile could be worshiped as a form of God, but no one seemed to be attached to any of them. On the other hand, the stone in the temple was consciously recognized to be a significant form of God and was worshiped by many as such. My friend then recited a common north Indian saying: *mano to dev, nahi to patthar*, "If it is seen or accepted as such it is God, otherwise it is just a stone." The difference is in the perspective, not in ontological status; divinity is in the eyes of the beholder. The world is shot through with divinity, but it is human nature to be more attracted to particular beings or forms than to some vague diffuse absolute. The *murti*, then, is that particular form of divinity with whom the worshiper can develop an intimate relationship through various acts of worship. Vasudha Narayanan explains the conception of the *murti* in terms of the Shri Vaishnava tradition: "This image [*murti*] is an actual and real manifestation of the deity, neither lesser than nor a symbol of other forms. It is wholly and completely God, though it does not exhaust his essence."[84] Because it is the most accessible form of God, many believe the *murti* to be superior to all other forms of God. *Puja*, the act of honoring or worshiping an embodied form of divinity, consists of loving activities such as waking the deity in the morning with affectionate songs, offering water for drinking, supplying a variety of tasty foods, bathing, decorating and dressing the body of the deity, lighting incense, and praising and entertaining with chants, music, and dance. These actions serve not only to please the deity but also to connect the devotee to the deity.

Two general types of *murti*s are found within Hindu religious practice. The first are embodied forms of divinity that are artistically crafted by human hands, generally guided by the traditions of production that have been maintained and passed down over generations. These are typically the iconographic forms of the various gods and goddesses found in Hindu temples and home shrines. The artistic forms are usually ritually installed through a procedure conducted by a Hindu priest known as *prana-pratistha* ("installation of the life breath") before the divinity is considered to be available as the *murti* for the worshiper. The second type of *murti*s are natural forms of divinity in which a god or goddess is assumed to be present without any human intervention. No installation ritual is necessary, since divinity is understood to be perpetually present in certain natural phenomena. Examples would include sacred stones, such as any stone from Mount Govardhan, which is considered to be a natural form of Krishna; natural Shiva lingas, which are often found in rivers or caves; or *shalagram*s, which are fossilized stones from the Gandaki River of Nepal that are considered to be natural forms of Vishnu. Natural *murti*s, also referred to *svarupa*s (perhaps best translated in this context as "innate forms" of God), would also include rivers, lakes, mountains, and of course, trees. In this cultural context, a tree is considered to be a particular manifestation of divinity or the embodied form of a specific god or goddess.

The History of Tree Worship in India

What makes the worship of trees in India exceptional among worldwide tree worship is the long history of uninterrupted practice that has continued there dynamically to the present day. Although the forests of India have been as ravaged by commercial logging and urban and agricultural clearings as anywhere else in the world, a reverential conception of trees can be traced back to the beginning of South Asian history that still informs many practices directed toward individual trees in India today. Since ethnographic data for earlier historical periods does not exist, it is difficult to determine how different the performance of tree worship was from what it is now. Presumably such things as the specific offerings made to trees would have been defined by the ritual customs and materials available during a particular time period. While it is important to acknowledge differences between ancient forms of tree worship and its contemporary practice, examination of some common features of Indian tree worship that cover a large expanse of time is useful to better understand tree worship as it is currently enacted.

In general, trees have been considered animate beings associated with growth, longevity, vitality, generosity, and fertility. The gifts they provide are physical—material well-being, excellent health, good luck, delightful marriage, vigorous children, and so forth—as well as spiritual—they aid in attaining religious healing, divination, heaven, liberation, or enlightenment. Moreover, trees are natural expressions of the seemingly inexhaustible ability of life to regenerate itself endlessly. Reflecting on this feature in Indian literature, Albertina Nugteren remarks: "Poets express their awe at this continuous flow of life force, and they stand in wonder before this constantly renewing life. Trees are images *par excellence* of this circuit."[85] The amazing abilities of trees were attributed to the fact that they are linked to all three realms vertically (roots in the underworld, trunk in the surface world, and branches reaching up to the heavenly world), and are thus a connector of these realms and an ideal place for people to meet with gods and spirits. Trees are therefore regarded as cosmic centers, but more mundanely are also often situated in the heart of a village or temple compound and provide a focus for a variety of social and religious activities. In addition to trees being recognized as a good place to meet the gods, they have long been considered the very bodies of various divinities. No matter how trees have been conceived, they have been approached for some kind of mutually beneficial exchange with the understanding that communication between humans and trees is quite possible.

The earliest evidence of tree worship on the subcontinent is found within the archeological remnants in the Indus River Valley, where an urban civilization flourished over four thousand years ago. All conclusions drawn from this ancient data are highly speculative, but archeological evidence from ancient Indus Valley settlements suggests that trees were regarded as divine beings, and many have argued that tree worship was an essential feature of Indus Valley religion. Sir John Marshall, one of the earliest archeologists to write on the Indus Valley Civilization, studied the pictorial images of trees on the pottery shards and clay seals found at various sites, and concluded that tree worship was prevalent among the early inhabits of the Indus Valley. He believed that two forms of tree worship were practiced there: the tree itself was worshiped and also tree spirits were worshiped in personified form.[86] The next scholar to take up the work of exploring and interpreting the archeological evidence found at the sites of the ancient cities in the Indus Valley was E. J. H. Mackay, who maintained that the early inhabitants of the Indus Valley worshiped both pipal and neem trees as divinities.[87] The scholar K. N. Sastri went so far as to declare, "The *pipal* god was the supreme deity of the Indus valley."[88] After recognizing the presence of tree-spirits on the seals found in the Indus Valley, the art historian Benjamin Rowland wrote, "Their appearance furnishes positive proof that the cult of tree-spirits mentioned in the *Yajur* and *Atharva Vedas* had its origin in the Indus culture."[89] After reviewing the evidence for early tree worship in the Indus Valley Civilization, Malla concludes: "Probably many religious beliefs and traditions of the Indus people were inherited by the Vedic Aryans. It may reasonably be deduced that the *pipal* god of the Indus people held similar position even in the remote pre-Vedic age."[90] It is difficult to evaluate the truth of these strong claims; however, archeological evidence does seem to indicate that trees were conceived of as divine beings and as such played a noteworthy role in the earliest religious activities of the Indus Valley.

Natural phenomena were worshiped as gods of nature in the early Vedic culture that superseded the Indus Valley Civilization; this included praise of the sun, fire, wind, water, and certainly trees. Early Rig Vedic hymns—dating back well over three thousand years—recognize the healing capability and sacred powers of trees and other plants, which are addressed as mother goddesses by healers: "Mothers, you have a hundred forms and a thousand growths. You who have a hundred ways of working, make this man whole for me.... You mothers who are called plants, I say to you who are goddesses.... In the sacred fig-tree [*ashvattha*] is your home; in the leaves your dwelling-place has been made."[91] For this reason the blessings of trees were sought in several Rig Vedic hymns.[92] The pipal, or *ashvattha* tree as it is known in Sanskrit, in particular was singled out for special metaphysical consideration. Malla remarks: "The *asvattha* tree was made the basis of a profound metaphysical doctrine in Vedic times....*Asvattha* is said to be abode of all gods.... In the later Vedic texts *asvattha* is regarded as *Brahma-taru*—the embodiment of knowledge and the Great creator. That is why *asvattha* is called on certain occasions as 'tree of life' or the 'tree of creation.'"[93]

The Upanishads give clear expression to the idea that all beings are interconnected and share in the same essence (*brahman* or *atman*); the unified reality of Atman or Brahman certainly includes trees. The Brihadaranyaka Upanishad identifies trees as being the hairs on the cosmic sacrificial horse from which came the entire world, and the Aitareya Upanishad identifies trees with the hairs on the cosmic Person (*Purusha*) from which all beings arose.[94] The Chandogya Upanishad identifies the "finest essence" of a tree with the finest essence that pervades the entire universe, animates all beings, and "constitutes the self of the whole world."[95] The Shvetashvatara Upanishad celebrates the "God who pervades everything," but who is identified specifically as the God who abides in all beings and natural elements, including trees.[96] Although no description of tree worship is found in the early Upanishads, all of these texts agree that there is no sharp ontological boundary separating trees, humans, or any other kind of being; they all share a common essence. Later Upanishads, however, such as the Bilva Upanishad, allude to tree worship directly: "To Bilvopanisad the *bilva*-tree is nothing but the form of Lord Siva.... the worship of the *bilva*-tree is referred to on par with the worship of the Lord Siva himself."[97]

It is in the context of temple Hinduism, however, that we encounter tree worship in unequivocal form. Some scholars maintain that in an early period gods were first worshiped in India in the natural form of a tree rather than in a form crafted by human hands and placed in a temple. The art historian Venkata Ramanayya, for example, contends:

> The various gods and goddesses whom the indigenous population of the peninsula worshipped were not accustomed to dwell in the secluded atmosphere of the temples; they loved the life in the open.... In a large number of villages, the *gramadevatas* [village deities] have no temples at all; they are lodged in the open air in the shadow of a big tree. In a good number of villages, no object is placed to represent the deity. In all these places, the tree itself is regarded as the embodiment of the deity.... These instances are enough to show that the gods of South India had no temples at the beginning. Almost all of them were worshipped in the form of trees.[98]

Once again it is difficult to assess such claims with any certainly; however, in the Puranic period—during a time when texts were being produced that discussed temple construction and practices—trees still continued to be considered as the embodied forms of gods and goddesses. It is in the Puranas that textual notions of trees and tree worship are most fully developed and articulated, though even here the descriptions of actual practices are few and brief. Nonetheless, this collection of Hindu texts remains the best source for scriptural notions about trees. Although there seems to be more diversity with regard to the theistic identity of particular trees in contemporary tree worship than in Puranic texts, there is much variety to be found here too, for the conception of divinity developed within Hindu theism includes both an assumed unity as well as a manifest diversity of divine being.

The Puranas—the term literally means "ancient"—are a group of early texts that date from the beginning of the first millennium and give expression to vital religious thought and practices. These fluid and developing texts are compilations of multiple authors over long periods of time (making them difficult to date) that reflect oral and living traditions. The Puranas constitute the principal scriptures of theistic, temple-based Hinduism and are a treasure house for cultural practices that stretch over a period of almost two thousand years. Concerning them, Ludo Rocher writes: "The Puranas are, first, important documents for the study and reconstruction of the history of Hindu India. In a more practical way, they have contributed to the continuity of Hinduism through the ages, and are indispensable for a correct understanding of Hinduism today. As a matter of fact, every Hindu is influenced by the Puranas, and his activities are guided by them."[99] Many Puranic texts explicitly express the notion that a tree is an embodied form of a deity. The Skanda Purana, for example, declares: "The great wonder is that gods take the form of trees."[100] And speaking specifically of the supreme deity Vishnu: "Visnu is the tree itself. It is the form of Visnu."[101] The Padma Purana states: "Oh! There is no other form of Visnu on earth like this tree-form, viz. the holy fig tree.... the god in the form of the holy fig tree is most adorable."[102]

Because trees are considered to be divine beings, the Puranas extol the virtues of planting them. Planting of trees keeps one from misfortune in this life and the next, and results in great karmic and heavenly rewards. Planting trees is considered to be so beneficial that the Matsya Purana announces that planting a tree is the most precious and fruitful gift possible:

> A pond is equal to ten wells;
> Ten ponds are equal to one lake;
> Ten lakes are equal to one son;
> And ten sons are equal to one tree.[103]

The Padma Purana declares: "Those who plant trees will attain the highest position."[104] Additionally, "By planting a tree a person does not fall from heaven."[105] This text further elaborates a list of the benefits of planting trees. These include long life, avoidance of hell, great prosperity, wealth, and healthy offspring. The Matsya Purana states that by planting just one tree, people obtain all their desires, achieve heaven, liberate their ancestors, and attain the highest perfection.[106] Concomitantly, the Puranas lay out the consequences of harming trees. A person who cuts an *ashvattha* tree, for example, is said to suffer for a long time in hell and then be reborn in a very low state.[107]

Expression of these ideas endured in some manner throughout history. In the sixteenth century, for example, the notion that various gods and goddesses took the form of trees to better observe Krishna's playful activities in the area of Braj was articulated in religious texts and continues to be expressed in literature down to the present. A seventeenth-century text describes how a devotee was given sight of the form of Krishna within every leaf on all the trees of Braj, and a twentieth-century hymn celebrates how various gods took the forms of trees in Braj to witness Krishna's play there.[108] Certain trees in Braj are never cut or harmed, since they are assumed to be the embodied forms of special beings who have assumed the bodies of trees to enjoy Krishna's ongoing activities there.[109] While living in Banaras I observed many signs posted on the protective cages placed around the trunks of trees. One in the residential neighborhood of Ravindrapuri reads: "God resides in this tree" (*vriksha me ishvar ka vas hai*). I spoke with Rana P. B. Singh, Professor of Geography at Banaras Hindu University, and asked him why trees are commonly worshiped in India. "Because," he told me, "people believe that they can communicate directly with the gods by approaching a tree." Discernable in all of this is a general cultural conviction about the divine and animate nature of trees.

Reverential attitudes toward trees in India are today sometimes exemplified—particularly by Chipko leaders—with the story of the early eighteenth-century heroine Amrita Devi and the Bishnois of Rajasthan.[110] According to this narrative, the Bishnois followed a code that prohibited the cutting of a live tree. Their children were raised to love trees and had their own special tree they would hug and talk to. Amrita Devi was one such child who carried these ideas with her into adulthood. One day the peace of her village was shattered when the king's axmen arrived to log the Bishnois' forest to fire the royal kiln. When Amrita Devi saw the men approaching the village trees, she rushed toward them, explained the Bishnoi faith, and pleaded with them not to cut the trees. Seeing that the axmen were unmoved by her pleas, Amrita Devi hugged the first tree marked for felling, uttering her famous words: "A chopped head is cheaper that a felled tree."[111] In anger an axman swung his ax into her body, and she fell to the ground dead. Her three daughters immediately took her place by hugging three more trees, and they too were brutally killed by the axmen. After some time more Bishnois joined in the protest, and by the end of the day 359 more were slaughtered while hugging trees. When the king heard what had occurred he was horrified and immediately halted the timber harvesting. While visiting the scene of the massacre the king apologized to the Bishnois and promised them that they would never again be asked to provide timber, nor would any of their special trees ever be cut. Forest-defending Chipko members, who not only hug trees to protect them, but also wrap them with sacred thread and recite sacred texts beneath them, draw both inspiration and determination from this story which gives testimony to the extremely high regard in which some people hold trees.

Sacred trees are known to give generously without ever becoming exhausted. For this reason virtually all sacred trees in India have been considered a *kalpa-vriksha*, the famous mythological "Wishing-Tree" that yields many kinds of favorable riches, insures fertile offspring, and fulfills all manner of desires, including spiritual enlightenment. The *kalpa-vriksha* is identified in the Puranas as one of the wonderful things that came out of the churning of the ocean by the gods and demons to secure the ambrosia of immortality. This tree has the power of giving anything that one wishes to receive. One of the earliest representations of the *kalpa-vriksha* is a piece of sculpture from the third century B.C.E. now housed in the Calcutta Museum.[112] At the base of the tree are pots, bags of money, a lotus flower, and a conch shell exuding coins. A tree sculpted into a stone railing in Bodhgaya that dates back to the first century B.C.E. depicts two hands of a tree god reaching out to give a man food and drink.[113] Although the *kalpa-vriksha* has a specific identity in Hindu mythology, many people regard any sacred tree as a type of *kalpa-vriksha* or Wishing-Tree. Nugteren writes of the Wishing-Tree: "The tree was considered the abode of a wish-fulfilling deity, male or female.... In order to have one's wishes granted one had to invoke the deity by name, offer words of praise as well as material gifts."[114] Nugteren believes the association of trees with wish-fulfilling abilities has to do with the fact that their roots stretch deep into the earth where precious substances such as gems, gold, and life-giving water are located. Regardless, the divine power of the Wishing-Tree is conceived of in a number of ways. "In this complex of ideas and practices the position of the tree itself varies: its wish-granting properties may be perceived as (a) coming directly and more or less naturalistically from the tree itself, (b) coming through the agency of a tree or its derivative, such as the sacrificial stake, and (c) coming from an anthropomorphized and personified tree deity to whom the tree provides merely an abode, a locus, and who has an existence independent of the tree. In some rare passages trees are spoken of as sentient beings who can feel, talk, act, even move."[115] My own sense is that the boundaries between these conceptions are not firm, and that a single wish-fulfilling tree might be viewed through a combination of these possibilities. However regarded, one appeals to the generosity of the Wishing-Tree by honoring or worshipping it with a variety of praises and offerings.

Puranic literature often identifies "Five Sacred Trees," or the Panchavati, as being the most worthy of worship. These typically include the *Ashvattha* or pipal tree (holy fig or *ficus religiosa*); the *vata* or *bargad* (banyan or *ficus indica*); the *bilva* or *shriphala* tree (bel, wood-apple or *aegle marmelos*); the *amala*, *ambla*, or *amlaki* tree (myrobalan or *emblica officinalis*); and the *nimba* or *nima* (neem, margosa or *melia azadirachta*). This remains a fairly standard and widely recognized list. I was speaking to a priest of a small Hanuman temple in Banaras one day about the sacredness of trees. I asked him how he views trees. "All trees are sacred [*pavitra*]," he informed me, "but five types are especially [*khas*] sacred." He went on to name the five species just mentioned. I came across a few sites in the Banaras region where these trees had been planted together intentionally as a group. A Shiva temple named Narmadeshwar Mahadev, for example, which is located in a village called Shivapur on the pilgrimage circuit around the periphery of city of Banaras, is surrounded by these five sacred trees. A neem tree stands before a Shitala shrine to the northeast side of the central Shiva temple, a banyan tree to the southeast, an amala tree to the south, a pipal tree to the southwest, and a bel tree—often considered to be an embodied form of Shiva, grows on the northwest side of the temple. One of the priests of this temple explained to me that all five are *pujaniya*—"worthy of worship." Clear signs of recent worship were present the day I visited this temple. The neem tree was wrapped with bright orange and red cloth, red sindur had been smeared on the trunk, and incense and flowers were scattered about its base. The banyan tree had old string hanging on it from previous ritual activity, as did the amala tree, and the trunk of the pipal tree was freshly smeared with sindur paste from recent worship. Many I spoke with attributed the sacred designation of these trees to the fact that they have beneficial medicinal qualities. Since I discuss the pipal, banyan, and neem trees in detail in the following chapters, here I illustrate some of the exemplary medicinal qualities and concomitant sacred conceptions of these five trees with the *amala* tree.

The amala tree (also known as *ambla, amlaki*) is a type of myrobalan whose scientific name is *emblica officinalis*, but is often called the Indian Gooseberry. It is commonly included in the Panchavati list of five sacred trees and has long been worshiped for its nourishing fruit and promise of spiritual blessings. The amala tree is a small tree with leathery leaves and ping-pong ball-sized fleshy fruit, which is a potent source of vitamin C and is used in many Ayurvedic medicines. Because of its beneficial medicinal effects, the fruit is also a favorite ingredient in many chutneys. The name amala literally means "pure," but due to the medicinal quality of its fruit, it is also taken to mean the "sustainer."[116] Moreover, the designation amala is a name of Lakshmi, linking this tree with the goddess of abundance, well-being, and good fortune. Because of the nurturing nature of its fruit, however, the amala tree is generally considered to be a form of the goddess Mother Earth, who is worshiped in this form to destroy sins, insure health and safety for the family, and help attain individually desired ends.[117] It is especially worshiped these days on Akshaya Navmi, the ninth day of the bright half of the lunar month of Kartik. This fell on October 31st in the year 2006 during the period I conducted most of my research in Banaras. A priest of the famous Annapurna temple in Banaras explained that on this day one is to take a bath in the Ganges, put on new clothes, and worship an amala tree with a variety of offerings.[118] As part of this ritual worshipers are to wrap the amala tree nine times with red and yellow *kalava* string and wave an honorific camphor flame before the tree with hopes of having their wishes fulfilled. Participants are then to prepare and enjoy a meal under this therapeutic wish-granting tree.

In addition to the five sacred trees identified as the Panchavati, other trees regarded and worshiped as sacred beings include banana and kadamba trees. Although not as common as the three main species that dominate tree shrines, these too demonstrate some general characteristics of conceptions of sacred trees in India, which are typically regarded as animate divine beings. Banana trees are frequently worshiped on Thursdays and are conceived of as the god Brihaspati, a planetary deity (Jupiter) associated with power, intellect, and leadership. I visited a banana tree shrine in the small compound of a Kali temple near Triveni Ghat in Rishikesh, for the banana tree is also linked to the goddess Kali.[119] Signs of worship were clearly evident: red strings had been wrapped around the tree's trunk, garlands of marigold flowers were strung in its branches, and incense and water offerings had been made at its base, around which several Shiva *linga*s and images of Ganesha had been placed. Because of the fluid nature of the religious ideas associated with trees in India, the identity of the god or goddess connected with a particular tree is not firmly set; a single species can be identified with more than one god or goddess. I asked a woman I encountered worshiping this tree about its identity. "This tree is Kali," she said. I spoke with the priest of this temple about the central tree, and he informed me that it was "an embodied form [*svarupa*] of Brihaspati Bhagavan." The reasons people approach these deities also vary. This same priest reported: "If people are having problems in their life, then this worship can take them away. For example, if a man cannot find a job he prays here and good work will come to him." The woman I met here told me she worshiped the banana tree to make her life "auspicious" (*shubha*). This banana tree demonstrates, then, that in the context of Indian tree worship a tree is considered to be a powerful and animate divine being, whose identity can vary, but is able in whatever form to nurture life and fulfill a variety of wishes for a person who approaches the tree respectfully with prayers and offerings.

The religious treatment of kadamba trees—a species closely associated with Krishna that is well-known for its fragrant spherical white and yellow flowers—is also illustrative of some general features of the conceptions of sacred trees in India. I had occasion to observe the worship of a kadamba tree in the context of women's rituals during the lunar month of Kartik, a month known to be particularly auspicious for religious practice. The fifth day after the end of this month is a special day for worshiping kadamba trees in the region of Banaras. During the entire month of Kartik women gather early in the morning at Assi Ghat and other places along the river, and sit in circles to worship Krishna and sing songs about his divine love.[120] Worship of a kadamba tree that grows above Assi Ghat serves as the culmination of the month's ritual activity for the women who assemble at this ghat. I was present for the concluding worship of the Assi Ghat kadamba tree in November 2006 and then again in November 2008.[121] On the latter occasion I reached Assi Ghat just before six in the morning as the eastern horizon was brightening; a crowd of women had already assembled at the tree. Many were circling the tree when I arrived, singing devotional songs to Krishna, wrapping the tree with red and yellow string, and decorating it with colorful pieces of cloth. At some point all of them poured water from an assortment of brass pots onto the roots of the tree and made an offering at its base. Each of the women made physical contact with the tree; many massaged its trunk with eager affection. Overall the atmosphere was festive and joyful.

The women I spoke with regarded this tree as the "Krishna tree." They referred to two narratives while identifying it as Krishna's favorite tree, since Krishna climbed into a kadamba tree on two important occasions.[122] In the first, he ascended a kadamba tree after stealing the clothes of a group of young cowherd women (*gopis*) who were engaged in an austere winter ritual bath in the Yamuna River aimed to secure Krishna as their beloved. Krishna—the ever-playful lover—snuck up on them, collected their clothes, and scampered up a kadamba tree before addressing the women and demanding that they come before him naked to retrieve their clothing. This story has great meaning for the Assi Ghat women who strive for a loving encounter with Krishna, and a kadamba tree is the favored site for such a meeting. On another special occasion Krishna sounded his alluring flute from high in a kadamba during the autumn full moon to call the cowherd women to a rendezvous for a night of dancing and love-making deep in the flowering forest of Vrindaban. In this incident too the kadamba tree is viewed as a special place to have an intimate encounter with Krishna. The women worshiping this tree informed me that they were here to experience and celebrate Krishna's love and their love for Krishna. One told me with a giggle, "Krishna is our boyfriend and we are here to dance with him."

The kadamba is associated with Krishna in at least two significant ways. Some of the women accounted for the specialness of the kadamba tree by the fact that it is a favorite residence of Krishna. One explained: "We are doing this worship [*puja*] because Krishna likes the kadamba tree. We do this once a year at the end of our Kartik puja. We tie cloth in the tree because Krishna put the gopis' clothes in this tree and also he sits in this tree to call the gopis (his female lovers) to him with his flute." But some of the women's understanding of the kadamba tree went much further than this; although a text such as the Bhagavata Purana does not state this in any explicit way, they identified this very tree as a form of Krishna. In one of my initial conversations two women told me: "We see this tree as Krishna. Just as Krishna called the gopis to him with his flute, this tree calls us to him for love [*prem*]. Many kadamba trees are worshiped on this day. But this one is *our* Krishna." When I asked a woman who had just finished worshiping the tree why she did this, she replied simply, "Because it is Krishna." Many women concurred by informing me, "This tree is Krishna Bhagavan." I questioned another woman who was participating in the celebration; she reported: "This is a kadamba tree. It is Krishna. So we are all here honoring [*manti*] Bhagavan in this way." In exemplary fashion, the kadamba tree illustrates another common feature of conceptions of sacred trees in India: some tree worshipers identify them as the residence (*vas*) of a deity, whereas others identify them as an embodied form (*rupa*) of that deity. Although there seems to be a very strong preference for the latter view, I found this difference reflected in both textual sources and my ethnographic interviews.

Much can be learned from a survey of the conceptions of trees in the context of tree worship worldwide: trees have not only been commonly thought of as animate beings but also as powerful divine beings who when approached in a respectful manner offer in return life-enhancing benefits to human beings. While a wide variety of tree worship has been practiced in virtually every part of the world, Indian tree worship assumes a particular mode that is informed by a specific worldview. Much Hindu tree worship is rooted in a widespread religious notion that all of life is interrelated and sacred. Trees are considered to be a vital part of the totality of reality and are closely associated with the great divinity who pervades everything. Moreover, trees are considered to be either the favored homes of powerful gods or goddesses, or more commonly, the embodied forms of such divinities. In addition to recognizing an unmanifest dimension of divinity, Hindus assert that divinity assumes a variety of physical forms. One of the most accessible types of these is a neighborhood tree. Trees in India are generally associated with vitality, generosity, fertility, and longevity, and are typically approached for good health, abundant life, overall well-being, and spiritual advancement. Although Hindu texts such as the Puranas express much about general notions of trees, they provide little specificity with regard to the theological identification of trees, and almost nothing by way of concrete descriptions of the worship of sacred trees. To understand tree worship in India as an actual lived practice, it is necessary to turn to contemporary ethnography, bearing in mind that contemporary practice may differ in some respects from that of the past. To accomplish this, I examine in the next four chapters three types of sacred trees with the aim of providing detailed accounts of a variety of tree shrines and the ritual worship that takes place at them, as well as the theological conceptions of the trees at the center of these shrines. Well rooted in the fertile context of Indian tree worship, I proceed with an eye on questions raised in the first chapter that are associated with animism, anthropomorphism, and other related issues frequently denigrated in modern discourse about religion.

Among all sacred trees the most important are the pipal, neem, and banyan, with the pipal tree occupying the preeminent position. During a conversation about sacred trees, a man sitting under a pipal tree in Banaras explained to me: "The pipal is the most important tree because it is Vasudeva [a common name for the All-Encompassing God Vishnu]. People worship it for the benefit of their souls [*atman*]. People worship the neem for good health, and they worship the banyan for long life. These are the three most sacred [*pavitra*] trees." Most people I spoke with in northern India readily agreed with this introductory statement; pipal, neem, and banyan trees are declared again and again to be the most sacred of all trees, and they are certainly the three most frequently found at the center of a tree shrine in this part of the world. I, therefore, move on to explore in the following four chapters the rich and varied world associated with each of these three primary sacred trees. Who are these trees for those who interact with them in significant ways in northern India? And what forms does this interaction take?

3

King of Trees

Among all trees I am the Ashvattha [Pipal].
—Krishna speaking in the Bhagavad Gita

O Ashvattha, I honor you, King of Trees,
who are the residence of sacrificial fire
and the perpetual abode of Govinda [Krishna].
May you remove all my misfortunes.
—Sanskrit mantra for worshiping the pipal tree

The Lord of the World [Buddha] worshiped you O Maha-Bodhi [Pipal] Tree.
I too worship you. All honor to you, O King of Enlightenment!
—Buddhist Pali Gatha

Somvati Amavasya Vrat

The early morning light filters softly through the verdant leaves of a large pipal tree growing near Assi Ghat in Banaras as a ring of eight women dressed in colorful saris gracefully circle round it. After pouring small pots of water on its roots, they circumambulate the stout tree clockwise 108 times; two wrap it with red and yellow cotton string. With each revolution the women stop at their own personal altar set up at the base of the tree, make an offering they had carried around it in their right hand, and then reach up and smear a dab of bright orange sindur paste to the trunk of the tree with the ring finger of their right hand. Incense from the altars fills the air. As they finish their 108 orbits, each woman squats at the base of the tree and massages it with attentive affection. The women are in high spirits, and the tree itself is radiant in its adornment of special multicolored string, bright flowers, and colorful pieces of cloth (figure 3.1).

Although pipal trees are worshiped every day of the year by many people throughout India, this day was special. It was a Somvati Amavasya, a day the new moon happens to fall on a Monday. Whenever this occurs women in the holy city of Banaras celebrate the Somvati Amavasya Vrat. A *vrat* is a votive ritual

Figure 3.1 Women performing the Somvati Amavasya Vrat in Banaras

conducted for the welfare of oneself and others, and usually has a specific goal, such as a happy marriage, healthy family, prosperity, or some other life blessing. Although in theory *vrats* can be performed by men, they are typically performed by women, and almost always involve fasting and the devotional worship of some deity.[1] Moreover, *vrat*s are usually accompanied by stories that narrate how someone—generally a woman—saved her family from some danger by the performance of the *vrat* vow. Women in Banaras performing the Somvati Amavasya Vrat take an early morning bath in the Ganges River, begin a fast for the day, and proceed to worship a pipal tree. I had two opportunities to observe the Somvati Amavasya Vrat during my year of residence in Banaras, since the new moon fell on a Monday twice while I was there: once on November 20, 2006, the new moon of the lunar month of Margashirsh, and the second time on March 19, 2007, the new moon of the lunar month of Chaitra. Both were grand occasions in which most of the numerous pipal trees in the city of Banaras were worshiped according to the conventions of the Somvati Amavasya Vrat.

I arrived early at Assi Ghat on both days this special *vrat* was to be performed, making my way to three pipal trees that grow here and are frequented by many tree worshipers. I watched a woman dressed in a turquoise and magenta sari, her long shiny hair tied neatly into a bun, remove her sandals and approach one of the trees reverently. Standing near the tree, she looked up into its branches for a few moments with her hands joined together in prayer. She then bent down and made a water offering, pouring it slowly onto the roots of the tree from a small copper pot while chanting "*Vasudevaya namah*" (All honor to Vasudeva!). She lit a few sticks of incense and pressed them into the ground at the base of the tree and then took some marigold flowers from a plastic wicker basket and placed these carefully near the incense. Once she had finished this, she took out a small piece of orange cloth and spread it out on the ground before the tree. She hung a garland of flowers just above the bright cloth, hooking it to a rough piece of bark on the trunk of the tree, and then offered two green guava fruits, some white sugar crystals, and several red bangles on her cloth altar. Next she got up, tied a red and yellow string around the tree, and walking round it clockwise seven times, wrapped the trunk of the tree to honor and establish a mutually protective relationship with it. Returning to her altar, she laid out a leaf bowl containing bright orange sindur paste and a bag of uncooked white rice. Taking a small amount of the rice in her right hand, she joined the colorful swirl of women circling the tree. Each time she returned to her altar she sprinkled the rice onto the orange cloth. She then reached down into the leaf bowl, took some sindur paste on the ring finger of her right hand, and stretched up to dab this onto the upper trunk of the tree (figure 3.2). (Sindur paste is a substance commonly placed between the eyes on the forehead of a person one wishes to honor.) Taking up another handful of rice, she repeated this ritual process 108 times. Once she had finished her revolutions of the tree, she went back to her personal altar, crouched down, and began massaging the foot of the tree with evident tenderness for several minutes. After this, she stood up, and placing both of her hands lightly on the sides of the tree, hugged it while touching her forehead gently to its trunk. Gathering into the plastic wicker basket her instruments of worship and taking one last look up into the upper branches of the tree, she turned and walked away.

I observed many women perform the worship of a pipal tree during both of the Somvati Amavasya Vrats I attended. Some wrapped the tree with white string, while others used plain red or plain yellow, but most swathed it with a red and yellow multicolored string. In addition to establishing a cloth altar at the base of the tree, one woman applied a piece of yellow cloth to the trunk of a pipal tree with a paste made of moist turmeric powder, and proceeded to make her offerings of sindur on this cloth with each of her 108 circumambulations. Some women added colorful pieces of cloth to the tree by weaving them into the abundant string wrapped around the tree. One woman touched her handful of rice offerings to the tree briefly before placing it on her altar of gold-colored cloth. A few waved tiny clay honorific oil lamps before the tree. And some intoned Sanskrit mantras as they circled the tree. I even saw a few women embrace and kiss the pipal tree they were worshiping (figure 3.3). Although each worshiped the tree in her own way, most women followed a procedure similar to the one described above.

Why do these women perform this ritual in which the central act is the worship of a pipal tree? And how do they conceive of the pipal tree? The most common answer I received to the first question was the single word "*suhag.*" This is a Hindi

Figure 3.2 Worshiper applying sindur paste to honor this pipal tree

version of a longer Sanskrit word: *saubhagya*. Both of these words mean "a fortunate or blessed state," but typically refer to the auspicious state of a happily married woman. Thus, the majority of women perform the Somvati Amavasya Vrat to experience marital love and domestic happiness and avoid the inauspicious state of widowhood through their ritual pursuit of the general welfare and long life of their husbands. But this is not true for all women performing this ritual. One woman I talked with explained: "Look, not all of these women do this for *suhag*. Yes some do, but others do it to get a good marriage, others for a child or to fulfill some personal wish, and still others for the good health of some family member. But all do it for the well-being of the family. To make all in the family healthy, happy, and peaceful [*shant*]."[2] To a large degree this is a ritual that aids the religious duties and desires of women, who are in charge of the well-being of the family.[3] Another woman who had just finished her 108 revolutions of a large pipal tree added: "We are doing this to be close to God [Bhagavan]. We worship this particular tree because it is big and old,

Figure 3.3 A Somvati Amavasya Vrat participant kissing a pipal tree

and has much power. Look, there are smaller ones, but for us this is the place to worship. Much peace comes from this worship. We also do this for the long life and good health of our family members, especially our husbands." Women expressed the idea that the worship of a pipal tree is an important aspect of their religious responsibility: "We do this to honor God. This is part of our Hindu religion [*dharma*]. We worship the pipal tree as God." Aside from familial goals, many women performing this ritual said that they do it for their own happiness and "peace of mind." One woman told me that she worshiped a pipal "to develop a positive relationship [*nata*] with the tree." Another told me something similar: "We do this to worship and honor God, to show our appreciation for life, and establish a beneficial relationship with the pipal tree. And this brings peace of mind."

In response to my inquiries, many of the women identified their theological conceptions of the pipal tree: "We worship Vishnu in the form of this tree. This tree is a part [*amsha*] of Vishnu, and the pipal is worshiped on this day for *suhag*." Another woman said: "We worship this tree as Vasudeva [Vishnu] to receive the blessings [*ashirbad*] of Vasudeva. We get our desires [*kamana*] fulfilled in this way." Others stated that they did not necessarily seek any specific personal results from this worship, but did it simply to honor Vishnu in the form of a pipal tree: "We do this to worship Vasudeva, who resides in this tree. We just honor him in this way." A woman standing nearby agreed, "Yes, we do this to show respect [*adar*] to Vishnu in the form of this tree." Another woman informed me: "The pipal is Vasudeva, but beneath it all the gods reside. We do this for peace [*shant*], that's all." Yet another woman explained to me that those performing this ritual worshiped not only Vishnu on this day but also his consort Lakshmi, the Goddess of Abundance. Others concurred: "This tree is Vasudeva, but Lakshmi is with him here too, so we worship them both. The red bangles are for her." One woman, who seemed to have had a good knowledge of Puranic accounts of the pipal tree, told me: "Brahma resides in the roots of the pipal, Vishnu in the trunk, Mahadeva [Shiva] in the branches, and all the gods on each and every leaf. This tree is very sacred [*pavitra*] and all good things come from it. Scientists have proven that it produces more oxygen than any other tree; therefore, good health and peaceful life for all beings come from it." Regardless of why they perform this ritual, then, the pipal tree is typically considered to be either the residence of Vasudeva (another name for Vishnu), or more commonly, an actual embodied form of Vasudeva by the women who worship it as part of their Somvati Amavasya Vrat. This is in line with the general notions of tree divinities introduced in the last chapter, and the fact that most people hold the latter view makes reconsideration of animism and related issues more relevant. The view that the pipal tree is a form of Vishnu is also more allied with the story to be told about this vrat below. Moreover, although the great majority of women performing the Somvati Amavasya Vrat regard the pipal tree as an embodied form of Vishnu, a range of other theological conceptions could be applied to this tree; in theory the pipal tree can be conceived of in the form of any divinity. Women participating in this ritual certainly view the tree as a powerful sentient being with whom they can establish a mutually beneficial relationship. They believe that by nurturing and honoring the pipal tree with conventional modes of Hindu worship they will in return receive life-blessings in a great variety of forms.

Following the advice of one of my informants, I purchased a small pamphlet describing the Somvati Amavasya Vrat and accompanying story.[4] Copies of this pamphlet are readily available at several of the outdoor stalls located at Assi Ghat, and I noticed a few women reading this text on the days the Somvati Amavasya Vrat was performed. The pamphlet contains a section of a Sanskrit text, the Bhavishyottara Purana, as well as a Hindi translation and commentary. The description of the ritual procedure is brief and fairly simple. This text advises the practitioner to begin observance of the *vrat* with a resolve (*sankalpa*) to worship Vishnu along with Lakshmi at the base of an Ashvattha or pipal tree in order to fulfill one's highest desire. After making a water offering (*udaka*) to the pipal tree, the text instructs ritual participants to wrap the tree with string, worshiping Vishnu at its base while circumambulating the tree 108 times. Like most pamphlets of this nature, it contains a story narrating how the *vrat* came into existence and illustrating the effectiveness of the *vrat*.

The epic narrator Suta tells the story of how King Yudhishthira approached his grandfather Bhishma as he lay dying on a bed of arrows at the end of the horrific Mahabharata War. The king sadly informs his grandfather that the great war had completely wiped out his family so that no one was left to carry on their lineage. He is immensely tortured by this and is particularly distressed by the death of his brother Arjuna's unborn grandson Parikshit, who had been killed by a powerful weapon while still in the womb of his mother Uttara. Accordingly, he asks the wise Bhishma what he can do to remedy this situation and insure that his family line will continue into the future. Bhishma tells him about a powerful votive ritual (*vrat*), and advises him to go to a pipal tree the next day the new moon falls on a Monday and worship Vishnu, making worthy offerings while circumambulating the tree 108 times. Pleasing Vishnu with this special form of worship, Bhishma claims, yields the most auspicious results. He assures Yudhishthira that by performing the Somvati Amavasya Vrat Parikshit will be revived and his family line will thereby survive. Yudhishthira then asks Bhishma how this *vrat* came into being. Bhishma responds with a story.

Once long ago there lived in the holy city of Kanchi a brahman by the name of Devaswami and his beautiful wife, Dhanavati. Over time the couple had seven fine sons and a virtuous daughter named Gunavati. All of the sons eventually married and lived happily with their lovely wives in the joint household. Seeing this, Gunavati too wished to live in such a happy married state. One day a holy man came to their house begging. Enthralled by the charisma of the holy man, the seven wives of the sons each made an offering to him, and he blessed them saying, "May you always live in the blessed state of marital bliss [*saubhagya*]." After witnessing this, Dhanavati sent her daughter Gunavati to the holy man for a blessing. Instead of blessing her for a long and happy marriage, however, he intoned: "May you always remain righteous." Disturbed by the obvious difference in the blessings he gave her daughters-in-law and her own daughter, Dhanavati confronted the holy man who revealed that on the very day of her daughter's wedding her daughter was destined to become a widow. Upon hearing this distressing prediction Dhanavati became anxious and pleaded for the holy man to tell her how her daughter could avoid this disastrous condition. The holy man counseled that a woman named Soma must be brought to their house and that Gunavati should honor her properly and do as she says; as a result of this she would destroy the defect of Gunavati's future widowhood. Dhanavati asked for the identity and location of this Soma. Informing her that Soma was a washerwoman who lived in Sri Lanka, the holy man departed.

Traveling to Sri Lanka with one of her brothers, Gunavati began her search for Soma. Once she had located Soma's house, Gunavati and her brother began serving the washerwoman secretly by cleaning her courtyard every morning before dawn. When Soma discovered who was doing this work she was horrified, since they were high caste brahmans and she was a low caste washerwoman. She demanded to know why they were performing actions contrary to caste custom, which became the opportunity for Gunavati to tell about her defect of widowhood. Soma agreed to return with Gunavati to her home and help her. Soon after, arrangements were made to marry Gunavati to a handsome and virtuous brahman named Rudrasharma. As predicted, he died during the wedding celebrations, but fortunately Soma was on hand to be of assistance. Although everyone else was greatly distraught, she remained calm and taught Gunavati the *vrat* by which she could bring her husband back to life. The day happened to be a Monday that coincided with a new moon. Gunavati bathed in a river, went to a pipal tree, and worshiped Vishnu in that form by circumambulating the tree 108 times with offerings of sugar crystals in hand. After Gunavati successfully revived her new husband by means of this ritual, Soma journeyed back to her home in Sri Lanka only to discover that her own son, husband and son-in-law had all died while she was staying with Gunavati. Luckily, however, she had given strict instructions not to cremate the body of anyone who died while she was away. This day too happened to be a new moon and a Monday. She then bathed in a river, proceeded to a pipal tree, and worshiped Vishnu in the manner she had taught Gunavati. As a result, she not only revived her dead family members, but also filled her town with beauty and her own home with unlimited wealth. When asked by a group of women how she had accomplished this, she informed them that she had worshiped Vishnu in the form of the pipal tree by circumambulating the tree 108 times. Soma told the women if they too practiced this ritual, they would never experience widowhood (*vaidavya*), but would live always in a blissful married state (*saubhagya*). She then taught them the Somvati Amavasya Vrat, and from there it spread. Soma lived a long and happy life, and when she died she went to the heavenly abode of Vishnu.

After narrating this story, Bhishma taught the ritual to Yudhishthira, and gave him two Sanskrit mantras to use.[5] The first was intended for honorifically circumambulating the Ashvattha or pipal tree, the second for worshiping the tree. Translated into English they are respectively:

> All honor to the Ashvattha [Pipal], whose roots are the form of Brahma, whose trunk is the form of Vishnu, and whose upper parts are the form of Shiva.

O Ashvattha, I honor you, King of Trees, who are the residence of sacrificial fire and the perpetual abode of Govinda [Vishnu/Krishna]. May you remove all my misfortunes.

Bhishma advised Yudhishthira to teach the Somvati Amavasya Vrat to the Pandava wives Draupadi, Subhadra, and Uttara, and assured him that as a result of this the promising child in Uttara's womb would come back to life. Indeed, Uttara gave birth to a healthy son, and Parikshit grew up to become a great king.

Several conclusions can be drawn from this story. First, it provides a blueprint and rationale for a special ritual that involves the rather unique feature of circumambulating a pipal tree 108 times while making offerings with each revolution. Second, the pipal tree itself—addressed as the "King of Trees"—is directly worshiped. Third, the pipal tree is here considered to be an embodied form of the supreme god Vishnu. And fourth, the pipal tree is regarded as a powerful presence and vital sentient being who can be approached with reverence to yield great benefits for domestic life, such as good health, well-being, and longevity for family members, as well as happiness, wealth, and overall abundance for the worshiper. These ideas are alive and well today, as the women of Banaras who participate in the Somvati Amavasya Vrat clearly demonstrate through their words and deeds.

The Pipal Tree

The pipal tree, also known as the Ashvattha in Sanskrit literature, as well as the Bo or Bodhi tree in Buddhist contexts, is a type of fig tree that is often considered in India the most sacred of all trees and is planted near temples or other religious places. Thus, its Latin botanical name is *ficus religiosa*, the "holy fig tree." This magnificent tree grows to very large proportions, providing abundant shade and shelter, and often towers above a village landscape where it is frequently planted to create a protected and special space for social and religious gatherings. It is also commonly found in urban environments where it is worshiped by a wide range of people for a variety of reasons. The trunk of the pipal is somewhat smooth when it is young, but develops vertical folds and rough bark as it ages. I have encountered pipal trees in Banaras with a trunk diameter of over ten feet. A pipal tree grows well with other trees, and its rope-like roots often wrap themselves around and intertwine with the other tree. It is not uncommon to see a pipal tree planted together with a neem or banyan tree. Carried by birds, the seeds of the pipal also can sprout in the cracks of walls and buildings, which it gradually splits open with its growing roots. The leaves of the pipal are truly remarkable; they are broadly round or heart-shaped with smooth edges, and narrow suddenly at the tip into a long tail. In her book *Plant Myths and Traditions in India*, botanist and cultural historian Shakti Gupta narrates an Orrisan myth that accounts for the unusually long tip of a pipal leaf.

> *Aswattha* is considered sacred by some tribes of the Ganjam district of Orissa. According to them, before the creation of the world Kittung and his sister used to live in a gourd. When the gourd broke, the two started living on the Kurabeli hill. This was a time when there were no trees on earth. When summer came, the sister complained of the intense heat. A squirrel bit off four fingers of the left hand of Kittung while he was asleep at night, leaving only the third middle finger. On hearing his sister complain of the heat, Kittung cut off his maimed left hand and put it on a stone, which grew into the *Aswattha* tree called *Onjerneban* tree by the tribal people. The apex of the leaf is prolonged into a long projection which to the tribal people represents the middle finger of Kittung's hand.[6]

The broad leaves of the pipal tend to hang down so that the slightest breeze causes them to quiver and rustle very much like the cottonwood or aspen trees of North America. For this reason, another name for the pipal tree is *cala-dala*, which means "with 'moving' or 'restless' leaves." Pipal trees are marvelous shade trees, affording cool relief during the challenging heat of a northern Indian summer (figure 3.4). Small figs appear on the tree, which turn reddish-purple when ripe. Birds are fond of the pipal fig; the seeds pass out of them undigested to grow both on the ground and on top of buildings.[7] The latter location is problematic, because there is great reluctance to cut or destroy a pipal tree. I have seen many growing on the upper walls of old buildings, slowly eating away at the structure, yet they seem to be left alone.

In addition to their ability to provide protective shelter from taxing weather, pipal trees have also been used in traditional Indian medicine. "Every part of *ashvattha* has medicinal value," declares Malla.[8] The pipal tree has been recognized in the Ayurveda system for a long time as a source of powerful medicine. Its powdered bark is used as a remedy against many diseases; it has been applied to burns, sores, wounds, and used to treat ear troubles, and uterine disorders. The pipal is considered to be a very effective collector of solar energy; several people told me that the pipal tree is the only tree that can absorb and use all colors of solar light. One text claims that it is "the abode of the Sun on Earth."[9] Therefore, parts of a pipal tree are used in Ayurvedic herbal medicines where one's constitution is judged to be in need of stimulating fire (*pitta*). It is a blood purifier and has also been utilized as an aphrodisiac and employed to cure infertility and impotency.[10] In addition to this, the pipal is used to treat mental disorders, problems with the eyes and teeth, and ailments affecting the internal organs. Remedies using the pipal tree are available in considerable detail within Ayurvedic literature.[11]

Figure 3.4 Large pipal tree growing on the outskirts of Banaras

Many people I spoke with throughout northern India told me that pipal trees are special because they are the only tree that produces oxygen (both Hindi and English speakers used this term) twenty-four hours a day. Whether pipal trees are unique in this fashion or not from a scientific perspective, the fact that people regard them so tells us much about how they are conceived. A physicist living in Banaras told me that pipal trees are "huge *prana* [life-breath] factories, that pump out more oxygen than any other tree. I believe that scientists will discover that oxygen coming out of a pipal is different than that coming out of other trees. If you sit under a pipal tree for an hour or so you get great peace. In my own study of Indian culture I have discovered that every enlightened person had sat under a pipal tree and achieved enlightenment there."

In addition to healing powers and spiritual knowledge, pipal trees are identified with truth. Monier Williams relays the following incident from nineteenth-century colonial India:

> A certain magistrate, well known for his energy and good nature, knowing that all Hindus regard it as a work of immense religious merit to plant these trees, hit upon the clever idea of trying to conciliate the good-will of the inhabitants of his district by planting some Pipal trees in the marketplace of a large town where a number of traders were in the habit of transacting their business. This he accordingly proceeded to

do, fully expecting to entitle himself to their gratitude, but imagine his surprise when a deputation of these traders made its appearance one day and entreated him to desist, urging with the most naïve candour that their business could not be carried on without a certain amount of deception, and that the neighbourhood of the Pipal trees would paralyze all their negotiations.[12]

In some ways, this links more contemporary notions associated with the pipal tree to the Vedic and Upanishadic notion of the Ashvattha tree as a "tree of knowledge" mentioned in the last chapter.

Pipal trees, also identified as "trees of life" in the Vedic and Upanishadic periods, can live for a long time. In his book, *Common Trees*, H. Santapau writes:

> Every villager knows that the Peepal has a very long life, compared with other common trees. There are records, however, of a tree taken to Ceylon from Northern India in 288 B.C.; at the end of the last century the tree was still living and doing well; in 1852 it was, not just supposed, but known to be 2147 years old! Such a tree was at the time either the oldest or one of the oldest trees of the whole world, it was certainly the oldest tree the records of whose growth had been carefully preserved all through the centuries to near the present time. There seems to have been a tradition in Ceylon that the ruling dynasty would last in power as long as the sacred Peepal remained alive; this accounts for the care with which the tree was looked after for so many centuries.[13]

The tree Santapau refers to was originally taken from a cutting of the famous Maha Bodhi tree in Bodh Gaya under which the Buddha achieved enlightenment. I cannot attest to the factuality of Santapau's report, and of course, his statement does not take into consideration such trees as the mighty coastal redwoods or bristle cone pines of North America, which can live over three and five thousand years, respectively; but nonetheless his point is that the pipal tree can live to a very old age. Although pipal trees are found in the forest, they grow much better in open landscapes where they receive plentiful space and sunlight. People have thus cultivated pipal trees in cleared spaces over centuries, and it seems that pipal trees would not have been as abundant if it were not for human cultivation. Pipal trees and human beings have long enjoyed a mutually beneficial relationship characterized by an exchange of gifts that are respectively valuable to each species.

The pipal tree is the real powerhouse among all sacred trees in India. It is considered to be the most sacred of trees and has been worshiped for several millennia on the subcontinent as an arboreal form of divinity. On the morning of the second Somavati Amavasya Vrat I observed, I talked with a woman I had gotten to know who sells flowers and other items used in worship near the largest pipal tree at Assi Ghat. I asked her why the women worship a pipal tree on this day. "Because," she explained, "the pipal is the most powerful and sacred [*pavitra*] of all trees." Although people articulated in different ways why they regard the pipal as the most sacred of trees, I never met a person in Banaras, or anywhere else in India for that matter, who disagreed with this point of view. The flower seller expressed a very common opinion that the pipal "is Vasudeva, and for this reason is the most sacred tree." I met a professor of pathology from the Banaras Hindu University medical school while he was worshiping a pipal tree; he told me that he worships this tree frequently "because all gods and goddesses reside in the pipal tree. It is our most sacred tree." While talking with a college student under another pipal tree, I asked him if all castes and types of people worship the pipal tree in Banaras. "Yes," he replied, "but not just in Banaras. All types of people worship the pipal tree everywhere in India. It is the most sacred tree for us." The botanical folklorist K. D. Upadhyaya agrees, reporting, "Pipal or the Bo (*Ficus religiosa*) is the most sacred tree in India."[14] Cultural historian Gupta goes one step further, declaring that the pipal tree is the most sacred tree in the entire world, with the longest history of worship: "For antiquity and veneration, the *Aswattha* (pipal) is unrivalled throughout the world."[15] This declaration comes from recognition of the continuity of the worship of the pipal tree from the present time stretching all the way back for more than four millennia to the era of the ancient Indus Valley Civilization. Seals have been uncovered from the ancient urban sites that according to some scholars depict worship of the pipal tree: "The cult of tree worship is as old or older than civilization, in fact almost the first objects held in reverence were trees. In India this is borne out by a seal discovered at Mohenjo-daro, now in Pakistan, which depicts *Aswattha* (pipal) being worshiped. This seal dates back to the third-fourth millennium BC."[16] Archeological data has even led one scholar to claim: "the *pipal* god was the supreme deity of the Indus Valley."[17] Regardless of the factuality of this latter assertion, the pipal tree has long been and continues to be widely recognized as the premier sacred tree in India.

Historical and Textual Views of the Pipal Tree

The pipal tree also played an important religious role during the Vedic period in which the natural world was believed to be animated with divinity; the sun, water, wind, earth, fire, and various plants, for example, were all worshiped as deities. The central religious rite during the Vedic period was the fire sacrifice, a means by which the practitioners communicated with and sent offerings to the gods by means of fire, deified as the god Agni, with the expectation that this would in return yield beneficial results. The use of the pipal tree and its wood was widespread in Vedic ritual; dead branches from a pipal tree, for example, were used to start the sacrificial fire.[18] In fact, Naveen Patnaik reports the belief that "the wood of the Asvattha or sacred fig was used to light the original sacred fire with which the gods granted knowledge to the human race."[19] The Ashvattha or pipal tree was also considered to be the residence of Agni, god of the sacrificial fire, who was brought out of the wood through friction: "The sacredness of the *Aswattha* tree comes perhaps from the old Vedic ritual of kindling the sacrificial fire at religious ceremonies by friction between two peculiarly shaped pieces of wood, one of which is the Aswattha, and the ceremony is called 'the birth of Agni.'"[20] The other piece of wood came from a sami tree; the friction drill was made from pipal wood and was considered male, whereas the friction pan was made from sami wood and considered female.[21] Moreover, Gupta reports that during the Vedic period:

> Brahmans worship the Aswattha tree daily during their evening prayer. They go to the tree and facing east repeat a prayer and sing hymns in praise of the tree which says: 'O Aswattha tree! You are a God. You are a king among trees. Your roots represent Brahma the Creator, your trunk represents Siva the Destroyer, and your branches, Vishnu the Preserver. As such you are an emblem of the *Trimurti*. All who honour you in this world by performing Upanayana, walk round you, adoring you and singing your praise, obtain remission of their sins in this world and bliss in the next. I praise and adore you. Pardon my sins in this world and give me a place with the blessed after death.' The worshipper then walks round the tree 7, 14, 21, 28, 35 or more times but always in multiple of seven.[22]

According to the Atharva Veda the Ashvattha or pipal tree was considered to be the abode of all the gods and was worshiped for victory over enemies and birth of a male child.[23] Malla maintains: "The *asvattha* tree was made the basis of a profound metaphysic doctrine in Vedic times."[24] The whole universe is considered to be a pipal tree with a thousand branches in the Rig Veda.[25] In later Vedantic philosophical texts the pipal tree is considered to be both the tree of knowledge (*brahma-taru*) and the tree of life (*jivana-taru*). "In the later Vedic texts *asvattha* is regarded as Brahma-taru—the embodiment of knowledge and the Great creator. That is why *asvattha* is called on certain occasions as the 'tree of life' or the 'tree of creation.'"[26] The Ashvattha is considered to be the highest reality of Brahman in the Maitri Upanishad.[27] The Katha Upanishad also identifies the Ashvattha with the pure and eternal ultimate reality of Brahman and claims that the whole world rests on it.[28] This understanding of the pipal as the world tree of life is continued in the Bhagavad Gita; the one who truly knows it is said to be the knower of all wisdom.[29] Many have noted that this tree is conducive to productive meditation. Patnaik writes, "So deeply is this tree associated with both the origin and the symbiosis of life that it is thought to induce illumination, and countless Indian legends tell of sages meditating in its shade."[30] The most well-known among these is, of course, the Buddha, a contemporary of early Upanishadic Hinduism.

The great epic *Mahabharata* also makes grand claims about the worship of the pipal: "According to the *Mahabharata*, the man who worships *Aswattha* daily, worships the whole universe."[31] Here is metonymic representational thinking at its best, where a vital part of the whole gives one access to the whole itself. In the Bhagavad Gita, a section of the greater *Mahabharata*, the Ashvattha or pipal is identified with the entire universe, and herein we find the famous statement made by Krishna that "Among all trees I am the Ashvattha."[32] It is in this extremely popular and well-known text that clear identification is made between the pipal tree and the all-encompassing god Krishna or Vishnu.

It is in the Puranas, however, that most textual information about the Ashvattha or pipal tree is to be found. This is particularly true of the eclectic Padma Purana, which claims: "A person gets more spiritual benefit from planting an Ashvattha tree on the bank of a pond than from performing hundreds of sacrifices."[33] Perhaps even more vehemently it declares: "Ah, there is nothing on earth as great as Vishnu in the form of an Ashvattha tree.... God in the form of an Ashvattha tree is considered to be worthy of the highest worship."[34] This text then goes on to enumerate the many benefits that come from worshiping a pipal tree.[35] One is freed from all misfortunes by merely looking at an Ashvattha tree and obtains good fortune by touching it reverently. A blessed long life is insured from honoring an Ashvattha tree by circumambulating it clockwise while chanting the mantra: "O Ashvattha, I honor you whose leaves are always moving, who are an enlightened being (Bodhisattva), and in whom Vishnu forever resides; for you are greatly worthy of worship at all times." Permanent residence in heaven is achieved by offering gifts of water, food, flowers, incense, and lamps to an Ashvattha tree. Worship of an Ashvattha tree is said to yield offspring, as well as eternal wealth, happiness, fame, success, honor, and prosperity. This type of worship is proclaimed to be infinitely more fruitful than any other type, yielding its results well beyond this life. Importantly, the supreme religious goal of ultimate liberation (*moksha*) is included in the list of benefits to be obtained from worshiping an Ashvattha tree. Considering all this, the Padma Purana asks: "Who in this world would not worship the Ashvattha in whose roots resides Vishnu, in whose trunk resides Shiva, and in whose upper branches resides Brahma?"

Alongside these claims, the Padma Purana asserts that cutting an Ashvattha tree is a great sin that brings much misfortune.

The Skanda Purana is another medieval text that has much to say about the Ashvattha or pipal tree. It too declares that the Ashvattha is "the most sacred [*pavitra*] of all trees" and adds that it "is accompanied with great auspiciousness [*mangala*]."[36] The Skanda Purana extols the benefits to be gained from worshiping it; these include the destruction of all misfortunes and the achievement of ultimate liberation (*mukti*). This Purana also declares that one incurs great sin by cutting an Ashvattha tree and as a consequence ends up in hell (*naraka*). The Skanda Purana agrees with other Puranas in identifying the Ashvattha (also called in this text the "tree of enlightenment" (*bodhi-druma*) as a form (*rupa*) of Vishnu).[37] In sum, the Puranas announce that there are great advantages to be secured from reverently approaching and worshiping a pipal tree, and every reason to avoid harming one.

Who is a Pipal Tree?

We are now ready to consider the question "Who is a pipal tree?" for the Puranic texts and the tree worshipers of northern India. Before addressing this query I want to set aside the question "What is a pipal tree?" When I first began my research on sacred trees in Banaras, I frequently asked people whether the tree they were worshiping had sentience or was animate (*sajiv*); whether it had consciousness (*cetana*), whether it had a soul (*jiv* or *atma*); whether it is a person (*vyakti*) or had personhood (*vyaktitva*). As time went on I asked these questions less and less. Not only did I always receive an affirmative answer to such questions, but people who seemed to assume the answers were completely obvious, typically treated my questions as so absurd that I began to feel foolish asking them. To ask someone who is worshiping a tree if that tree has sentience makes one liable to suspicions of madness. Regarding the personhood of a tree, a cloth merchant who worships a pipal tree daily at Tulsi Ghat in Banaras informed me as we stood under the tree: "This tree is a man [*admi*], who can speak and think just like you and me." When I asked him further about this, he said: "This tree is talking all the time, but since our hearts are not clean, but full of impurities, we cannot hear it. Only people with very clean hearts can hear the tree. These are special people; they can hear it." Another Banaras tree worshiper told me something similar. He agreed that trees communicate, but said that you have to worship trees with sincerity for a long time to be able to hear what they have to say. He informed me that once the pipal tree he worships most frequently told him "through inner words [*antar shabda*] that my life would be successful [*saphal*] and this made me feel very peaceful [*shant*]." After meeting a priest of a Hanuman temple located under a large pipal tree that stands near the bank of the Ganges atop Chauki Ghat, I asked him if this tree has personhood (*vyaktitva*). "Yes," he assured me, "much [*bahut*]." I asked him if it has soul (*atma*). "Yes, of course!" he responded incredulously. Pushing my point further, I asked him if this tree ever talks. "Yes," he answered, "but only rare people can hear trees talk. And for most of these, they hear and see the tree move and talk only with their minds eye" (he pointed to the third eye between his eyebrows).

I concentrated on the issue of consciousness in some of my interviews. A Hanuman temple located near a famous pond dedicated to the goddess Durga is crowded with people worshiping a pipal tree in its courtyard on Saturdays. I had many occasions to discuss worship of pipal trees with one of the priests of the temple while the two of us stood under this tree. When I asked him if this tree had consciousness (*cetana*) he replied emphatically, "Yes, of course!" I then asked him how he knew this. "Because all life has consciousness. You, me, this tree, all life forms. He has soul [*atma*] just like you and me." I pressed him further, asking for specific signs of this tree's consciousness. "I know this because he [the pipal tree] accepts peoples' offerings. Look, here is what people do. (He began to massage the base of the tree.) This is like massaging the leg of a man. This awakens and draws the attention of the god, and then he accepts what people offer to him and hears and responds to their requests. I have seen the results many times. This is how I know that this tree has consciousness." On another occasion I spoke with a man who had just made a water offering to a huge pipal tree on the edge of the Pushkar Pond in Banaras. I asked him whether the tree had consciousness. "Yes, certainly!" he replied, and went on to tell me that he comes to this tree every morning and evening and has established a close relationship (*sambandha*) with this tree. "This tree," he said, "has life [*jivan*] just like me and you. It is a person [*vyakti*] like you." Accordingly, the question "Who is this tree?" made complete sense to the tree worshipers I spoke with and they answered it without hesitation.

The pipal tree in Indian Hindu culture is clearly assumed to be an animate, sentient being with feelings and consciousness; it is experienced as a living presence with whom one can establish a meaningful, mutually beneficial relationship. More than this, however, the tree is considered to be a powerful deity. Who is the divinity of the pipal tree? I received many different answers to this question. A few people I spoke with explained that Brahman—the general term for ultimate impersonal reality—pervades the pipal tree. A man I talked with in Rishikesh called the pipal "Bhagavan," a common name for the personal form of God. I asked him which form of Bhagavan. "Whichever form one sees it as," he answered as a Hindu who assumes a plurality of divine forms. While Hindus recognize that God is one, they also recognize great diversity in both divine manifestations and in human dispositions and concomitant perceptions. Therefore, while acknowledging the oneness of God, it is typical for many Hindus to develop a specific relationship with a particular manifestation or conception of divinity to which they are most attracted. This is often called one's "preferred deity" (*ishta devata*). From this perspective, the pipal tree can be considered to be any form of divinity to which one is drawn, though we will see that one identity in particular is paramount.

A few people I spoke with simply identified the divinity of the pipal tree as *pipal-devata*, or "pipal-god." Numerous people informed me that the great multiplicity of all gods reside in the pipal tree. When I asked an attendant of a Hanuman temple beneath a large pipal tree at Chauki Ghat to identify the divinity of the pipal tree, he responded by saying that all goddesses reside in the pipal tree, naming specifically Sarasvati, Lakshmi, and Durga. Several people told me that Lakshmi resides in the pipal tree, and many more said that Lakshmi resides in the pipal tree with her consort Vishnu. Early one morning I was walking upstream from Assi Ghat and I came upon a priest of a small Shiva temple worshiping a medium-sized pipal tree in the courtyard of the temple compound by waving the honorific *arati* lamp before it. After he finished with this brief ritual he invited me to sit with him on the porch of the temple, where he explained that this was a very special tree. When I asked him if it was a god (*devata*), he said, "Yes, many." I then asked if they resided within it or if the tree itself was their body. He replied that the tree was their body (he used two Hindi words while expressing this: *sharir* and *rupa*), and took me over to the tree to illustrate his point. The roots and trunk of the tree had unusual shape and form. Within the tree's twisted limbs he showed me Ganesha, the elephant-headed god of fruitful beginnings; Hanuman, the monkey god who is the devoted servant of Lord Ram; Lakshmi, the auspicious goddess of abundance; Shiva, patron god of Banaras; and Bhadra Kali, a powerful form of the Great Goddess—all highlighted with red paint. He also showed me an area on the tree that he said had all the remaining gods and added that taken as a whole the tree is Vasudeva (Vishnu). He went on to say that he himself had established (*sthapita*) the stone Shiva lingam worshiped in the temple, but that the gods in the pipal tree had manifest on their own (*svayam pragata*) in this natural form (*prakriti rupa*). For this reason, he said, this tree was a much more powerful (*shakti*) divine form to worship than a temple image (*murti rupa*).

The notion that all gods reside in or near the pipal tree is fairly common. One man I spoke with under the large pipal tree at Assi Ghat confirmed this by declaring: "All gods and goddesses reside in a pipal tree." A woman worshiping the same tree told me, "The pipal is Vasudeva, but here beneath it are all gods: Shankar (Shiva), Hanuman, Devi (the Goddess), and others." I even met a man who regards the pipal tree as the goddess Durga, although I found his view to be somewhat rare. I asked this man, a desk clerk at a hotel just downstream from the

Dasashvamedha Ghat in Banaras with a large pipal tree growing out front that is worshiped daily by many people, why this tree was considered to be so special. "Because," he replied, "this tree is God. You know, people believe that if you worship this tree you will have a happy and healthy life. You must have seen many people worshiping this tree." I inquired whether he himself ever worshiped this tree. "Yes," he said, "every morning before I come into the hotel I stop and worship this tree. I worship it because it is a god." When I asked him which god, he said, "Devi, I worship it as the goddess Durga." The anthropologist Ann Gold reports that some people in a Rajasthani village she visits also consider the pipal tree to be a natural form of the goddess.[38]

The pipal tree is considered by some to be a *trimurti*, that is, a compound form of the three major Hindu divinities Brahma, Vishnu, and Shiva. A pipal tree worshiper in Banaras explained to me that "Brahma is the roots of a pipal, Vishnu its trunk, Shiva its upper parts." And yet when I asked if just these three reside in the pipal, he said, "No, 33,000 gods reside in the pipal tree." There are several fairly well known Sanskrit mantras that express this idea. Besides the mantra (used in the Somvati Amavasya Vrat) translated on page 66, here are three more examples:

> All glory to you, O King of Trees, who are Brahma in your roots, Vishnu in your trunk, Maheshvara [Shiva] in your branches, and Lord of all gods in each and every leaf.[39]
> Glory to you, Supreme God, who are Brahma in your roots, Vishnu in your trunk, Maheshvara in your branches, and all gods in each and every leaf.[40]
> All glory to you, O King of Trees, who are in the form of Brahma in your roots, the form of Vishnu in your trunk, and the form of Shiva in your upper parts.

Rana P. B. Singh, a professor of geography at Banaras Hindu University, told me during a conversation that a pipal tree is a *trimurti*, just like a Shiva linga, and sketched this out for me as we sipped tea together one afternoon at an outdoor restaurant at Assi Ghat. He drew in my field notebook a Shiva linga next to a pipal tree and illustrated that the roots of the pipal and the base of the linga are both Brahma, the trunk of the tree and the column that supports the linga are both Vishnu, and the upper branches of the tree and the upper portion of the linga are both Shiva. To further understand this conception of the linga (and pipal tree), he invited me to consult one of his books. In *Banaras Region: A Spiritual and Cultural Guide,* Singh quotes the Agni Purana to support his *trimurti* view of the Shiva linga: "From the foot up to the knees should be Brahma's portion, from the knees up to the navel should be Vishnu's portion, and from the navel up to the top of the head should be Shiva's portion. The portion assigned to Brahma is buried in the ground, that for Vishnu is within the Pithika, and that for Shiva is above the Pithika."[41] As with a Shiva linga, he claims, so it is with a pipal tree; they are a combined form of the gods Brahma, Vishnu, and Shiva.

Sometimes foreign gods too find a place in pipal tree shrines. I discovered that even in Khan Market, one of the most westernized of New Delhi's upscale markets that cater to the foreign embassy crowd, pipal trees are worshiped. One morning while I was visiting this market I noticed that incense and flowers had been placed at the base of a pipal tree, and that the ground was moist from recent water offerings. These particular signs of worship were rather routine. What captured my attention, however, was a poster of Jesus exposing his bleeding heart attached to the tree; a fresh garland of roses had been placed around the poster. It seems in this case that Jesus is easily absorbed and included within the sacrality of the pipal tree. The pluralistic view of the god of the pipal tree provides exemplary illustration of Hindu conceptions of divinity that can encompass a multiplicity of deities, including foreign gods. Having a long and varied history, the pipal tree seems well suited to serve as a somewhat blank screen onto which a particular face of divinity can be projected; it is a potent divine form that can be conceived of in a great variety of ways. Nonetheless, the most common conception of the pipal tree identifies it with the supreme god Vishnu.

While multiple possible conceptions of the pipal tree exist, by far the most frequent answer I received to the question "Who is a people tree?" was that the pipal tree is "Vasudeva," another name for Vishnu. The Indian botanist Gupta states succinctly, "The tree is believed to be Vishnu himself."[42] Certainly, the overwhelming textual claim is that the Ashvattha or pipal tree is some form of Vishnu. The Skanda Purana, for example, identifies the Ashvattha as the "tree named Vishnu."[43] Not only is the pipal designated Vishnu, but is itself considered to be an embodied form of Vishnu. The Skanda Purana clarifies this point, stating explicitly, "The tree itself is a form [*murta*] of Vishnu."[44] Whereas some texts identify the three major parts of the Ashvattha with the *trimurti* Brahma, Vishnu, and Shiva, the Skanda Purana identifies them with various forms of Vishnu: "Vishnu is forever present in its roots, Keshava in its trunk, Narayana in its branches. Moreover, Lord Hari is in its leaves, Achyuta in its fruit, and it is connected with all gods."[45] The Vayu Purana also identifies the pipal tree as a form of Vishnu: "I bow down to Hari, lord Vishnu who has assumed the form of the Ashvattha tree."[46] In the *Vishnu-Sahasra-Nama*, a text that extols the thousand names of Vishnu, Vishnu is identified as the "Ashvattha, chief among all trees."[47] This statement is similar to the one made in the popular Bhagavad Gita quoted in the epigram at the beginning of this chapter that identifies Krishna with the Ashvattha tree. While the Ashvattha tree is clearly identified in the Padma Purana as Vishnu, this text also refers to it as the residence of all gods, a place to connect with dead ancestors, and the abode of the planets.[48] The identification of the pipal tree with Vishnu or Vasudeva provides another aspect for understanding why this tree can so readily be viewed as a multitude of divinities. The eleventh chapter of the renowned Bhagavad Gita, for example, involves a revelation of the universal form (*vishva-rupa*) of Vasudeva that makes it clear that Vasudeva encompasses all gods and goddesses.

Nearly all the women worshipping pipal trees on Somvati Amavasya told me that they considered this tree to be a form of Vasudeva. A woman who had just offered a pot of water, some incense, and flowers to a large pipal tree at Chauki Ghat spoke for many of her fellow worshipers, explaining: "Vasudeva resides within the pipal tree. That is why I honor it with worship (*puja*)." A man worshiping a large pipal tree that stands before a newly constructed hotel, which was built so as not to destroy or harm the tree, identified the tree as "Bhagavan Vishnu, or Krishna." I asked him if the tree and Krishna were different. "No," he responded, "they are one and the same. The pipal is a *svarupa* of Krishna." In my many conversations with tree worshipers in Banaras, hundreds of people informed me that the pipal tree is Vasudeva. Additionally, I witnessed numerous tree worshipers praising the pipal as Vasudeva while circumambulating it and chanting "*Om Vasudevaya namah*" (All Glory be to Vasudeva!). Once again, two views appear to be operative here. One is that the pipal tree is the residence (*vas*) of Vasudeva, the other is that the tree is an embodied form (*rupa* or *svarupa*), or body (*sharir*) of Vasudeva. Of the two, I found the latter view to be by far the most common. This is not surprising, as the understanding that the pipal tree is an embodied form of Vasudeva/Vishnu is also the dominant view expressed in Hindu scripture.

A religious booklet I collected in Banaras states, "The pipal is an actual form [*rupa*] of Bhagavan Vishnu."[49] I spoke with a man worshiping a pipal tree in Banaras who told me "the pipal is a *svarupa* of Vasudeva." Many people made this same point, including a theologian I spoke with in Braj who told me that the pipal tree is a "*svarupa*" of Krishna. In line with this view, a fascinating story was reported in the news in the fall of 2005. The BBC announced that a senior police officer in Lucknow was dressing as a woman, a strategy sometimes employed by men to identify with the gopis, the female lovers of Krishna: "TV news channels flocked to his home to film him worshipping Hindu deity Lord Krishna in the form of a tree.... He has been spending his time embracing a peepal, or holy fig, tree in his garden, chanting mantras to his beloved Lord Krishna."[50] It is evident from this report, a variety of texts, and the many testimonies of tree worshipers in northern India that the pipal itself is typically regarded as an embodied form or *svarupa* of Vishnu, also known as Krishna or Vasudeva.

Fundamental to the theology of the well-known Bhagavad-Gita is the view that the entire universe is an aspect of Vasudeva, the highest divinity who encompasses the totality of all reality.[51] Therefore, it is not surprising that the pipal tree is regarded as part of Vishnu, especially considering that it is held to be the greatest of all trees in India, often addressed as "the King of Trees." Not only is the pipal considered to be a part of Vasudeva, but more specifically a *svarupa*. A *svarupa*—literally "own form"—is a particular, concrete, and potentially intimate form of divinity that is accessible for worship. The Gita recognizes that it is difficult for embodied beings to worship God as the disembodied absolute.[52] Therefore, God—while unified and nondifferent from everything that exists—assumes through the creative processes numerous concrete forms that are available for worshipful relationships. As we stood together admiring a large pipal tree that grows near the Ganges in Banaras a tree worshiper used this tree to explain to me that God is one, but assumes many names (*nama*) and forms (*rupa*). "Brahman, Bhagavan, and Devi are one, but take many forms, just like this tree. He is one tree with a single trunk, but look how many different leaves he has. Just like this, God is one but appears in many different forms." Vasudeva is one, and has an essential dimension beyond all physical manifestations, but for the purpose of worship assumes many tangible forms. This is a central feature of Hindu theism: although divinity is ultimately one, it can be conceived of and identified in multiple ways. Importantly, as we have seen, one of the most significant embodied forms Vasudeva assumes is the pipal tree. The Christian missionary Abbe Dubois discovered this about the pipal tree in the early nineteenth century: "It is consecrated to Vishnu, or rather it is Vishnu himself under the form of a tree."[53] In short, while both Hindu scriptures and contemporary tree worshipers identify it in a variety of ways, the overwhelmingly dominant view of the pipal tree is that it is a form of Vishnu. What might be some of the practical consequences of this perspective?

One of the reasons that the pipal is the most esteemed tree in India is that its practical and medicinal value is enormous; for this reason alone many people are dedicated to protecting this species. Much more relevant, however, its identification as an embodied form of the supreme Vasudeva himself leads to a great reluctance to harm it in any way. The botanist Santapau writes: "Hindus consider the Peepal a sacred tree, so that to cut a tree or its branches is to them as wrong as to ill treat one of the sacred cows of the country. Even when the tree is causing much damage to buildings and in the forests, the Peepal is respected and will not be cut down by orthodox Hindus."[54] This was certainly confirmed by many people I talked with in Banaras and elsewhere. I encountered a group of men one morning who had gathered under a large pipal tree on the bank of the Ganges to perform yogic exercises. I talked with them about the tree. The eldest among them said: "The pipal is the most sacred [*shuddha*] of all trees. It is Vasudeva. All the gods reside in this tree. In each and every leaf. That is why we never pluck even a single leaf from this tree with our hands." A man who daily worships a pipal tree in the interior of Banaras told me: "We never cut a pipal tree. For us it is God. It gives us so much. It gives oxygen for twenty-four hours. Therefore we feel great affection [*sneha*] for this tree. Besides, the gods would be angry with you if you cut down a pipal tree and only trouble would come of this." I was talking to a man in Rishkesh about pipal trees when he pointed to a young pipal tree growing nearby and said: "See that small pipal tree growing near that building. It will most likely grow into that building, but no one will cut it because we believe God resides in this tree." Several sawmills are located on the Sonarpur Road in the city of Banaras; I visited a few of them to ask the owners if they sold wood from a pipal tree. All informed me they did not. In response to my question one sawmill owner explained to me "the pipal tree is *pujaniya* [a Hindi word meaning "worthy of worship"]. Therefore, we never cut or sell pipal wood." I will explore other reasons for not cutting a pipal tree in the following chapter, but in this context the prohibition to cutting pipal trees is motivated by an understanding of the tree as an embodied form of God, an honor and respect for this awesome divinity, a desire to keep the mutually beneficial relationship positive, and an affection that grows out of worshipful interaction with and care for the tree. Such ideas are expressed, generated, and enacted especially in the context of a tree shrine.

Types of Pipal Tree Shrines

Tree shrines are some of the most spectacular features of the religious landscape of India. Pipal tree shrines are quite common and come in many shapes, sizes, and colors. There appears to be a progression of tree shrines from the most basic platform to complex structures; this often represents a chronological development of a particular shrine. The simplest shrine is just a bare patch of ground at the base of an unadorned tree where water offerings are poured, flowers or other offerings are placed, and into which sticks of incense are inserted. Additionally, offerings such as honorific vermilion (*sindur*) or flower garlands might be applied directly to the tree's trunk. Here the abundant shelter of the tree serves as a natural temple. I visited several large pipal trees of this kind upstream from the densely inhabited parts of Banaras and observed people on a number of occasions make offerings of water, incense, and marigold flowers at the base of the trees. A natural opening or crevice in the folds of the trunk of a large pipal sometimes serves as a preferred place to leave offerings (figure 3.5). Next in the sequential development of a pipal tree shrine, a circular planter-like container is often built around the sacred tree. The planter is usually constructed out of stone or concrete and is typically capped with some kind of platform on which various embodied forms of divinity such as Shiva lingas are commonly placed. As a

Figure 3.5 Flower offering left at a simple pipal tree shrine

shrine develops, small temples are built beneath the tree. It is not uncommon to find a temple dedicated to Hanuman, for example, standing under a pipal tree. Hanuman murtis and temples are often painted bright orange, adding color to the site (figure 3.6).

A good example of this type of shrine is one that has developed around a large and extremely popular pipal tree growing near the bank of the Ganges River at Assi Ghat in Banaras. This is an active shrine, and besides being a favorite site for fulfilling the Somvati Amavasya Vrat, the pipal tree here is worshiped by hundreds of people every day (figure 3.7). The trunk of this pipal tree is around four feet in diameter and has a crown that stretches out in a circular span approximately eighty feet. The tree is surrounded by a round cement enclosure that is about thirty inches high and twelve feet in diameter. The lower portion of the retaining wall has been painted yellow and the rim has been painted orange. On the west side of the tree stands a bright orange Hanuman temple that is nearly

King of Trees

Figure 3.6 Stone images of Hanuman smeared with orange sindur paste at a pipal tree shrine near the confluence of the Yamuna and Ganges in Allahabad

Figure 3.7 Popular Assi Ghat pipal tree shrine in Banaras

eight feet tall. A small white marble temple dedicated to the goddess Durga is located on the surface of the platform on north side of the tree, a similar one has been established for the goddess Ganga Devi on the south side, and a stone form of the elephant-headed god Ganesha rests against the tree looking out on the east side. There is a series of twelve black stone Shiva lingas that ring the tree on all sides. Every morning a steady stream of tree worshipers approach this shrine and offer such items as water, marigold flowers, incense, bright red sindur powder, and uncooked white rice to the pipal tree and the various gods and goddesses who reside in its shelter. Many women come here early in the morning carrying plastic wicker baskets full of items to use in their worship at the tree shrine. Typically they first worship the tree directly, pouring water on its roots at a special spot on the east side of the tree. They then continue by making offerings to the assembly of gods and goddesses on the platform beneath the tree in a manner that is determined by personal preference. As this is a "people tree," there is no official priest in charge of the shrine, and all worshipers are free to worship in their own particular style as long as they do not harm the tree or interfere with the worship of others.

Pipal trees are sometimes so much a part of a temple complex that they seem to blend into the buildings of the temple. Thirty yards down a narrow alley that leads off the east side of Sonarpur Road near the busy commercial center of Godolia in Banaras, there is a temple called the "Prachin Shri Hanuman Mandir." This temple is frequented by people from the neighborhood and provides a peaceful sanctuary from the nearby hubbub of the Godolia markets. A small flight of stairs ascends to a platform upon which is located the main temple of Hanuman, who looks upon another small temple housing Rama, his consort Sita, and his brother Lakshman. Looming high over the temple of Hanuman stands a huge pipal tree with a trunk of about seven feet in diameter. Although the roof of the temple complex does not enclose this tree, it is so close that worshipers can make their offerings under the shelter of this cover. A unique feature of this particular pipal tree shrine is its rather humbling path for performing its honorific circumambulation. One must pass through a narrow passage between the tree's trunk and the Hanuman shrine, circle around the back side, then duck under a massive branch of the tree by bowing and squeezing between the tree and a pillar holding up the roof of the temple complex. The "face" of the tree looks toward the interior of the temple platform. A large knot about four feet off the ground has been coated with orange sindur paint; this protrusion is a favored part of the tree around which to hang offerings of jasmine and marigold garlands. Below this there is an old statue of Sarasvati, goddess of the arts. Next to her is a Shiva linga and a stone featuring a pair of intertwining snakes. Tucked into a crook in the tree is a stone Ganesha. All have been smeared with orange sindur paste. Early one morning I watched a man dressed in a white shirt and dark trousers remove his shoes to ascend the stairs to the platform and engage in ritual movements that I came to learn are rather standard here. He approached the tree, offered water and a garland of jasmine flowers, and then waved an *arati* lamp before the tree to honor it. He put the lamp down and then circumambulated the tree eleven times through the humbling passage around the tree, and ended his worship by massaging the trunk of the pipal tree and placing his forehead to it reverently.

The next stage of the expansion of a pipal tree shrine entails building a temple enclosure around the entire tree, leaving a hole in the roof of the structure for the trunk to penetrate. In almost all cases, I found these temple structures with pipal trees towering high above them providing housing for an embodied form of Hanuman, the great monkey devotee of Vishnu in his incarnation as Rama, in addition to the pipal tree. Perhaps the most worshiped pipal tree in Banaras is one that stands inside the Senapati Vanakati Hanuman temple near Durga Kunda, a famous pond and temple complex. The story is told that the Hanuman now housed in the temple was found here when men were clearing the forest long ago for a king, and that the temple was established by the renowned sixteenth-century Banaras saint Tulsidas. Several people told me that it is the most important Hanuman temple in Banaras, although most people give this position to the Sankat Mochan Hanuman temple. The existing temple building is a rectangular structure measuring approximately twenty-five feet by sixty feet. On the west end of the temple is a shrine housing Hanuman, and on the east side is a shrine accommodating the divine couple Sita and Rama. There is a small shrine housing a Shiva linga just to the south of the Sita-Rama shrine. In between this temple and the Hanuman temple and enclosed in a raised circular container is a large pipal tree, now situated inside the temple structure with its upper trunk and canopy poking out of the roof. Every day, but especially on Saturdays, crowds of people jostle with one another to get into a circular queue and place their right hand on the tree as they circumambulate the pipal tree clockwise—usually seven times—after offering it water, flowers, and small clay oil lamps. I watched two women circle this tree one Monday afternoon. After finishing their seven revolutions they paused to massage the trunk of the tree and then placed their foreheads to the tree with their hands gently embracing its flanks.

Wherever I traveled in India I found pipal trees marked, surrounded, and honored by some kind of shrine. In the southern India states of Karnataka and Andhra Pradesh pipal trees are frequently paired with neem trees; placed beneath them are naga stones, forms of snake divinities whose presence brings fertility, health, and long life (figure 3.8). Many pipal trees grow on the banks of the Ganges at the famous Triveni Ghat of Rishikesh; all are contained within stone planters and worshiped daily by the large number of pilgrims visiting this site (figure 3.9). In the courtyard of the ancient Lakshmi-Narayana temple complex in Chamba

Figure 3.8 Serpentine naga stones under a pipal tree in the southern state of Karnataka

Figure 3.9 Pipal tree shrine at Triveni Ghat in Rishikesh

located in the mountainous state of Himachal Pradesh, I observed a small pipal tree that was kept in a pot on an elevated pedestal and honored with various offerings and wrapped with white string. Pipal trees are also found along the bank of the Yamuna River in the pilgrimage centers of Mathura and Vrindaban; most of these have had sacred stones (either Shiva lingas or rocks from Mount Govardhan) placed beneath them, and many are wrapped with red and yellow string on a Somvati Amavasya.[55] Although pipal trees are revered in a great variety of ways at countless pipal tree shrines throughout India, some standard features of their worship can be delineated.

Daily Worship at a Pipal Tree Shrine

What does daily worship look like at a pipal tree shrine? A sizable pipal tree with deep folds in its large trunk grows in the center of Chitaranjan Park located just above the central and famous Dasashvamedha Ghat in Banaras. The tree is enclosed in a low cement planter that serves as an altar; orange-painted shrines for Hanuman and Ganesha have been added to the platform. Early one morning I watched a woman dressed in a dark red blouse and a light green sari with gold trim, her oiled black hair tied neatly into a bun, remove her sandals and approach this tree. She began her worship by pouring water onto the base of the tree from a brass pot with a curved spout that she carried in her right hand. After extracting items for her worship from a plastic wicker basket, she first smeared orange-red sindur paste on the trunk of the pipal tree. Then she offered the tree uncooked white rice, pressing it to its bark. Next she filled a small clay dish with oil, added a cotton wick, lit it with a wooded match, and waved this flaming *arati* lamp before the tree to honor it. Taking a garland of jasmine flowers from her puja basket, she hung it on a piece of the tree's rough bark. After this she placed an offering of red sindur powder, uncooked white rice, and sugar crystals on a large green leaf and inserted it into a hollow in the base of the tree. She then circumambulated the pipal nine times chanting *"Vasudevaya namah"* (All glory to Vasudeva!). She concluded her ritual by massaging the trunk of the tree and pressing her forehead gently against it while embracing it reverently. She glanced up into the upper branches for a few moments, gathered the various worship utensils in her basket, retrieved her sandals, and departed.

Portrayed in the actions of this woman are some common features of pipal tree worship, all of which assume that a majestic animate being is fully present in or as the tree. Deferential attitude is shown by such gestures as purifying one's body and removing one's shoes before approaching a pipal tree. The heart of tree worship involves a variety of valued offerings; the gifts necessarily include water, but also regularly flowers, fruits, and other foods, such as sugar crystals and uncooked rice. The smearing of sindur paste and the waving of an *arati* lamp are favorite ways of showing honor to a respected being within Hindu religious practice, and both are frequently employed in worshiping a pipal tree. Reverential circumambulation and intimate bodily interactions with the tree often conclude the worship. Three features of pipal tree worship stand out as worthy of further comment.

The most basic offering made to a sacred tree at a tree shrine in India is a water offering (*udak; jalanjali*); practically this is tantamount to watering a plant. Many people told me that a water offering is the most important and essential gift one can give a tree. As one woman I spoke with at a pipal tree shrine in Banaras put it, "Of all the offerings, this is the one the trees like most." The Skanda Purana declares that "water [*jala*] is said to be nectar [*amrita*] for trees."[56] When pressed for time many people offer only water as a quick form of worthy worship. Water is poured onto the roots of a tree, for one of the Sanskrit names for a tree is *pada-pa*, that is, "one who drinks with the feet." Water is an essential element for life; it is vital to the well-being of all living beings. Water is the first thing offered to a guest and is a regular offering in Hindu puja. Water, for example, is offered in conch shells to the divinities in temples several times everyday, it is poured from brass or copper pots on Shiva lingams and other deities in simple outdoor shrines, and it is presented to the rising sun every day by many Hindus.

An important characteristic of Indian tree worship is—as observed in the performance of the Somvati Amavasya Vrat, but done on other occasions as well—wrapping a tree with cotton string, usually colored red and yellow. This method of tree worship is fairly unique to India. The string is called variously: *kalava, nara,* or *raksha* in Hindi. The first two words simply connote the red and yellow string used in religious ceremonies. The last term, *raksha*, means "protection, protector, protective armor, or a safeguard."[57] Early in my year of research in Banaras I became friends with an auto-rickshaw driver I had employed to visit tree shrines beyond walking distance from my house. Nagendra grew up in a brahman family in Banaras and graduated from Banaras Hindu University. Since he showed great interest in my research project I used him frequently for transportation and relied on him as a conversation partner between and after interviews. Nagendra had observed tree wrappings with me on several occasions and asked his parents why this was done. He reported to me what they told him: "The pipal tree is wrapped with *raksha* for two reasons: to make a cloth offering [*vastra-dan*] to Vasudeva, and like in Rakhsha Bandhan, it is also a way of both protecting the Vasudeva tree and asking Vasudeva in the form of a tree for protection in return."[58] These two explanations were confirmed by several other people I spoke with about the meaning of tree wrapping.[59] The cotton string is, then, considered to be a simple form of clothing; it is a *vastra-dan* or "cloth offering" to the tree divinity and is used to adorn the tree as a means of honoring it.[60] Moreover, the string used to wrap the tree is the same kind of string that is used by girls and women to wrap the wrist of their brothers on the Hindu festival of Rakhsha Bandhan. On this occasion, a girl or woman honors and demonstrates loving care for her brother by wrapping his wrist with *raksha* or a *rakhi* (both words mean a "protector"); the brother in return accepts a protective role toward his sister. Thus, the exchange is mutually beneficial. In a similar manner, a tree worshiper who wraps a pipal tree—typically understood as an embodied form of Vishnu—honors and demonstrates loving care for the tree while seeking the protective blessings of the tree. Tree wrapping, then, is a ritual exchange that illustrates the mutually beneficial relationship between the tree and the tree worshiper.[61]

Another striking feature of pipal tree worship in India is the affectionate interaction with the tree. Although the original "tree huggers" who inspired forest protection activists worldwide were Indian,[62] the reasons tree worshipers in northern India hug trees are quite different than those who hug trees to defend them from the loggers' axe. During my year of research, I witnessed many tree worshipers massage the base of a pipal tree, hug its trunk while placing their forehead against it, and on a few occasions I observed a tree worshiper even kiss a pipal tree. Although in the context of home shrines bodily contact between the worshiper and deity is not uncommon (in contrast to temples maintained by brahman priests in which ordinary worshipers rarely are allowed physical contact with the deity), this level of intimacy is somewhat unusual. A living tree seems to be a particularly available form of divinity with whom one can establish a wide array of relationships. These range from regarding the tree as a majestic master to an intimate lover. Tree worshipers told me that they massage pipal trees to please (*prasanna*) them. They place their heads against trees to honor them and receive their blessings. And the kiss certainly demonstrates an affectionate relationship with a being that is considered to be intimately present for close relationship. Some people perform these affectionate acts to get some kind of blessing from the tree, whereas others do them simply out of appreciation or gratitude for the tree. Many tree worshipers explained to me that they have developed a close relationship with their favorite tree just like they do with a friend or family member. The various Hindi words they used to describe this were *nata*, *rishta*, or *sambandha*. These are all terms employed to denote a close "connection" or "relationship" with another. A man in Banaras described to me how his mother had broken into grateful tears one morning while telling some family friends how a pipal tree she cares for in her backyard had given so many blessings to her family. The specific acts of tree worship, then, both express and generate the intimate relationship many tree worshipers have with sacred trees in India.

Reasons for Worshiping a Pipal Tree

Besides the specific objectives expressed by the women who worship pipal trees during the Somvati Amavasya Vrat, there are a variety of reasons Hindus worship pipal trees in northern India. Many report that they worship pipal trees to receive blessings (*ashirbad*) for a successful, abundant, and healthy life. A number of people I spoke with said that they worshiped pipal trees to be happy (*sukha*). Others, recognizing the pipal tree as a type of *kalpa-vriksha* "Wishing Tree," maintain that all desires are fulfilled by worshiping a pipal tree. I met a cloth merchant at the Tulsi Ghat pipal tree who told me that he worships this tree every day before he opens his shop in the morning to insure gainful business for the day. Generally, worship of a pipal tree is believed to drive away all one's problems and result in a good life (*accha jivan*). In this sense, the contemporary view of the pipal tree is in line with the ancient view that the pipal tree is a "tree of life." One morning I was sitting beneath a huge pipal tree that grows before an old Jagannath Temple near Assi Ghat in Banaras, when a woman came to worship the tree. After informing me that the tree is Vasudeva, she went on to say: "If you worship this tree all your troubles [*takliph*] will go far away. I have gotten rid of many troubles here." Sometimes very specific things are attributed to the worship of a pipal tree: a satisfactory marriage, a healthy child, high scores on a college exam, a new car, and so forth. I met a young man who worships a pipal tree every week in the temple complex within the Dasanam Juna Akhara in Banaras. He explained to me that as a result of this worship he has not been sick for two years and had obtained his current lucrative job without paying any money, a very unusual situation at a time when many people in India have to pay a handsome sum to secure good employment.

While some people worship pipal trees for specific personal gain, others do it out of appreciation for the gifts a pipal tree gives naturally. Although not all tree worshipers would accept this, a hierarchical assessment of motives exists within certain discourses related to Hindu worship. The distinctions rest on the degree to which someone seeks personal gain in the act of worship, opposed to performing it just as an act of affectionate admiration. When the act is motivated by the desire for personal gain it is called *sakama* (with desire), when it is performed for appreciation alone it is called *nishkama* (without desire). Although many use the word *puja* (worship) for both, some convey this distinction by calling the first *puja* and the second *seva* (loving service). In many ways *sakama puja* is linked historically to the pursuit of power and life blessings through the performance of the ancient Vedic fire sacrificial ritual: offerings are poured into the mouth of the fire with the expectation of some kind of fruitful return (*phala*). The devotional practice of *karma-yoga* as expressed in the Bhagavad Gita and elsewhere rejects this approach in favor of a form of spiritual practice that encourages one to perform actions without attachment to the results or fruit of those actions (*karma-phala*). This assessment of the hierarchy in the motives of worshipers in some Hindu traditions is evident in the following words from a contemporary commentary on the Bhagavad Gita: "The upper class devotees do not desire anything, including *mukti* from the Lord, except for one boon: The devotion to the lotus feet of the Lord birth after birth. Lower class devotees use God as a servant to fulfill their material demands and desires. A true devotee considers oneself the servant, the Lord as the Master [other options also exist; for example, one can consider oneself as a friend or lover of the Lord as the Beloved], and the entire creation as His body."[63] The higher path according to this way of thinking involves a show of appreciation and asks for nothing except a devotional relationship, while the lower path involves requesting particular things for oneself. Both paths, however, assume and foster a close relationship with the deity being worshiped.

Perhaps they were just expressing an ideal, but many tree worshipers I spoke with told me they were not worshipping the tree for any benefit (*phayda*), but rather simply as an act of appreciation (often using the Hindi word *adar*). As I arrived at a Shiva temple complex within the city of Banaras one day, a priest was watering a pipal tree that grew within the temple compound. When I asked him about the tree, he told me that it is "Vasudeva," and that he was doing "*jal-seva*" (water service or worship) to the tree. I enquired about the benefits of caring for this tree. "Listen," he said, "I am doing service (*seva*) to this tree. I honor the tree in this way, and in return it gives me shade. Shade is the main benefit I get from honoring this tree. I honor it because it gives shade—to all beings, not just me. And it gives shade to all without asking." On another occasion I watched a man conduct a rather elaborate puja of a large pipal tree that stands at the top of Chauki Ghat. When he finished I asked him if he worshiped this tree everyday. He affirmed that he did so each day before work. When I asked him what benefit (*phayda*) comes from this, he pointed to his heart and said: "I'm not looking for anything. I just honor [*manta*] this tree." Similarly, I observed a man worship a pipal tree at a shrine in Rishikesh with water, marigold flowers, and an *arati* lamp offering, without making any offerings to the gods assembled at the base of the tree. As he was putting his sandals back on I asked him what benefit he gets from this. He answered: "This tree is sacred [*pavitra*] and gives many good things. Therefore, I just honor it. I do not do this to seek any special thing for myself. Good things just come naturally from this tree. It is wonderful and very worthy of worship [*pujaniya*]." A man worshiping the pipal tree at the Senapati Vanakati Hanuman temple in Banaras put it this way: "Listen. We don't come to worship asking for anything in particular. Maybe some people do, but I am speaking for myself. I don't come asking for anything. I come just to honor God." I asked a woman worshiping a large pipal tree that grows in front of a hotel on the bank of the Ganges in Banaras if she worshiped this tree every day. "Yes," she responded, "this tree is Vasudeva." When I asked her what benefit [*phayda*] she derives from this worship, she answered: "Benefit? I don't look for benefits. All is in his hands. I just honor him for all that he has given to me and my family. That's all." The mother of one of my friends in Banaras told me that her mother began everyday by first bathing and then offering fresh water to a huge pipal tree that grew in the front yard of their house, which was built so as not to disturb this ancient tree. Every evening she lit an oil lamp and placed it before this tree "to thank and honor this tree for all the shade, oxygen, and other blessings that it gave to our family."

Other pipal tree worshipers eschew material benefits for more enlightened experience, such as peace or as an expression of spiritual devotion. While visiting Bodh Gaya, the place where the Buddha achieved enlightenment under a pipal tree, I spoke with a Hindu man who was circumambulating a pipal tree near the Maha-Bodhi Temple. When he had finished, I asked him if this tree was sacred (*pavitra*). He assured me that it was, remarking "This tree is Vasudeva." I inquired about the benefit he receives from worshiping it, and he replied: "People worship this tree to bring them peace [*shanti*]. If there is peace in your heart then you don't need anything else." A similar statement was made by a man worshiping a pipal tree in front of an old mosque near Panchaganga Ghat in Banaras. After pouring water on the base of the tree and circumambulating it fourteen times, he explained to me that he comes to this tree every day right after taking his morning bath. He told me that for him this tree is a "*svarupa* of Vishnu." When I asked him what benefits accrue from this worship, he said: "It brings one peace, and with peace [*shanti*] nothing else is desired." I spoke with a young man who comes to worship a pipal tree in the Senapati Vanakati Hanuman temple every day and asked him what experiences (*anubhava*) came from this worship. "What to talk about experiences?" he responded, "I just do this for devotion [*bhakti*]." Likewise, I watched a man offer perfumed water to the large pipal tree that stands atop Tulsi Ghat and circumambulate it several times, massage its base, and place his head reverently to its trunk. He informed me that he does this daily. When I asked him why, he answered, "Because all we have comes from God [Bhagavan], and it is necessary for us to show our respect [*adar*] and appreciation for this."

Talks with pipal tree worshipers reveal a wide range of the resulting relationships cultivated through worshipful acts and attitudes. I spoke with a man at the Senapati Vanakati Hanuman temple in Banaras who had been coming to this temple every day for the past forty years. He told me "many people worship this tree just to honor it, especially on Saturdays, the most auspicious day to worship a pipal tree."[64] When I pointed out that this was Monday and that he had still come, he continued: "Everyone is in a big hurry these days. There is no peace in life in this situation. I leave enough time every morning on my way to work to worship here. In this way I start each day with a peace of mind that leads to good health, whereas rushing around leads to disease. When you honor a powerful being like a pipal tree you will develop a relationship with it, and in return that being will treat you well. Without this honoring [*manna*] nothing happens between two beings." A man I encountered in Rishikesh seemed to agree: "If you honor me then I will treat you well. If you don't then I won't. It's the same with a tree." Both of these men expressed the idea that if you respect a tree it will in return enter into a positive relationship with you and bless you with good things in life, such as peace of mind.

While living in Banaras I made friends with a man who had received a Ph.D. in physics from an American university. His parents were both professors at Banaras Hindu University, one taught chemistry and the other nutrition; he therefore grew up on the wooded BHU campus where his family lived with his paternal grandmother. He told me that his grandmother had worshiped a pipal tree on the corner of their block, making at least a water offering to the tree every morning. Over the years she developed a close relationship with this tree. A decade after she had died a peaceful death, her son was riding his motorcycle home and lost control of it, crashing into a ditch containing a pile of bricks. It just so happened, however, that he crashed underneath the pipal tree that his mother had worshiped for years, and the sharp-edged bricks were covered with a thick layer of the tree's leaves, cushioning his fall so that he walked away from the crash unscathed. The family attributed his good fortune to the fact that his mother had worshiped this tree with great affection; the tree was watching out for her son. Over the years my friend himself had also developed a close relationship with this pipal tree. Every time he passes by it, he stops his motorcycle and hugs the tree and talks to it. "It is my friend," he told me. "Whenever I am depressed I go to this tree and hug it and talk to it. I always come away feeling much better.... Since I started worshiping a pipal tree every day, my life has changed dramatically. Many wonderful things have come into my life. My career as a singer really took off as a result of my relationship with this tree. I felt that I have been loving this pipal tree and it said to me, 'Here is a gift for you.'" He went on to declare, "I have personally felt the presence of God more in a tree shrine worshiped by sincere people than I have in the most popular of temples, such as the Kashi Vishvanath Mandir [the most important temple in Banaras]."

According to many accounts and traditions in northern India, worship of pipal trees also results in achieving the highest spiritual blessings. The following story involving the famous poet-saint Tulsidas is told about the large and popular pipal tree at Assi Ghat.[65] As a young man, the great saint Tulsidas spent much of his early life in Banaras with an intense desire to see Lord Rama. At that time the Assi Ghat area was covered with a jungle. Every day Tulsidas would come here to empty his bowels and bathe, and every morning he would pour any water that remained in his water pot onto the roots of this pipal tree. After some time, the god (*devata*) of the pipal tree appeared to him and told him that he was so pleased with the water offerings that he would grant Tulsidas a boon. The saint had only one desire: to see Lord Rama. The tree divinity informed him that he could not give him this power, but Rama's devoted servant Hanuman could. The tree divinity reported that Hanuman came to Assi Ghat every morning to bathe in the Ganges disguised as a leper. Tulsidas waited for him the next morning, and when he approached grabbed onto his feet. The leper yelled at him to let go, warning that he would catch leprosy. Undeterred, Tulsidas hung on for a long time, forcing Hanuman finally to reveal his true form. Tulsidas's discovery of Hanuman, which led to his saintly attainment of Lord Rama, was due to the blessing of the pipal tree. For this reason, my informant explained, there is a Hanuman temple under the Assi Ghat pipal tree. Several people I spoke with insisted that this is why Hanuman temples are frequently found beneath pipal trees. Contemporary stories about the ability of a pipal tree to grant the highest spiritual blessings are very much in line with the ancient view of the pipal tree as the "tree of knowledge." For the most well-known case of all, and to encounter what must be the most renowned of all pipal trees, it is necessary to travel to Bodh Gaya.

Buddhist Views of the Pipal Tree (at Bodh Gaya)

As the story of Tulsidas and other narratives associated with pipal trees indicate, according to many Hindus the highest kinds of spiritual rewards can come from worshiping a pipal tree. In a sense, any pipal tree will do—the one just down the block is an embodied form of Vishnu and if approached appropriately can yield great results. No need for lengthy pilgrimage to worship a pipal tree, for one likely is nearby. The situation is different, however, for Buddhists. There is one pipal tree that stands out amongst all others, and many Buddhists expend much effort to visit it. The Maha-Bodhi Tree under which the Buddha is believed to have achieved enlightenment is almost certainly the most famous pipal tree in the world, and many Buddhists travel great distances to see, touch, worship, and meditate under this legendary tree. Guidebooks available at Bodh Gaya observe that the Bodhi Tree is the most sacred of all sites for Buddhists; accordingly, this particular pipal tree is a major pilgrimage destination for Buddhists worldwide. A pamphlet published by the Bodh Gaya Temple Management Committee, for example, declares: "This [Bodhi Tree] is the most important of all places for a devout Buddhist. The Jataka tales reveal that the Bodhi Tree is an object of veneration as the Buddha himself sanctioned it and is regarded as a symbolic representation of the Buddha."[66] No consideration of the positive attitudes associated with the pipal tree, then, would be complete without taking into account the world-famous Maha-Bodhi Tree at Bodh Gaya.

The Maha-Bodhi Temple compound in Bodh Gaya is a remarkable space. It consists of a huge square courtyard filled with many ancient stone Buddhist images, stupas, and shrines. Much religious activity occurs amongst its sacred objects and gardens of trees and flowering plants. Tibetan monks clad in gold and maroon robes perform countless prostrations inside the walled compound during the winter months, and a wide array of Buddhists from around the world can be seen meditating or performing rituals of various sorts within its stone walls. Three concentric circumambulatory paths allow for continuous movement around the compound. At the center of all this is the towering Maha-Bodhi Temple—built right next to the Bodhi Tree—celebrating the foundational experience for Buddhism: the enlightenment of the Buddha (figure 3.10). Although the temple itself is quite impressive, housing an image of the Buddha in the Earth-touching posture he assumed as he sat under the tree, the central attraction here is the Maha-Bodhi Tree itself. Temple authorities acknowledge that the Bodh Gaya tree has died or been destroyed a few times throughout its long history, but the current tree is said to be a direct descendent of the original tree under which the Buddha sat.

Buddhist chronicles record that Buddhism was introduced into Sri Lanka during the time of King Ashoka in the third century B.C.E. At the request of the Sri Lankan ruler, Ashoka's daughter was sent to Sri Lanka with a sapling produced from a cutting of the original Bodhi tree in Bodh Gaya: "The cutting of the sacred Bodhi tree, brought from Bodhgaya to Sri Lanka by Asoka's daughter (the nun Sanghamitta) at the request of King Devanampriya Tissa (247–207 B.C.), was transported to Anuradhapura with great pomp and planted in the Mahameghavana park."[67] Whenever the Bodhi tree in Bodh Gaya expired, cuttings from the tree in Anuradhapura were used to replant it.

The current Bodhi tree in Bodh Gaya is immense: its five-foot diameter trunk supports a colossal crown that branches out to the west side of the temple. Supports have been added to some of the more massive limbs to insure that they do not break from their own heavy weight. The trunk of the tree is completely surrounded by an ornate light-pink sandstone fence about eight feet high, which is often decorated with colorful bits of cloth, prayer flags, and strings of marigold flowers. From time to time the entire stone fence is wrapped with huge pieces of gold cloth, a favored offering for honoring the tree by Thai Buddhist pilgrims who visit this site in large numbers.[68] Within this enclosure and up against the east side of the tree is the Vrajasana Jnana Sthali, the seat upon which the Buddha achieved enlightenment. The seat is sheltered with an ornate gold covering, and is often strewn with a colorful

Figure 3.10 Maha-Bodhi Temple in Bodh Gaya

variety of flowers that have been offered by the pilgrims. Aromatic smoke from numerous sticks of incense left by Buddhist devotees surrounds the seat with sweet fragrances (figure 3.11).

People from all over the world visit Bodh Gaya to pay their respects to the Maha-Bodhi Tree using the ritual procedures of their own country. When I visited Bodh Gaya to observe the veneration of this sacred tree, I encountered Buddhist pilgrims from Tibet, Japan, Thailand, Sri Lanka, Korea, India, Burma, Vietnam, Europe, and North America. It would be difficult to generalize about the kind of worship that goes on here, but it is common for Buddhist pilgrims of many nationalities to make water offerings to the tree, and almost all of them circumambulate the tree and bow to honor it. It is also common to witness pilgrims scrambling to catch leaves floating down from the tree, especially before they touches the ground.[69] These will be carefully safeguarded and taken home as sacred souvenirs.

Figure 3.11 Bodhi Tree under which the Buddha achieved enlightenment

More elaborate forms of worship of the Maha Bodhi tree, however, can also be observed here. I watched a group of Thai pilgrims offer bottles of water to the roots of the tree, apply small pieces of gold leaf to accessible places on the rough surface of the roots, and then tie some marigold garlands to the fence that surrounds the tree and wrap it with a large gold cloth that matched the color of Thai monastic dress. They then sat beneath the tree and chanted prayers of praise to the Buddha and Bodhi tree. One of the women in this group told me that they offered the large gold cloth to the tree "to bring good things into our lives." A group of Sri Lankan pilgrims offered uncooked white rice at the base of the tree, in addition to water and flowers. They wrapped the tree railing with a large piece of orange cloth, the same shade Sri Lankan monks wear. A group of Tibetans wrapped the railing with multicolored prayer flags, while a few fastened pieces of white cloth on the railing. As these examples show, some pilgrims who visit the Bodh Gaya worship the tree itself directly. Others, however, honor what the Buddha accomplished under the tree, but the distinction between these two is often difficult to determine.

Some scholars insist that the Bodhi tree itself is not worshiped, but is only honored because of its association with the Buddha's enlightenment. My own research, however, has caused me to question this claim, at least for certain types or nationalities of Buddhists. Thai and Sri Lankan Buddhists, for example, face the tree during their chants and worship the tree itself. Since saplings from the

Bodhi tree were carried by Buddhists throughout Burma, Southeast Asia, and Sri Lanka, pipal trees grow in Thailand and Sri Lanka and are worshipfully honored there too. On the other hand, Japanese Buddhists, who come from a land where pipal trees do not grow, face the temple during their chants and do not seem to make many offerings to the tree directly. All Buddhists agree, however, that this tree is very special or sacred, and that pipal trees in general should be honored. I spoke with one of the chief caretakers of the Maha-Bodhi Temple, who believed that the Bodhi Tree is sacred because the Buddha achieved enlightenment beneath it. He refused to recognize it as a god (*devata*) or divine being, intentionally distancing himself from Hindu views of pipal trees. "It is only a tree," he insisted. "For Buddhists it is very special; it is sacred [*pavitra*]. Buddhists would never cut a pipal or Bodhi tree or use its wood to build anything, but it is not a *devata*." Other Buddhists disagree with this position, not hesitating to identify the Bodhi tree as a divine being, or even as a form of the Buddha himself.

I acquired a book in the temple bookstore in Bodh Gaya titled *Vandami Bodhi-Vriksham* ("I Worship the Bodhi Tree").[70] This book, written in Hindi by the Buddhist historian Madhukar Pipalayan, is a treasure house of information about Buddhist views of the Bodhi Tree. Pipalayan claims that the Bodhi Tree is supremely sacred (*parama-pavan*) and is the very basis and center of Buddhist culture; in fact, he argues, it has been considered an integral form (*ekibhuta-rupa*) of Buddha himself.[71] In his book he traces a long history of pipal tree worship in India and cites evidence of pipal tree worship in the ancient Indus Valley Civilization and in early Vedic culture in which the pipal is considered a "form of god" (*deva-rupa*). According to Buddhist traditions, however, all previous Buddhas achieved enlightenment under a tree, and many of these did so under a pipal tree, which has long been known as a "tree of knowledge." Following this Buddhist view of history, Pipalayan pushes Buddhist association with the pipal tree far back before the time of either the Indus or Vedic cultures. Although he acknowledges that Shakyamuni Buddha lived after the time of both of these cultures, he credits the presence of pipal tree worship in them to the worship of pipal trees by former Buddhas, whom Buddhists believe easily pre-date both of these ancient cultures. He argues that worship of the pipal tree was then taken up in later Indian traditions that became associated with Hinduism. He highlights the identification of the pipal tree with Vishnu in the Puranas, particularly in the Padma Purana, but attributes this to the fact that Buddhist ideas became absorbed into Vaishnavism in later Hinduism, whereby Buddha was regarded as an incarnation of Vishnu. Later Hindu conceptions of the pipal tree, Pipalayan contends, are therefore greatly influenced by earlier Buddhist conceptions of the Bodhi tree.

The historical accuracy of this overtly Buddhist agenda is debatable; based on evidence in early sculptural remains many art historians present a different account. "The tree, like the other (Buddhist) symbols," writes David Snellgrove, for example, "was already in pre-Buddhist times an object of miraculous efficacy, and therefore worthy of worship (puja)."[72] The art historian M. S. Randhawa supports this position: "It seems that tree worship was widely prevalent in India before the rise of Buddhism.... Buddhism adopted the cult of tree worship from the older religions which prevailed in the country."[73] The art historian Klemens Karlsson concurs, arguing that Buddhism absorbed preexisting notions of the sacrality of the pipal tree: "What seems to be worship of trees is found already in the Indus Valley civilization. This can be seen on several seals both from Mohenjo-daro and Harappa.... There was already a cult of sacred trees before the time of the Buddha.... Both Buddhists and Jains adopted this tradition of worshipping trees.... Finally, the tree became associated with the enlightenment of the Buddha and used as an indexical sign pointing to the Buddha Sakyamuni and his enlightenment."[74] Whatever account one accepts, Pipalayan's primary point remains: the pipal tree has been identified with Buddha for a long time.

Pipalayan examines in detail the previous lives of the Buddha as represented in the Jataka stories, for these stories reveal much about Buddhist conceptions of trees. He draws attention to the fact that in no less than thirty of the Jataka stories, the Buddha appeared in his former lives as a bodhisattva in the form of a tree god (*vriksha-deva* or *vriksha-devata*).[75] Moreover, according to Pipalayan, a Bodhi tree can be understood as a bodhisattva in the form of a tree god.[76] He points out, for example, that in one of the Jataka stories the future Buddha took the form of a tree god to preach compassionate nonviolence toward all beings.[77] Two other Jataka stories provide a glimpse of both early tree worship and of the generosity of the future Buddha in the form of a tree divinity. In the first story we meet a group of villagers who on the occasion of a special festival prepare to make offerings to their favorite trees. Prosperous people offered flower garlands, incense, and rich foods to the trees; however, a poor man who was devoted to an Aranda Tree—the very tree the future Buddha had embodied—had nothing to offer his tree except a modest cake and a coconut shell full of water. Feeling the inadequacy of his own gifts in comparison to those of others, the poor man turned away from the tree without leaving his offerings, but the tree divinity called out to the man, requesting him to return and hand over his gifts. After the poor man had presented his cake and water to the tree, the tree divinity asked him why he was conducting this worship. The poor man told the divinity of the tree that he did so to alleviate his misfortune. The tree then blessed him with a fabulous treasure that put an end to his poverty.[78] In the second story the future Buddha becomes another tree divinity, and in this form showers great wealth on a poor brahman who swept the ground around the tree and worshiped it regularly with prayers, flowers, incense, and honorific lamps.[79]

Honorable personhood in these Buddhist stories is certainly not limited to the human. Another Jataka story illustrates the nobility and sentience of a tree being as a bodhisattva. While dwelling in the Jetavana forest, Buddha told the following story to the monks gathered around him. King Brahmadatta, who once ruled the region of Banaras long ago, desired to build a new palace supported by a single stout, tall column. He commanded his workers to search his kingdom for the perfect tree to construct such a palace. They did so and located in the king's own park a huge and ancient tree, which the king ordered them to cut down. The workers went to the tree and worshiped it with flower offerings and honorific lamps, wrapped it with string, and apologized for what they were about to do, informing the tree god that the king had commanded them to cut it down within seven days. The tree reflected on the disastrous consequences of his falling on the young trees growing around him and thought to himself: "Now my life only lasts as long as this my abiding place. And all the young sal trees that stand around this, where dwell the deities my kinsfolk, and they are many, will be destroyed. My own destruction does not touch me so near as the destruction of my children: therefore I must protect their lives." Stirred into action by his compassion for the young trees around him, the tree divinity went to the king's sleeping chamber one night and stood before him weeping sadly. The king awoke and asked the radiant being to identify himself. The tree spirit informed the king that he was the very tree slated to be felled for construction of the new palace. His name was Lucky Tree, a tree that had stood within what is now the king's park for sixty thousand years and had been worshiped over the years by multitudes of people. During all this time no one had dared to harm him. The king listened to this, but nonetheless told the tree spirit that he intended to use his trunk to build a magnificent palace. Understanding that the king would not change his plan, the tree divinity requested that the workers cut him up branch by branch, rather than by a single cut at the base of his trunk. The king realized, however, that this would be a very painful death for the tree, and asked why the tree would willingly choose such a death: "First hands and feet, then nose and ears, while yet the victim lives, and last of all the head let fall—a painful death this gives. O Lucky Tree! O woodland king! What pleasure couldst thou feel? Why, for what reason dost thou wish to be cut up piecemeal?" The tree answered that by being felled in this manner the smaller trees around him would not be crushed to death as they would if he were to come down in one huge crashing fall. The king then realized that the tree was willing to endure a very painful death to save his friends and relatives who grew around him. Moved by such noble compassion, the king told the tree to have no fear, for he would now abandon his plan to utilize a tree to support the new palace. From his encounter with this tree, the king was morally transformed and spent the rest of his life doing good deeds. After narrating this story to the monks, the Buddha revealed, "I was myself Lucky Tree, the king of the gods."[80]

Prince Siddhartha, who became the Buddha under the Bodhi Tree, maintained a close relationship with trees his whole life. He was born between a pair of shala trees in the Lumbini forest; he first meditated under a jambu tree at Kumaravastha; after renouncing his home he practiced asceticism under an amra tree near the town of Anupiya; once he abandoned harsh asceticism, he accepted some rice pudding from the cowgirl Sujata under a banyan tree;[81] and he made a vow to sit under a pipal tree on the bank of the Niranjana River until he had achieved full awakening. Once he had achieved full awakening and had become Buddha, he made his decision to preach the Dharma—and thereby establish all future Buddhist practice—under a pipal, and most of his later preaching at the Deer Park in Sarnath and elsewhere took place under a tree.

Very importantly, Pipalayan insists, Buddhists believe that Buddha himself worshiped the Bodhi Tree, thereby setting a model for all later Buddhists. He quotes a famous Pali Gatha to illustrate his point: "The Lord of the World [Buddha] worshiped [*pujita*] you O Maha-Bodhi Tree. I too worship you. All honor to you, O King of Enlightenment!"[82] According to Buddhist tradition, Buddha had a special relationship with the Bodh Tree. A white marble sign that stands today within the Maha-Bodhi compound in Bodh Gaya to mark a special place where the Buddha meditated reads: "After enlightenment Lord Buddha spent the second week in meditation here gazing unwinking at the Bodhi Tree." Based on his reading of early Buddhist literature, Pipalayan maintains that the Bodhi Tree was commonly viewed as a kind of tree god or bodhisattva who provides protection for those who sit beneath it and nurtures the attainment of the highest knowledge.[83]

Worship of the Bodhi Tree has been portrayed in much Buddhist art. Although there has been a hesitation on the part of many art historians to call this tree worship, this is exactly what it seems to be for many practicing Buddhists, past and present. Numerous surviving sculptural representations show people worshiping the Bodhi Tree. A piece of the stone railing in the Bodh Gaya Museum, for example, depicts worship of the Bodhi Tree. In a manner reminiscent of pipal tree worship in India today, a human figure kneels at the base of the tree, bowing in a reverent posture with his head touching the tree. Above him is a winged celestial figure shown offering a flower garland directly to the upper portion of the tree (figure 3.12). Both figures seem to be worshiping the tree itself. While acknowledging that the Bodhi Tree was used in some Buddhist contexts to represent the enlightenment of the Buddha, based on my own interviews and observations of Buddhist pilgrims in Bodh Gaya, and my reading of Pipalayan and others,[84] it seems likely that the tree is also represented in Indian art as being worshiped directly. This is very much in line with the understanding of the Bodhi Tree as some kind of divinity, or perhaps even a compassionate, helpful bodhisattva.

In addition to highlighting the view that the Bodhi Tree is a divinity in its own right, some historians find evidence in Buddhist literature for claims of an identification between the Buddha and the Bodhi Tree. The art historian Malla, for example, writes: "Buddha is known to have told that 'He who worships it

Figure 3.12 Early Buddhist sculpture of Bodhi Tree worship

[the Bodhi Tree] will receive the same reward as if he worshipped me in person.'"[85] Pipalayan explains that according to Buddhist belief: "The Maha-Bodhi Tree was also born on the very day that Prince Siddhartha was born in the Lumbini Forest. So the holy Bodhi Tree is the exact same age as Gautama Buddha."[86] For Pipalayan this indicates an identity between the two. Furthermore, he calls the Bodhi Tree an "integral form" (*ekibhuta*) of the Buddha. It is to a large degree because of this identity, Pipalayan maintains, that great honor is conferred on the Bodhi Tree.

The celebrated emperor Ashoka is said to have established a significant historical example for both Buddhist conceptions and worship of the Bodhi Tree. Buddhist records indicate that the emperor made a pilgrimage to the Bodhi Tree in Bodh Gaya and worshiped it by offering it copious amounts of water. These records also indicate that Ashoka looked upon the tree as a form of the Buddha: "It is known that King Ashoka regarded the Bodhi-tree as the Buddha himself."[87]

Pipalayan too strongly emphasizes this point, maintaining that Ashoka considered the Bodhi Tree an aspect of the Buddha.[88] Buddhists accounts report that Ashoka is to have said, "When I looked at the king of trees, I knew that even now I was looking at the Self-Existent Master."[89] A story is told that Ashoka so loved the Bodhi Tree that one of his queens became exceedingly resentful of it and tried to have it destroyed: "As he treated it just like he did the queen, the real queen Tisyaraksita had even tried killing the 'Bodhi' out of jealousy."[90]

In sum, there are four reasons why Buddhists have honored the Bodhi Tree with reverent worship throughout the ages and continue to do so today. First, the tree nurtures the quest for ultimate knowledge and protects those seekers who take its shelter. Second, it has been viewed as the body of some kind of divinity: either a tree god (*vriksha-devata*) or a helpful bodhisattva. Third, the Buddha himself worshiped the Bodhi Tree, establishing a paradigm for this practice as part of the Buddhist path. And fourth, the tree is considered by some Buddhists to be a form of the Buddha himself. Combined, these rationales have provided sufficient motivation for many Buddhists to become devoted tree worshipers.

Hindus also visit the pilgrimage site of Bodh Gaya, for the elastic theology of Hinduism easily encompasses Buddha, and many Hindus consider Buddha a form of Vishnu. Since there is a small Shiva linga inside the contested site of the Maha-Bodhi Temple, a Hindu priest is included among the officials who make up the Maha-Bodhi Temple Committee. After observing him offer a brass pot of water to the Bodhi Tree—which he does every morning—I spoke with him about his understanding of pipal trees. He reported: "For us Hindus all pipal trees are sacred [*pavitra*] and worthy of worship [*pujaniya*]. The pipal tree is Vasudeva, but this one is very special because Buddha attained enlightenment beneath it." I asked him if Buddhists worship all pipal trees. "No, only this one," he replied, "but they would not harm any pipal tree. They respect them all because of this tree." He later amended this statement, informing me that Sri Lankans do worship pipal trees in Sri Lanka. Other Hindus I met in Bodh Gaya shared this priest's views. Two workers in charge of sweeping the temple compound who identified themselves as Hindu and seemed to share an interest in different views of the Bodhi Tree told me: "For us, all pipal trees are sacred [*pavitra*] and are the same [*sab pipal ek hi hai*], but for Buddhists only this particular tree is sacred."

Although they recognize the specialness of the Maha-Bodhi Tree, Hindus in Bodh Gaya seem to hold the more general understandings of pipal trees shared by Hindus in other regions of northern India. While in Bodh Gaya I visited a sizeable pipal tree that stands about a kilometer from the Maha-Bodhi temple and shelters a small Shiva temple beneath it. I arrived at this shrine as a man was worshiping the pipal tree; when he had finished I asked him if this tree was a god (*devata*). "Yes," he said, "it is Vasudeva." I asked if this pipal tree was significantly different from the Maha-Bodhi Tree. He replied: "No. They are the same [*ek hi hai*]. All pipal trees are sacred [*pavitra*] as they are a form of Vasudeva." I met a resident of Bodh Gaya one evening after observing him circumambulate another large pipal tree growing in the Maha-Bodhi compound. This man explained to me that for him the tree he was circumambulating, as well as all pipal trees, are sacred because they are all forms of Vasudeva. He told me that he worships a pipal tree "to get peace in his soul [*atma*]," and preferred to worship the Maha-Bodhi Tree "because of its great power [*shakti*]," but because of the crowds there this evening had decided to worship this pipal tree instead. "After all," he remarked, "all pipal trees grant peace." For Hindus, then, the Maha-Bodhi Tree shares in the same sacredness of all pipal trees, however, most acknowledge that this tree is special because of its association with the Buddha.

The Hindu pilgrimage center of Gaya is located very near Bodh Gaya. The *Gaya Mahatmya*, a text that celebrates the greatness of this Hindu site that is presumed to include Bodh Gaya, provides illustration of another specifically Hindu understanding of the specialness of the Maha-Bodhi tree while praising this tree. In this text the tree of Buddha's enlightenment is represented as a prime place for performing the death ritual of *shraddha*: "Obeisance to you king of Asvatthas, of the form of Brahma, Vishnu and Shiva, the tree of enlightenment [*Bodhidruma*] for the performers (of Shraddha) and the redeemer of the Pitrs (ancestors)."[91] Once again, the special quality of this tree is recognized, while at the same time it is represented in a fashion that ties it into more general Hindu notions of pipal trees.

People I spoke with in Bodh Gaya were not in agreement about whether Buddhists honor all pipal trees or just the Maha-Bodhi Tree in the Bodh Gaya temple compound. One merchant who lives in Bodh Gaya and makes his living selling souvenirs to Buddhist pilgrims insisted that both Buddhists and Hindus might worship any pipal tree: "Both Buddhists and Hindus conduct worship [*puja*] to the Bodhi or pipal tree. This one here is the most special for Buddhists, but they honor all pipal trees. For Hindus the pipal is Vasudeva, but not for Buddhists. For them too the pipal is a divinity [*devata*], but for them is *jnana-prapti-devata* [a "god for obtaining knowledge or enlightenment"]. But neither Hindus nor Buddhists would harm any pipal tree." On the other hand, an Ayurvedic doctor who lives in Bodh Gaya informed me that Buddhists worship only the Maha-Bodhi Tree in Bodh Gaya: "Hindus worship any pipal tree, but Buddhists worship only the Bodhi tree here. The Buddha chose to sit under a pipal tree to achieve enlightenment because there are two great things available in its shade: one, a large amount of oxygen that gives mental peace, and two, a great power [*shakti*] that can be used for both physical and mental power." Hybrids of the two positions also seem to exist. I met the owner of a small tent-like restaurant in Bodh Gaya with a medium-sized pipal tree growing within it who identified himself as a Buddhist. He had placed a small Buddha image in a crevice of this tree, and every day he worships the tree by offering water and incense to it and chanting the threefold Buddhist refuge before it. When I asked him how he viewed this tree, he replied, "This tree is a *devata*." I then asked him to identify the god. "It is different for different people. All *devatas* reside within the Bodhi tree."

In general, however, two distinctive views emerge: one Hindu and one Buddhist. Hindus typically regard pipal trees as sacred (most commonly viewing them as an embodied forms of Vishnu) wherever they are found, but acknowledge that the Maha-Bodhi Tree is special because the Buddha achieved enlightenment beneath it. Buddhists tend to focus more exclusively on the Maha-Bodhi Tree—or some relative of it—because of its association with the Buddha. Regardless, both Hindus and Buddhists share a common ethic by endorsing the view that a pipal tree should be venerated and protected from injury. Lay Buddhists who worship the Maha-Bodhi Tree often report that they do so to honor the tree and bring good things into their lives; in this sense they have much in common with Hindu worshipers of pipal trees. In sum, although Hindus and Buddhists differ in their understanding of the sacred qualities of a pipal tree, they agree that the pipal is a divine sentient being who as a source of a variety of life blessings should be revered and certainly never harmed. Regarding attitudes associated with the pipal tree, Monier Williams wrote in the nineteenth century: "Yet no native of India would venture to cut down or in any way injure or interfere with the growth of this tree."[92] This certainly remains true today. What all worshipers of pipal trees share is the notion that a pipal tree is not only a conscious, sentient being, but also a powerful divinity with whom one can have a beneficial relationship if treated properly. But the account of the pipal tree as a benevolent being for whom worshippers feel much appreciation and affection is not the full story. For a more complete understanding of the conception of a pipal tree's power, we need to move into the more frightening abode of ghosts and Saturn.

4

Abode of Ghosts and Saturn

> I worship pipal trees in the morning.
> I never go near a pipal tree at night.
>
> —woman in Banaras

> Ghosts live in pipal trees.
> That's why we never go near them after dark.
>
> —man in Banaras

> All glory to Shani [Saturn],
> who is situated in the shelter of the pipal tree.
>
> —mantra to Shani

The pipal tree, as mentioned in the last chapter, is the most powerful of all sacred trees in India. Power, however, has two aspects. In *The Idea of the Holy*, the historian of religions Rudolf Otto delineates two different dimensions of the human experience of the sacred: the *mysterium fascinans* is the attractive, charming, and nurturing side of divinity, while the *mysterium tremendum* is the more frightening, dreadful, and chastising side of divinity.[1] To grossly oversimplify the variety of religions for the purpose of better delineating the different human responses to these two aspects, we might say that there are roughly two types of religiosity that by and large correspond to these two sides of divinity: a religion of love, which involves an attitude of appreciation and often leads to surrender in life, and a religion of fear, which involves an attitude of vigilance and often leads to an attempt to control or manipulate life. The conceptualization of the pipal tree as Vasudeva falls primarily within the first category, whereas the conceptualization of the pipal tree as the abode of ghosts or Shani (the god Saturn) is associated mainly within the second. Yet the same pipal tree might be viewed in both ways, even by the very same person. Sacred power, as the pipal tree demonstrates, is highly ambiguous.

Although much in his book is questionable, the early twentieth-century Christian missionary J. Abbot noted perceptively, "There is no manifestation of power which illustrates better than does the power of trees all the complex and often contradictory ideas associated with power."[2] In a chapter titled "The Power of Trees," Abbot contends that trees in India contain power (*shakti*), which can be a beneficial power associated with protection, healing, and fertility, or a threatening power related to illness, misfortune, and ghosts. Likewise, in his study of late nineteenth-century "popular religion," W. Crooke notes that "trees often develop into curious or uncanny forms which compel fear or adoration."[3] A woman I talked with in Banaras about pipal trees said to me: "People honor the pipal tree because it is the abode of God [Bhagavan]; but they also fear it because it is the abode of ghosts [*bhuts*]. In the daytime God resides in the pipal, but at night ghosts are there. Therefore, people only visit and worship the pipal tree during the day—especially during the morning hours." Abbot notes the possibility of this binary view of particular trees: "Certain trees are the abode of gods and some are the abodes of spirits, and it may be that the same tree shelters a god in the morning and a spirit in the evening."[4] My companion and auto-rickshaw driver Nagendra, who accompanied me on many of my outings to visit tree shrines, told me one day: "All people want a neem tree in front of their house because Mother is good to us. But no one wants a pipal tree in front of their house because although it has a good side it also has a frightening side. People like it, but also fear it. The pipal tree is Vasudeva, but it is also Shani. There are also ghosts on the pipal tree. People are attracted to Vasudeva, but they are afraid of Shani and the many ghosts on the pipal tree." Although some previous scholars have recognized a connection between the pipal tree and Vishnu or Vasudeva, to my knowledge there is no study that recognizes the close relationship between the pipal tree and the Hindu god Shani. Yet I encountered the worship of Shani at pipal tree shrines wherever I traveled in northern India; the pipal tree in this part of the subcontinent today is intimately linked to this divinity, who commands a great deal of fearful respect.

Shani: King of the Planets

A large pipal tree stands within the walls of an impressive shrine atop Chauki Ghat in Banaras that is connected to a Hanuman temple allegedly established by the sixteenth-century saint Tulsidas. A sign on the gateway leading into this temple complex informs us that the name of the temple is the "Shri Vasudeva Baba Hanuman-ji Mandir." This name is telling, for it associates the temple with Vasudeva. Inside the temple complex is a *murti*, or embodied form, of Hanuman, and also a small shrine containing a Shiva lingam. There is no form of Vasudeva here other than the tree. A man who grew up near this shrine told me that this tree was identified as a "Vasudeva tree," and for this reason a holy man who lived here became known as Vasudeva Baba, thus the name Vasudeva Baba Hanuman

Temple. The identification of this pipal tree with Vasudeva is further indicated by old white marble plaques that were installed at the base of the huge tree. One of them reads: *Shri Shri Vasudevaya Namah* ("All Glory to Shri Vasudeva!"); another features a Sanskrit mantra praising Vasudeva Krishna.[5] Clearly, this tree maintains a strong identification with Vasudeva. Today, however, changes are taking place at this tree shrine.

The tree has a massive trunk around six feet in diameter and reaches a height of about sixty feet. The main Hanuman temple is just to the west of the tree, and the entire complex is contained within a high wall that is covered with white marble and inscribed with many different chants and prayers. A three-foot high octagonal enclosure measuring approximately sixteen feet across surrounds the tree. The octagonal enclosure is painted bright orange and is capped with a white marble top. Many deities are located on this marble platform. On the east side are two small orange shrines each housing murtis of Hanuman; on the south side are three naga stones featuring hooded serpents, two intertwined snakes, and a small shrine accommodating three black stone Shiva lingas; on the west side is another shrine containing a Shiva linga; and on the north side are river stone Shiva lingas beside the figure of Ganesha and a few naga stones that have been dabbed with red sindur powder and yellow turmeric paste. I had stopped by this shrine several times over the decade prior to 2006, and noticed the presence of all of these deities during my previous visits. The priest of the Hanuman temple told me that they have all been here "a long time." In the year 2006, however, nine new black stone images were added to the other deities on the marble platform (figure 4.1).

The new deities are the *nava graha*, the nine heavenly bodies that according to Indian astrology greatly influence a person's life.[6] Budha (Mercury), Brihaspati (Jupiter), and Sukra (Venus) now sit on the north side of the tree, Surya (Sun) is on the east side between the two Hanuman shrines, Chandra (Moon), and Mangal (Mars) are situated on the southeast side among the naga stones, and on the southwest side of the octagonal platform is Shani (Saturn), flanked by the shadow planets Rahu and Ketu (the two lunar nodes where solar and lunar eclipses occur). At the base of the octagonal enclosure, just below Shani, is an opening that is encased with blue and white tiles and leads back into a dark space in which a section of the roots of the colossal pipal tree are exposed. Embedded in these roots is a black stone. This stone is regarded as a form of Shani, and has been there much longer than the new black stone image of Shani on the platform above. Prior to the new additions on the platform, this Shani had certainly received worship, but the *nava graha* added to this tree shrine indicate a recent increase in the worship of the *nava graha*, and particularly of Shani.

Worship of a pipal tree to mollify the negative effects of Shani and the other planets has historical precedents and is mentioned in some of the Puranas.

Figure 4.1 Black stone images of *nava graha* planetary deities beneath the Chauki Ghat pipal tree in Banaras

A story is narrated within a chapter of the Brahma Purana, for example, in which Shani destroyed a demonic force that had assumed the guise of a pipal tree. Once he had finished this, he announced: "The tasks of the people will be accomplished when they touch the holy fig tree (pipal) on my day after observing all holy rites. They will not have any trouble arising from me."[7] After giving a mantra that is worshipfully addressed to a pipal tree and is designed to elicit the aid of this tree to insure good health and protection from enemies, Shani provided instruction to overcome the negative effects of the planets: "On Saturdays men should get up early in the morning, O divine sage. They should meditate on Shiva. Repeating this mantra they should touch the holy fig tree. Thus the evil effects due to adverse planets will be dispelled."[8] Shani has clear connections with the pipal tree; in fact, one of the names for Shani listed in the Skanda Purana is Pipalayana: "the one who occupies the pipal tree."[9] The worship of Shani is on the rise in India today. As Shani is increasingly associated with pipal trees, so too there is a surge in the worship of these trees.

During my year of research on sacred trees, sets of *nava graha* were added to several other important pipal tree shrines in Banaras. My sense is that these additions have something to do with the rise of a religion of fear and control within India that is part of a larger global religious response for coping with the trepidation caused by an increasingly uncertain and terrifying world. But whatever the reason for their increased worship, the *nava graha*, and especially Shani, are very much associated with pipal trees in that they are thought to reside within or beneath a pipal tree. To gain a better understanding of the *nava graha* and their connection with pipal trees, it would be useful to include consideration of another tree shrine in Banaras, for the *nava graha* are depicted somewhat differently at each site and comparison of the two sites provides a more complete picture of these planetary deities.

Perched atop Hanuman Ghat is the site of the old Shri Dasanam Juna Akhara Hanuman Mandir, a prominent Hanuman temple surrounded by the residential compound of an ascetic order of Hindu mendicants. One enters the spacious courtyard of this compound through an entrance off a narrow alley that runs parallel to the river. The courtyard floor is covered with dark gray slate and all the buildings are painted light orange. At the center of the courtyard stands the main Hanuman temple; just to the west of it is a tree shrine that is open to public worship. A stout pipal tree is enclosed within a square planter that is about four feet high and ten feet across. The sides of this enclosure are painted bright orange with white tile trim on top and capped with a cement platform. On this platform stands an array of deities; primary among them—and the focus of much worship—are the nine heavenly bodies of the *nava grahas* (figure 4.2). Although all of the planets are identified with a particular tree, the pipal tree seems to be able to house them all.[10]

Circling this pipal tree shrine clockwise and beginning on the northeast side one comes before Brihaspati, or Jupiter. All of the *nava graha* are associated not only with a planet or other heavenly body, but also a day of the week (three of the nine are associated with Saturday), a direction, a color, and an animal.[11] Jupiter's day is Thursday, his direction is northeast, and his color is yellow. Although all of the *nava graha* are made from plain black stone at the Chauki Ghat shrine, here Jupiter is painted yellow. This deity faces away from the tree, is seated in crossed-legged posture, and features four arms—as do all of the other *nava graha* here. The *nava graha* are all in a seated posture in the temple compound at Hanuman Ghat, but at the Chauki Ghat pipal tree shrine they are depicted riding animal mounts; Jupiter at the latter site is riding an elephant. Most of the *nava graha* deities under the pipal tree in the Hanuman Ghat compound hold weapons in their hands, but Jupiter holds lotus flowers with his upper pair of arms and a string of meditation beads with his lower right. Jupiter has a keen intellect and is considered to be an expert in all types of knowledge. Known for his profound wisdom, he is the guru of the gods. He, therefore, is approached for strength of mind in all forms of learning.

In the center of the north side of the tree is Budha, or Mercury. Mercury is colored green, and his day is Wednesday. His direction is north, and although he is sometimes associated with a cat, at the Chauki Ghat shrine he is depicted riding a horse. Mercury is known for the dexterity and subtlety of his mind and

Figure 4.2 Nava graha deities under the Hanuman Ghat pipal tree; the figure in red is Mars; the head of Rahu is next to him

rules over astute judgment in both spiritual and worldly affairs. Moving on to the east side of the tree, we come first to Surya, the Sun. The Sun is considered by some scholars to be "the most important and oldest of the deities" long recognized as "the primeval creative force in the universe,"[12] but today seems to be increasingly eclipsed in importance by the rise of Shani. Although his color is commonly a brilliant pink, the Sun deity here is painted bright red. His day is Sunday and his direction is the east. At the Chauki Ghat tree shrine he is riding in a chariot pulled by seven horses. The Sun is the source of all light, energy, and illumination. He is king of the sky and ruler of time; those who worship him are freed from disease and all obstacles to their desires. To the right of the Sun is Shukra, or Venus. His color is white, his direction is southeast, Friday is his day, and at the Chauki Ghat shrine he rides a buffalo. Venus is a friendly divinity associated with beauty and brightness who can help his worshipers achieve their beloved desires. After Venus we come to Chandra, the Moon. The moon here at the Hanuman Ghat pipal tree is white and faces toward the tree, the opposite direction from the Sun, for he is overpowered by the Sun. He too is white. Although his direction is sometimes considered to be the northwest, here he appears on the southeast side of this tree shrine, as he does also in the Chauki Ghat shrine. His day is Monday and he rides an antelope at Chauki Ghat. The Moon is lord of growth and is associated with plants and the world of the ancestors. Turning the corner one comes to the south side of the tree where Mangala, or Mars, is encountered. Mars is colored bright red and rules over Tuesday. His direction is the south, and although he is sometimes associated with a ram, in the Chauki Ghat shrine he rides a lion. Mars is an energetic god of war, but he too can grant his worshipers many life blessings.

Situated in the southwest corner is Rahu, who rules over the southwest direction. Here his form is only a head, black in color. According to Hindu mythology Rahu was a serpent demon who drank some of the nectar of immortality the gods had produced by churning the ocean. Before the nectar could pass beyond his throat, however, he was beheaded by Vishnu in the seductive female form of Mohini. Rahu's head, nonetheless, remained immortal, and it is believed that this immortal head occasionally swallows the sun or moon, thus causing eclipses for the time it takes either celestial body to pass through the bodiless head. Ketu, on the other hand, is the resulting headless body. Rahu and Ketu, considered to be chaotic and inauspicious deities, are associated with the nodes where the spherical orbits of the sun and moon intersect, since this is where both solar and lunar eclipses occur. Regarded as a shadow planet in India, Rahu is associated with no planet of his own, but has a close relationship with Saturn and is therefore related to Saturday. Rahu rides a tiger mount at the Chauki Ghat shrine. The other part of his body is nearby; Ketu, whose direction is also southwest, is portrayed here as a black headless body. At the Chauki Ghat shrine he rides a crow, as he too is closely associated with Saturn.

Finally, on the west side of the pipal tree shrine, one comes at last to Shani, or Saturn. Although I have chosen to describe Shani last, people worshiping here typically begin with Shani and then move clockwise around the shrine to visit the other *nava graha* deities. While the other deities sit out in the open, Shani is housed in a small distinct temple located on the platform under the tree. Shani is the only one of the *nava graha* who is honored with his own temple, signifying his exalted position among the *nava graha*. He is the most important of all the *nava graha* and is commonly referred to as the chief or king of the *nava graha*.[13] The temple dedicated to him is a small block structure about three feet high that is crowned with a pyramidal top and painted orange. Inside the temple is a black form of Saturn glistening with a coating of sesame oil offerings, indicating a great deal of worship; indeed, more attention is given to Shani than any of the other *nava graha* located beneath this pipal tree. Shani's direction is the west and his day is Saturday; at the Chauki Ghat temple he rides a crow mount. This powerful divinity determines one's opportunities and one's misfortunes, and as the younger brother of Yama, Lord of Death, the length of one's life. Of all the *nava graha*, Shani is considered to have the greatest influence over human lives. He is, therefore, looked upon by many Hindus with much trepidation.

Shani's presence at the base of a pipal tree is common. Within the courtyard of a temple dedicated to Hanuman located across the street from the Tulsidas Mandir near the famous Durga Kund in Banaras, stands a medium-sized pipal tree. Inscribed in the Devanagari script on the wall behind this tree are the words *Shri Shanivas Deva Vriksha-ji* ("The holy tree god in which Shani resides"). This is a popular site for worship on Saturdays, the days the courtyard is filled with people making offerings to the pipal tree (figure 4.3). I met a man worshiping this tree one Saturday morning and asked him to identity the divinity of the tree. He answered simply, "It is Shani." I then asked him to tell me about the nature of Shani. He replied: "Shani is the son of the Sun [*Surya ka putra*], and brother of Death [*Yama ka bhai*]. He is very powerful. He is number one! He is the king of all *grahas* [*graha-raja*]. He can take away all your troubles if you please [*prasanna*] him. But he can cause you much grief if you do not." After consulting a priest in the nearby Hanuman temple this same man came back to modify what

Figure 4.3 Worship of a pipal tree associated with Shani near the Tulsidas Mandir in Banaras

he had told me earlier, now informing me that the pipal tree is Vasudev, but that Shani comes and resides here on Saturdays. Therefore, he explained, he had come here today to worship and please Shani by offering him a clay dish lamp fueled by sesame oil at the base of the pipal tree.

Many informative stories and a complex theology are associated with Shani. Early Puranic texts narrate his birth as the son of the Sun.[14] The solar luminary wished to marry and so approached Vishvakarma, the cosmic architect, who offered his own daughter Samjna ("Consciousness") to the Sun. From this union came the progenitor Vaivasvata and the divine twins Yama, god of righteousness and death, and Yamuna, goddess of a mighty river of love.[15] Samjna, however, could not tolerate her husband's brilliance for long, and so produced a double of herself called Chaya ("Shadow") to take her place. The union of the radiant Sun and the shadowy Chaya produced three more offspring: Manu, the first human; the river goddess Tapti; and Shani, the planet Saturn. Shani, son of a powerful father and shadowy mother, is considered in Indian astrology to be the divinity in charge of fate, the length of one's life, and the overall nature of one's experience in life. He is said to be unforgiving, even cruel, in his judgmental authority. Shani's nature is articulated in the *Shani-Mahatmya* ("The Greatness of Saturn"), a text that extols his capabilities. This text declares: "Saturn, who rules both longevity and prosperity, can make a king into a pauper, and vice versa. When Saturn is happy he causes good fortune to sweep through your life, and when he is angry he destroys everything. He controls everyone's destiny. No one can escape from Saturn's grasp, no matter where he might be in the world."[16] No other planet can determine the outcome of one's life experience as can the mightily influential Shani. Many people in India are very conversant with astrology and have strong fear of the consequences in their lives of Shani's harsh anger; therefore, they do what they can to appease him. The main story found in "The Greatness of Saturn" illustrates the power he holds over individuals.[17]

King Vikrama led a prosperous and happy life, until the day he insulted Shani just as he entered the seven-and-a-half-year astrological period when Shani dominates one's life. Soon after, Shani took the form of a wealthy horse merchant and visited the king's town of Ujjayani. The king was fascinated with one of the merchant's horses and mounted it to try it out. The horse turned out to be a magical horse that carried the king unwittingly far from his own land. Now lost, King Vikrama found his way to another merchant's house, and while staying there was falsely accused of stealing a pearl necklace. Consequently, the king was beaten by the merchant's men and taken to the local ruler, who had his executioner chop off King Vikrama's hands and feet and leave him to die in a desolate forest. The king somehow survived, and for two years was cared for by several people from a nearby town. One day a woman who had been born in the king's city of Ujjayani happened by and recognized the king. Feeling great pity for him, she took him home with her. The woman was married to a sesame oil-presser, and a bargain was struck whereby in exchange for food and clothing the king would sit as a weight on top of the oil press while the oxen turned it. He passed five years performing this menial task. Toward the end of his time as the oil-pressing weight the king began to sing so beautifully that he attracted the attention of the local ruler's daughter, who moved him into the palace for her entertainment. As time passed this princess fell in love with the king and determined to marry him. About that time the king's seven-and-a-half year period of Shani's torment came to an end, and Shani appeared before him. The king bowed respectfully to Shani and praised him profusely; as a result the powerful divinity became pleased and restored the king's severed limbs. Now blessed by Shani, King Vikrama married the beautiful princess, returned to his own kingdom and lived a long and happy life.

The scholar of Indian astrology, Robert Svoboda, maintains that Shani—like all the *nava grahas*—is a "Face of God," that is, a particular aspect of the supreme unified divinity.

> The rishis (sages) teach that though there is but One Reality, this True God has Many Faces, each a personality of the Godhead. Though each Face is superficially independent, all are identical behind the persona. From the perspective of Universal Reality every Face of God is a limited expression of divinity, but from the point of view of that Multiplicity which is the Universe, each deity can be taken as Supreme in every sense. Differing systems of theology assign different roles to the various deities, but the ultimate sum of each system remains the same Absolute One-Without-A-Second. Each Face of God is a *deity*, a portion of God, and each plays an important role in the Great Cosmic Drama.[18]

Shani can be understood, then, as a specific facet of the supreme divinity whose domain is the fortune or misfortune of everyone. Many people in India, therefore, seek to affect Shani's influence on their lives through a variety of ritual means. And one of the most important places to placate Shani is the base of a pipal tree. I met a pipal tree worshiper in Banaras who told me: "Astrological problems related to Shani and others can be helped by wearing rings with certain stones. The stones are like umbrellas against harmful rain. But the pipal tree is so powerful that it can turn off harmful rain altogether."

I encountered many people in northern India who informed me that they were worshiping at a pipal tree to appease Shani. I discovered several views regarding Shani's relationship with the pipal tree: some identified the tree itself as Shani, whereas others identified it as a favorite haunt of Shani. A priest who attends a popular Hanuman temple sheltered by a large pipal tree in Banaras told me "the tree itself is a form of Shani [*Shani ka svarupa*]." On another occasion, a man who had just finished worshiping this tree on a Saturday with water and a sesame oil lamp offering and seven circumambulations also maintained, "This tree is Shani." I visited a pipal tree located in the courtyard of a Hanuman temple near the main rail station in Banaras that has a Shiva linga situated beneath it. I asked the priest of this temple who the tree was: "The tree is Shani and Mahadeva [Shiva] resides beneath it."

The great majority of people I spoke with, however, identified the pipal tree as the favorite residence of Shani (*Shani ka vas*); some kind of embodied form of Shani—typically made from either black stone or iron—is often installed at the base of a pipal tree where he is worshiped. One of the priests attending the Hanuman temple adjacent to the Shri Shanivas Deva Vriksha-ji tree shrine explained to me: "The pipal tree is always Vasudeva. People worship this tree as Vasudeva every day. But on Saturdays Shani also resides here in this tree and people worship Shani on Saturdays to mollify any negative effects of Shani that have come into their lives." I met a woman one Saturday who had just finished worshiping the tree and circumambulating it seven times. She told me: "This tree is always Vasudeva, but on Saturdays Shani comes here. On Saturdays the tree is Maha-Vasudeva. We worship here on Saturdays to please Shani so that he will take away all our troubles." Many agreed with this common viewpoint, regarding the tree as an embodied form of Vasudev and the preferred dwelling place of Shani. Not everyone, however, restricted Shani's residence beneath the pipal tree to Saturdays alone. I spoke with a man who was worshipping at a pipal tree on a Tuesday with a well-established Shani shrine beneath it in front of the famous Bharata-Mata temple in Banaras. He stated this succinctly, "The pipal is Vasudeva and Shani always resides beneath it." A few people I spoke with even regarded the tree as both divinities. Another man who had just finished worshiping a large pipal tree that stands above Tulsi Ghat in Banaras told me "the pipal tree is both Vasudeva and Shani. We worship it every day, but mostly on Saturdays to pacify Shani so that our lives go well." Regardless of their understanding, people worship the pipal tree itself as a means of pacifying Shani and seeking blessings in their lives.

A small temple near Dasashvamedha Ghat in Banaras is divided into two sections: one half houses Hanuman and is called the Shri Sankat Mochan Hanuman Mandir, the other half envelops a large pipal tree and is identified as an old Shani temple called the Shani Bhagavan ka Ati-Prachin Mandir. This pipal tree shrine is very active, particularly on Saturdays. The tree is surrounded by a low platform capped with cement and slabs of white marble. In addition to a number of Shiva lingas and an image of Ganesha, a black stone form of Shani has been placed on the platform on the side of the tree nearest to Hanuman. The platform is crowded on Saturday mornings with honorific lamps that consist of small clay dishes flaming with cotton wicks that are fueled by sesame oil.

Offering a sesame oil lamp is considered to be an especially effective means of pleasing Shani (figure 4.4). The black image of Shani is usually draped with flower garlands and surrounded by burning sticks of incense. After making an offering of water and other presents, worshipers circumambulate the pipal tree with Shani residing at its base. Many of them conclude their worship by massaging the base of the pipal tree and bowing their head to its trunk. A priest of the Hanuman temple next door informed me: "Shani resides at the base of this tree, but the pipal tree itself is Bhagavan Vishnu. These people please Shani by worshiping Vishnu in the form of this tree."

On the bank of the Ganges at the famous Triveni Ghat in Rishikesh stands a large pipal tree that is the site of the Shri Shanideva-ji Maharaja Mandir. As is often the case, the tree itself is the temple. Near this pipal tree is a small pond named Rishi Kund. A sign placed by the pond identifies the water of the pond

Figure 4.4 Worshiper offering a sesame oil lamp to Shani at a pipal tree shrine near Dasashvamedha Ghat

as "Yamuna jal," that is, water from the Yamuna River. A priest of a nearby Shiva temple told me that this is because the goddess Yamuna is a loving and compassionate goddess and is the older sister of Shani. Accordingly, she makes Shani favorable toward anyone who approaches her with reverence.[19] A Sanskrit mantra posted on a sign at this tree shrine reads: "I honor Shani, who appears bluish-black in color, is the son of the Sun, the younger brother of Death [Yama], and was born from the mother Shadow [Chaya]." Strips of black cloth had been tied in the tree directly above a large black stone image of Shani that rests against it. The tree itself was wrapped with string and ringed with several Shiva lingas. I sat near this tree shrine on a Saturday one October morning, observing a steady stream of people making offerings. A woman dressed in a dark-blue sari first offered water to the tree from a brass pot. She hung a garland of marigold flowers on Shani, and placed a sesame-oil lamp, two bananas and some marigold flowers at the base of the tree. Next she hooked a piece of black cloth on a string tied around the tree. After this she circumambulated the tree seven times, stopped to massage its base and bow her head to its trunk, and then walked away from the tree. When I asked her why she performed this ritual, she replied, "To lessen the ill-effects of Shani and make my life better."

Inexpensive pamphlets available in northern India explain how one is to worship Shani on Saturdays.[20] These advise the worshiper to build an altar to Shani at the base of an old pipal tree. In addition to worshiping Shani with offerings of sesame oil lamps, incense, dark flowers, and black items, one is instructed to worship the pipal tree by offering it water and circumambulating it seven times while wrapping it with cotton string. While I rarely saw people wrapping colorful string around a pipal tree that is the site of a Shani shrine (except on a Somvati Amavasya), I noticed many circumambulating the tree, often seven times. The pamphlets that describe the worship of Shani declare that by performing this worship all troubles and diseases will be destroyed, and happiness and wealth will be obtained. Overall, such worship results in a life full of happiness (*sukh-purvak jivan*).[21] One of the most common names of Shani listed in all of these pamphlets is Pipala-Ashraya-Samsthita, "The One Who is Situated in the Shelter of the Pipal Tree."[22] The worship of Shani in India, then, is clearly and intimately linked to the pipal tree. Why is this so?

Shani's multifaceted connection with pipal trees is accounted for in a variety of ways. Many people explain Shani's association with the pipal tree by the fact that Shani is considered to be a loyal devotee of Vishnu, and pipal trees are regarded as readily accessible forms of Vishnu. On the day before Shani's birthday celebration of Shani Jayanti in the year 2007, an article appeared in the *Dainik Jagaran*, one of the local Hindi newspapers available in Banaras. This piece was written for the occasion of Shani Jayanti by the scholar Atul Tandan to explain the nature of Shani.[23] Within his article Tandan quotes a Sanskrit mantra that reads: "All glory to Shani, who is situated in the shelter of the pipal tree." He uses the occasion of elucidating the meaning of this mantra to explain the reason for Shani's connection to the pipal tree. A translation of his exposition follows:

> The meaning of this mantra is that Shani has a very close relationship with the Ashvattha or pipal tree. In the Nagara-Khanda section of the Skanda Purana, the greatness of the spiritual form [*adhyatmik svarupa*] of the pipal tree is introduced in this way: "Vishnu is forever in the roots of the Ashvattha tree, Keshava is in the trunk, Narayana is in the branches, Shri Hari is in the leaves, and Bhagavan Achyuta is in the fruit along with all gods.[24] This tree is the embodiment of Bhagavan Vishnu. Great souls offer water to the auspicious roots of this tree and worship it." The powerful lord Shani seeks to be situated in the shelter of a pipal tree with the loving wish that he remain always near his favorite deity, Shri Vishnu. It is probable that for this reason the sages established the methods for offering water to the pipal tree, for presenting it with lamps, and for circumambulating it on Saturdays to pacify Shani.

Tandan's point is that since the pipal tree itself is identified as an embodied form of Vishnu, Shani resides in its shelter out of loving devotion for his beloved Lord Vishnu. Any worship of Vishnu in the form of a pipal tree, then, will greatly please his devotee Shani, thereby bringing protection and blessings to the worshiper of the tree. Although this may be an overly easy way to gloss over any possible historical competition between these ancient divinities, many pipal tree worshipers I spoke with corroborated this explanation. One in Banaras told me: "The worship of Vasudeva pleases [*prasanna*] Shani very much. Therefore, when we worship the pipal tree form of Vasudeva, Shani is favorable towards us." A man who had just finished worshiping the large pipal tree that stands atop Tulsi Ghat informed me: "I worship this tree every day because it is a form of Vasudeva. I also worship it on Saturdays to help with the bad effects of Shani, who is his devotee. I am now in my Shani astrological period. This worship brings me peace of mind." My friend Nagendra explained Vasudeva's protection from the more negative aspects of Shani this way: "When someone is frightening you, it is good to go to someone who is stronger for protection. Vasudeva is the supreme God. He is stronger than Shani. Therefore, we worship Vasudeva as the pipal tree—with Shani looking on—to protect us from Shani's harmful effects."

In addition to Shani, it is quite common to encounter some form of the monkey god Hanuman beneath a pipal tree; his bright orange temples are a very familiar sight under the expansive green canopy of many of these trees. A priest of a Hanuman temple nestled under a pipal tree on the corner of a busy intersection in Jaipur informed me, "Shani resides in the pipal tree, while Hanuman resides beneath it." In the previous chapter, we learned that Hanuman stays near pipal trees because of his devotion to Rama, one of the most important incarnations of Vishnu or Vasudeva, the supreme deity most commonly identified with pipal trees. Although Shani and Hanuman meet under the pipal tree as fellow devotees of Vasudeva, a direct connection also exists between these two. A story is told in northern India that accounts for the connection between the two deities.[25] As the mighty demon Ravana, Rama's archenemy, ascended to power he captured Shani and bound him face down beneath the royal throne. When Ravana sat on his throne he would rest his foot on Shani's head. Shani remained helplessly trapped in this insulting position for a long time. After Ravana abducted Rama's wife Sita and took her captive to his kingdom on the island of Lanka, Rama's most trustworthy servant, Hanuman, flew to Lanka to deliver a message of hope to Sita. Hanuman was captured by Ravana's troops in Lanka, but being immensely powerful was able to get away. During his escape he freed Shani, and Shani was so grateful that he promised that he would never harm any person who worshiped Hanuman.

Other accounts have it that Shani is a devotee of Shiva, and that Shani is controlled by Hanuman because the latter is considered to be an incarnation of Shiva. Regardless, Hanuman is almost always present beneath a pipal tree, the abode of Shani, and many say this is to mollify the wrath of Shani. As the head priest of a Hanuman temple located under a large pipal tree near Godolia in Banaras explained to me, "Hanuman resides here to keep Shani peaceful." I met a professor of pathology who teaches at Banaras Hindu University just after he had finished worshiping a pipal tree at the Senapati Vanakati Hanuman temple in Banaras. He told me: "Shani can give you a lot of trouble. Therefore, we worship him here at this pipal tree with Hanuman, because Hanuman can free you from the ill-effects of Shani." The priest of a Hanuman temple located near the Tulsidas Manas Mandir explained to me: "In the decadent age (*kali yug*) the two most important gods to worship are Hanuman and Shani. Hanuman is the guru of Shani, so he will not harm anyone who is a devotee of Hanuman. For this reason, Hanuman is always present at a pipal tree because the pipal tree is the residence of Shani." Such views, then, tie both Shani and Hanuman to the pipal tree, whether the latter is associated with Vishnu or Shiva.

A story narrated in some of the Shanivar Vrat ("Saturday Vow") pamphlets connects Shani directly both to the pipal tree and to Shiva.[26] Once upon a time a group of sages who had gathered in the Naimisha forest asked the epic narrator Suta to expound on the greatness of the Saturday vow. In response Suta told them the story of a prosperous king named Gandharva who lived in the Garhwal Mountains. The king's wife was an accomplished yogini named Yogasiddha, who bore him a virtuous son named Dharmapala. When the king entered into his Shani astrological period he was advised to perform the Saturday vrat ritual that would ward off the negative effects of Shani. The king, however, did not pay attention to this advice, and as a result, disaster came upon him in the form of a massive attack on all sides of his territory by his enemies. In the ensuing battle the king was killed and his enemies took control of his kingdom.

The king's wife and son managed to escape, taking the son of the court's chief minister with them. They wandered helplessly in the forest for a long time, until one day they came to the hermitage of the sage Sandiliya on the bank of the Yamuna River. When the sage asked what had happened to them, the king's wife recounted their misfortune. Hearing their tale of woe, the sage informed them that it was all due to the fact that Shani had become angry with all of them because the king had failed to suitably honor him with the Saturday vrat. Therefore, he advised the two boys to perform this ritual and worship Shani properly. The king's son and the minister's son followed the sage's advice and began to worship Shani along with Shiva. Every Saturday they fasted all day beneath a pipal tree while conducting their worship and praise of Shani. They passed three months in this manner. To test the boys, Shani mounted a bull buffalo and set off for Sandiliya's hermitage. The day Shani arrived the minister's son was going for his daily bath in the Yamuna River. Shani secretly placed a pot full of money on his path and hid nearby to watch in the branches of the pipal tree the boys had been worshiping. The minister's son discovered the pot and stood waiting for its owner to return. Leaves of the pipal tree suddenly began to rustle and a voice came from the tree telling the boy that the money was his, and that he was to take it home with him. With great delight the boy returned home with the pot of money and told his foster mother that the god of a pipal tree (*pipal deva*) had given it to him. The king's wife instructed him to share it with his foster brother, the king's son. The boy went to the king's son and told him that he had acquired a pot of money due to the kindness of Pipaleshvar Mahadev ("Shiva as the Lord of the Pipal Tree") and wanted to share it. The king's son refused to take any of the money, however, not wanting to be distracted from his own pursuits. He sought nothing less than the return of his father's kingdom.

The king's son continued his ritual practice of fasting and worshiping at the pipal tree on Saturdays. On the 33rd Saturday, Shani called out to him from the pipal tree, saying: "King's son! I am Shani. I am pleased with you because of your vrat. I am the one who completely destroyed your father. I also ruined Hiranyakashyapa, Hiranyaksha, King Bali, King Nala, and King Harishchandra. Whatever boon you choose, I will grant it." To this the king's son responded:

> O God! My efforts are now successful from direct sight [*darshan*] of you. I heard that you are afraid of Shiva. Therefore, I became a worshiper of Shiva. I also heard that you are afraid of sage Pippalad, who is a great devotee of Shiva, and of the Pipaleshvar Mahadev linga he

established on the bank of the Yamuna River. Pippalad's father used to live here on the bank of the Yamuna. During his Shani period you made him poor and sick, and he died because of you. For this reason the sage's powerful son Pippalad became very angry with you and began looking in the direction of a pipal tree, which is your residence [*nivas*]. Pippalad acquired a magical mace from the power of his ascetic practice, and prepared to kill you with it. You fled into the sky out of great fear, but the sage pursued you and struck your legs with the mace. Seeing that Pippalad was about to kill you Shiva appeared on the scene, and said: "Son Pippalad, do not kill Shani as he is also my devotee. Choose whatever boon you wish instead." Pippalad agreed not to kill Shani, and addressed Shiva: "Because I broke his legs, Shani will not be able to run so fast. Now he will be called Manda Devata—the 'slow god.' Here is my wish: that you will protect those people who have *darshan* of you as Pipaleshvar Mahadev at the temple established by me."

After narrating this story, the king's son said to Shani: "I heard this from my mother, and so worshiped Pipaleshvar Mahadev. Thus, your powerful cruelty has no effect on me." Shani acknowledged the truth in what the king's son had said and gave no injury to him because he was a fellow devotee of Shiva. Instead, over the next few days, due to the grace of Shani, who resides in the pipal tree, and Pipaleshvar Mahadev, the form of Shiva situated beneath the pipal tree, the king's son received his father's kingdom back, married a beautiful princess, and lived a long and happy life with the minister's son serving as his own minister. In this way, the narrator Suta tells the sages who had gathered in the Naimisha forest, the king's son's wish was fulfilled by the power of the Saturday Shani vrat. He concludes by declaring that those who perform the Shani vrat on Saturdays will achieve their desired results.

This story indicates that the pipal tree is a residence (*nivas*) of Shani that is sometimes associated with Shiva. Understood from this particular religious perspective, an individual pleases or pacifies Shani by worshiping him and Shiva at a pipal tree on Saturdays. One Saturday I talked with a man worshiping the large pipal tree at the Senapati Vanakati Hanuman temple in Banaras by making an offering of water and a sesame oil lamp. A small stone Shiva linga has been installed on a low platform at the base of this tree. The man kept his right hand on the pipal tree as he circumambulated it; every time he went around the tree he stopped and respectfully touched the base of the Shiva linga with his right hand and then deferentially touched his forehead with this hand. After finishing his worship of the tree and linga he told me, "I worship the tree and the linga because Mahadev resides beneath the pipal in this form and he pacifies Shani." A woman doing much the same on another day told me: "This tree is Shani and

Mahadev resides beneath the tree. I worship them together here for powerful results."

As the deity in charge of the length of one's life, Shani is also related to death. In the story of the king's son, Shani rides a bull buffalo, the vehicle of his elder brother Yama, Lord of Death. Shani is sometimes directly identified with Yama; indeed, one of his ten names is Yama.[27] Shani's birthday celebration of Shani Jayanti falls on the new moon of the month of Jeshtha. The scholar Tandan explains that this is the new moon in which deceased ancestors are honored. He maintains: "In ancient texts Shani is said to be connected with the world of the ancestors and the ancestors themselves. As the younger brother of Yama, Shani is his representative among the *nava graha*."[28] Shani's connection to the dead, relates to another aspect of the pipal tree: it is considered to be the abode of ghosts, both benign and malevolent. The latter kind is usually referred to in Hindi as *bhuts,* and as dangerous spirits they are the source of much dread. A tantric text warns that one should never use pipal wood for a cooking fire because ghosts reside in the pipal tree.[29]

Residence of Ghosts

The association between trees and the dead is certainly not limited to India. In his lengthy study of tree worship, Frazer writes, "Sometimes it is the souls of the dead which are believed to animate trees."[30] Literary references to the connection between the dead and trees are ancient in India; however, here it is more the case that the dead reside in trees rather than animate them. In the Rig Veda, for example, a tree is associated with death and is called the "home of the gods"; this tree is where the souls of the dead are said to rest.[31] Today it is a fairly common site to see clay pots hanging from a pipal tree that is a bit out of the way, as pipal trees are considered to be the residence of ghosts (*prets*) (figure 4.5). These pots are filled with water and hung in a pipal tree to care for the recently dead. A small hole is punched in the bottom of the pot and a grass straw is sometimes inserted in it to allow for a slow and steady dripping of water that can be drank without the use of arms. There is reference to this practice in the Puranas; the Matsya Purana, for example, says that a pot filled with water should be hung from a pipal tree for ten days to alleviate the suffering and fatigue of the newly departed.[32] Several people explained to me that the pots are hung from a pipal tree because of the quantity and quality of oxygen the tree provides, as many maintain that the pipal is the only tree to produce oxygen twenty-four hours a day. The souls of the recently deceased are believed to hover around for ten days waiting for a new transformation. The purpose of the post-cremation mortuary rites (*shraddha*) is to "convert the marginal *pret*-ghost into an ancestral-*pitr*, and to facilitate

Figure 4.5 Clay pots of water hanging from a pipal tree in Banaras to care for the dead

the arduous journey of the deceased to the 'abode of the ancestors' (*pitr-lok*)."[33] These rites are designed to liberate the deceased from a ghostly condition and ensure the attainment of a good state after death. During the time immediately after death the soul is vulnerable and still in need of water and air. A pair of pots hanging in a pipal tree provide both. One man explained to me that "this is done to make the soul peaceful [*atma shant*]." From his ethnographic research on death rituals in Banaras, Jonathan Parry reports:

> After cremation, a water-pot is hung in the branches of a *pipal* tree. *Pipals* are described as 'the residence of ghosts,' and the pot as the 'house of the *pret*.' Morning and evening the chief mourner offers water into this pot with a verse which proclaims that he is cooling the *pret* down because he was burnt in the fire. The pot has a small hole drilled in the bottom so that the water drips slowly out. The *pret* waits on the

ground below. Each drop shatters into atoms and some of these fall into its microscopic mouth.[34]

The pipal tree in this context, then, is considered to be the abode of the recent dead, who are for the most part benign. Far scarier forms of ghosts, however, are believed to haunt pipal trees. These are known to be *bhuts*—dangerous and malevolent spirits—and are the source of much anxiety.

Many people I spoke with told me that they avoid pipal trees at night out of fear of an encounter with *bhuts*. I struck up a conversation with a resident of Banaras while we were both waiting to catch a plane at the local airport and mentioned that I was conducting research on the worship of pipal trees. "Be careful!" he warned me. "Dangerous ghosts live in pipal trees. Best to stay away from pipal trees at night. I would never go near a pipal tree at night." I asked a man worshiping a pipal tree one morning if he ever worshiped this tree at night. "No! Never!" he exclaimed. "Ghosts are here at night." This attitude is fairly common. "I never go near a pipal tree at night," a woman living in Banaras told me, "because one night when I was young I passed beneath an old pipal tree and I could hear the ghosts talking. I became so frightened that I ran all the way home. I'll never go near a pipal tree at night again!" Another woman told me of one of her neighbors who sat under a pipal tree one night and became possessed by a ghost. As a result, this neighbor became ill and had to be taken to an exorcist to be healed. "I stay far away from pipal trees at night myself," she concluded. "I am very afraid of the ghosts that might be there." These stories make it clear that pipal trees are considered to be the nightly haunt of ghosts, thus associating them with a very different kind of power than was encountered in the previous chapter.

Bhuts are sometimes known to concentrate in certain trees. There is a temple complex in Banaras with a large pipal tree that is covered with hundreds of rupee coins nailed to it. A few photos of different people have also been nailed to this tree. The name of this temple is Pishach Mochan, which means "He who Frees one from Evil Spirits." The priest attending this pipal tree shrine explained to me that a person who is possessed by a *bhut* is brought here. The *bhut* is drawn out onto a rupee coin by an exorcism specialist, and then the rupee is nailed to the tree to fix the *bhut* there and keep it away from the previously possessed person. Photos on the tree represent people who died a tortuous death and had been haunting others; they were nailed to the tree to hold them here. This particular tree is considered to be a tree loaded with *bhuts*, and what better place to keep dangerous *bhuts* than on a pipal tree, the dwelling place of ghosts. My friend Nagendra drove me to this site in his rickshaw. Usually he accompanied me as I wandered around pipal tree shrines, but he would not come near this particular tree; he chose instead to remain at a safe distance in the shelter of his rickshaw.

While other pipal trees are not considered to be as laden with *bhuts* as this one, many pipal trees are believed to be home to *bhuts*.

While visiting me in Banaras, my daughter Meagan discovered a Hindi comic book for sale in a newspaper and magazine stand entitled *Pipal ka Per* (*The Pipal Tree*) (figure 4.6).[35] This comic book—really more of a graphic novelette, since it is frightening, not humorous—appeared in a popular series; it contains a story that is indicative of cultural notions associated with the pipal tree and shows how they can be paradoxically associated with both gods and ghosts. The cover of the booklet depicts an anthropomorphized and terrifying pipal tree spirit who has just seized a young woman. The opening page portrays a large pipal tree, and the caption reads: "A tree gives fruit. A tree gives shade. There is a certain tree that gives death." The story begins with a high-ranking police officer informing his wife that the front door of their house is old and weak and needs to be replaced with a stronger one. He is concerned about the door because a

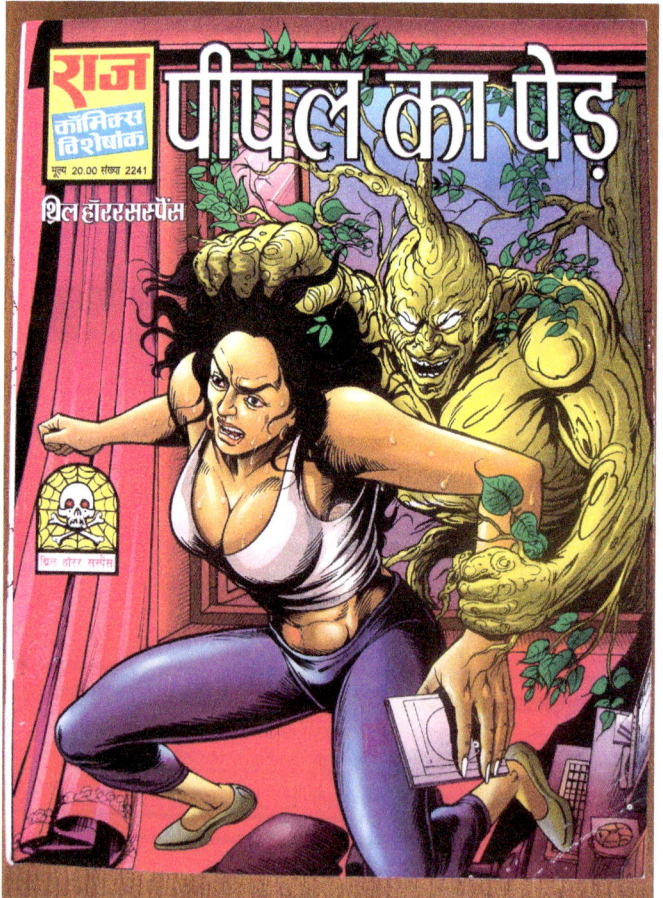

Figure 4.6 Cover of a comic book titled *The Pipal Tree*

notorious criminal named Pig he had sent to jail had just escaped and was now threatening him with revenge. "Wood from a pipal tree is not used for making furniture," he tells his wife, "because for Hindus the pipal is a tree worthy of worship [*pujaniya vriksha*]. It is the abode of the gods. But by chance a carpenter came into possession of the sacred [*pavitra*] wood of a pipal tree."[36] The policeman places an order with this carpenter to make him a door out of the wood from this pipal tree. After it has been installed he assures his wife: "The gods dwell in the pipal. Now the gods dwell in our door. If some trouble comes the gods will protect us." Anxious about the safety of his wife, he has their house watched over by a sentry, a guard dog, and a close circuit camera. The crafty criminal, however, is able to get past all of these and when he approaches the front door of the house it opens by itself. He enters the house and there fatally shoots the policeman's wife. The policeman chases down the criminal and kills him, but now realizes his life is ruined, for his wife is dead. He returns home, and cursing the door for failing to protect his wife, smashes it to pieces with an axe, thinking: "I had faith in this door, but it has broken my trust. It has failed me. The gods are not in it; evil spirits dwell in it."[37] He then drags the remnants of the door outside and sets them afire.

Two days later the police officer visits the lumberyard that had supplied the pipal wood for the door and tells the owner about the great misfortune that resulted from the door. The owner informs the policeman that he had bought the large trunk of a pipal tree, and not knowing that the wood was unlucky, had it cut up to make many different things, including the door. While driving away from the lumberyard, the policeman comes upon the scene of an automobile accident. A truck carrying a piano has crashed, injuring both the driver and the man accompanying the piano. The latter asks the policeman to make sure that the piano is delivered to the National Stadium for a very important concert. The policeman agrees to take it there himself and discovers that the pianist for this concert is a relative of his dead wife. The officer decides to stay and listen to the performance, and during the concert the piano sprouts tentacle-like roots that wrap around the pianist and strangle him to death. After witnessing this horrifying scene, the officer goes to the music store from which the piano was purchased to investigate the new fatality. He discovers that the piano was constructed out of the very same pipal tree from which his door was made.

In rapid succession, the policeman encounters many more deaths of his wife's relatives, all who die from some kind of interaction with an object made from the pipal tree: a destructive spirit emerges from a computer desk and kills one, a bed crushes another, wood scraps from the tree catch on fire and kill another, and a wooden candle holder bursts into flames and incinerates all the remaining family members. It turns out that a year prior to these events a young woman in this family had fallen in love with a classmate in her college and had eloped to marry him. A little while later she returned with her new husband, and the young couple asked for forgiveness and blessings from the elders of the family. The elders told them that they could receive forgiveness only under a pipal tree they said was the chosen deity (*ishta deva*) of the family. After they all had assembled at the pipal tree, the elders instructed the newly weds to bow down before the pipal tree. The couple did so obediently with reverence, but as they knelt with their heads bowed, an elder woman of the family rushed forward and slipped nooses around their necks and two men quickly yanked the ropes to hang the couple from the tree. The tree was then cut down and its wood was sold to the lumberyard; the various troublesome items were then made from this wood. Readers of the graphic novelette are informed that the souls of the murdered couple had inhabited the pipal tree, and through its wood had sought revenge on this family on the anniversary of their murder. The family had made two grave errors: they killed the lovers, who became avenging ghosts residing in the pipal tree, and they violated the sanctity of a pipal tree whose wood was then used for common lumber. Granted this is only a comic-book story, but it expresses some important notions regarding pipal trees in northern Indian culture: *bhuts* dwelling in pipal trees are dangerous and the abuse of a pipal tree leads to much bad luck.

Destroying a Pipal Tree

Many stories circulate in India about the bad luck that results from the abuse of a pipal tree. One of the first of several I heard was from a Hindi teacher at the Landour Language School in the Himalayan hill station of Mussoorie. "A few years ago a man living in Dehra Dun ordered some Hindu workers to cut down a pipal tree for him on a Saturday. When the workers refused to do this, the man hired some non-Hindu workers to fell the tree. Within a year of this, the man experienced the loss of his son, his wife, his job, and all his money. People attribute his great loss to the fact that he had a pipal tree cut down, and on a Saturday at that." A merchant in Banaras told me of another man who had a pipal tree cut down. Soon after this both he and his wife became sick and died. I heard another story about a manager of an ashram who had his workers chop down a pipal tree; within a year he too died. A woman living in Jaipur related how a neighbor of hers decided to cut down a pipal tree by himself; as he cut the tree it fell back on him crushing him to death. She attributed this to "bad luck from cutting a pipal tree." A physicist in Banaras told me that Hindus believe a pipal tree should not be cut, otherwise "shit happens." To illustrate his case, he narrated this story:

> Behind my house is a large garden that belongs to a neighbor. They had a huge, beautiful pipal tree growing in their garden, but wanted to cut

it down to make money. I myself told them that this was a very bad idea, and reminded them that it is illegal to cut living trees in the city of Banaras. However, they went ahead with their plan and had the tree cut down. Soon after they cut the tree, the man responsible for having the tree cut down, as well as several other members of the family, died and the surviving wife now has a bad skin disease. Cutting pipal trees is not a good idea; it leads to much bad luck.

There is an implied ethic at work here with regard to pipal trees. No worshiper I spoke with would dare harm a pipal tree. In the last chapter, we saw that pipal trees are not injured out of a general appreciation, respect, or even affection for them. Here, however, the motive seems to be one of fear. I spoke with the owner of a sawmill in Banaras and asked him if he ever sold wood from a pipal tree. "No!" he replied emphatically, "Hindus are afraid of it, so we never sell it." I spoke with a manager of a guesthouse in Banaras that was built so as not to disturb a large pipal tree worshiped everyday by many people. He told me that great care was taken during construction to preserve the pipal tree: "If we would have cut down this tree it would have destroyed our business." Speaking for many, another man told me: "I would never cut a pipal tree. The gods would be angry with me if I did and only bad things would come from this." Pipal trees are unquestionably considered to be animate, sentient, and powerful beings. The way that power is regarded, however, varies considerably: whereas the conception of pipal trees as embodied forms of Vasudeva leads to intimate relationships with them, the conception of them as the abode of ghosts or avenging spirits leads to avoiding certain kinds of interaction with them that is believed to cause much misfortune. Fear of bad luck restricts particular modes of behavior toward pipal trees, both ethically (harming them is discouraged) and ritually (they are approached only during specific times).

Bad Luck

In India bad luck has a name; in fact, she is a goddess. Her name is Alakshmi (she is also known as Daridra or Jyeshtha[38]) and she too is associated with pipal trees. Her tale is told in a number of the "Kartik Mahatmyas" found in several Puranas.[39] The story begins with a sage asking the epic narrator Suta why a pipal tree should be touched only on Saturdays, as several Puranas declare that a pipal tree should not be touched except on this day. The Skanda Purana, for example, declares that one should worship an Ashvattha on Saturdays by touching it, but not on other days as by doing so one will become poor (*daridra*).[40] Ethnographic evidence demonstrates clearly that many tree worshipers in India do not accept this, for I have seen many bow their heads to a pipal tree or touch it reverently with their right hand every day of the week. Nonetheless, the belief that a pipal tree should not be touched except on Saturdays is not uncommon, and the story of Alakshmi is framed within the context of this assumption. Here is Suta's tale.

Long ago, when the gods and demons came together for the purpose of churning the ocean to extract the nectar of immortality by using Mount Meru as the dasher and the enormous serpent Vasuki as the rope, both marvelous as well as frightening things came out of the ocean. Among these were the two goddesses, Lakshmi (good luck, prosperity, or auspiciousness) and her opposite Alakshmi (bad luck, poverty, or inauspiciousness). Since Alakshmi was born first, she is considered to be the elder sister of Lakshmi. Indeed, one of the names for Alakshmi is Jyeshtha, which means the "Eldest." The beautiful goddess of abundance Lakshmi was given to Vishnu, who fell in love with her immediately and wanted to marry her. Lakshmi readily agreed to this, but reminded Vishnu that it was improper for a younger sister to marry before her older sister. Therefore, she requested Vishnu first to arrange a marriage for her elder sister Alakshmi. Accepting this challenge, Vishnu convinced the sage Uddalak—or by some accounts tricked the sage—to marry her.

Taking his new wife with him, Uddalak set off to return to his ashram. As they approached, Alakshmi smelled the sweet scent of a sacrificial fire and heard the Vedas being chanted. She threw a fit, informing Uddalak that she could not live in any place where the Vedas are being chanted, where religious rituals are being performed, where people are living together in harmony, or where the gods are being worshiped. She could only live where religion is not practiced, where husbands and wives quarrel day and night, where theft happens regularly, and where all sorts of sins are being committed. Hearing these words, Uddalak was stunned and ordered Alakshmi to remain sitting in the shade of a nearby pipal tree while he went to look for a suitable place for her to live. Whether he could not find such a place, or whether he now realized the true nature of his wife and had no intention of coming back, Uddalak never returned to Alakshmi. The miserable goddess sat under the pipal tree for a long time, and when she understood that her husband was not coming back, she began to cry. Hearing her sobs from Vishnu's heavenly abode of Vaikuntha, the younger sister Lakshmi took pity on her and approached Vishnu for help. The compassionate Vishnu agreed to alleviate Alakshmi's sorrow. Arriving with his consort Lakshmi at the pipal tree on a Saturday, Vishnu addressed Alakshmi: "Hey Alakshmi, always remain in the shelter of the pipal tree; for indeed, it is a part [*amsha*] of me. Therefore, I give it to you as a place for you to live. I will bring Lakshmi with me here every Saturday to meet with you. Lakshmi will bless and dwell in the house of any person who worships the pipal tree on this day." Saying this, Vishnu returned to Vaikuntha with Lakshmi, and Alakshmi began her residence under the pipal tree. This story certainly accounts for why many people worship a pipal tree on Saturdays to seek the blessing of Lakshmi, as well as for the belief that the pipal tree can be a source of bad luck if approached in the wrong manner at the wrong time. Coming into the presence of Alakshmi without the auspicious influence of Lakshmi can lead to great misfortune. A priest of a Hanuman temple situated beneath a huge pipal tree near Godolia informed me "Lakshmi resides in this tree on Saturdays. That is why so many people come here to worship the tree on Saturdays. They seek the blessing of Lakshmi at this tree." A man I met on a train to Haridvar elaborated on this point: "Lakshmi resides in pipal trees on Saturdays. On all other days Alakshmi resides there alone. Therefore we only make contact with a pipal tree on Saturdays." Once again, the notion is expressed that pipal trees are a source of wonderful blessings, as well as a potential threat.

Care should be given, however, not to consider the frightful side of the pipal tree (and concomitant divinity) too negatively. It is simply one of the two powerful faces of the same nature, and the source of its power is ultimately nondifferent from that of its positive side. The dreadful facet is still a part of the divine world: Shani is considered to be an aspect of the one Lord Bhagavan and Alakshmi is the elder sister of the radiant goddess Lakshmi. One simply has to know how to deal with this side of power to prevent injury. The pipal tree, as we have seen, is sometimes believed to be a presence that can cause great harm, but the remedy for all harm it might cause is present in the very same powerful being that causes the harm. Shani can hurt one, but worship of the pipal tree can prevent this; death creates many problems, but the dead can be cared for properly with a pipal tree; dangerous *bhuts* inhabit pipal trees, yet the pipal tree is employed to exorcise menacing *bhuts*; Alakshmi can make one a pauper, however, worship of the pipal tree can bring about the blessing of Lakshmi's abundance; and cutting a pipal tree can cause complete ruin, but proper care of a pipal tree results in copious blessings. In sum, the pipal tree is a very mighty being in whom the two faces of divine power are well portrayed. Here is concrete expression of the existential fact that life paradoxically includes its opposite; the positive attracts the negative. A common tenet of Hindu theological thinking is that death is an ingredient of life; pots of death hang from the tree of life. The animate beings associated with the pipal tree, therefore, range from life-enhancing divinities to life-threatening ghosts and other potentially negative presences, like Shani. Although it is quite rare, a copper facemask of Shani is sometimes attached to the trunk of a pipal tree; much more common, however, is the face of the goddess on a neem tree.

5

Faces of the Goddess

> Mother Neem [*Nima Mai*] takes good care of us.
> —neem tree worshiper in Banaras

> The seven sisters are swinging on a branch in the neem tree.
> They enchant our minds as the easterly wind blows gently.
> The faces of the seven sisters are glowing.
> A sandalwood-like fragrance comes from their bodies.
> The seven sisters are swinging on a branch in the neem tree.
>
> No one has ever before seen such beautiful ornamentation.
> The hair of the seven sisters touches Earth.
> They take her into the tender shelter of their affection,
> And it appears Mother Earth too is completely fulfilled.
> The seven sisters are swinging on a branch in the neem tree.
> —Bhojpuri folk song

> This neem tree is the Goddess. It is her body.
> The face on her makes it easier for us to connect with her.
> —neem tree worshiper in Banaras

A narrow lane runs off a busy intersection in the heart of the city of Banaras. Not far from this intersection is a small shop that makes and sells milk sweets. Directly behind the shop is a cubical temple that measures about eight feet on all sides. The crown of a large neem tree pokes out of the top of this temple, for it was built to house the goddess of the neem. The outer walls of the temple are pale yellow; a large four-armed form of the goddess Durga dressed in a red sari and riding her tiger mount has been painted just to the left of the blue cage-like door that leads to the interior of the temple. Inside the temple is the double trunk of the neem tree or perhaps two trees are growing side by side; no one seems to know for certain. But no matter, for I was told that though the goddess has many forms, she is really one. The two trunks are enclosed in a low square encasement capped with dark grey slate, where offerings of incense, flowers, and fruit are placed. So far none of this is unusual, for we encountered these features of tree shrines at the site of pipal trees. What makes this tree shrine different, however, is that the two trunks are each draped in bright red cloth bordered with gold tinselly trim, the ornate cloth typically used to adorn a goddess. While pipal trees are wrapped with string on special occasions, neem trees such as this one are dressed continuously with large pieces of decorative red cloth. Even more noteworthy, a silver face of a goddess has been attached to each of the tree trunks on the top edge of the red clothing (figure 5.1). Garlands of flowers are draped over the two facemasks; on one the garland hangs down onto the breasts of the tree. This is a fairly common scene at a neem tree shrine in Banaras. Why is the face added to a neem tree? What experiences become possible by affixing a facemask to the trunk of a tree? And how is this tree conceived? Many of the conversations I had with people who worship neem trees indicated that this tree is commonly considered to be an embodied form of Devi, the Great Goddess, and that the face and permanent garments are added to help make connections with her stronger and more intimate.

Figure 5.1 Twin neem tree shrine featuring cloth ornamentation and facemasks

The neem tree (*Azadirachta indic*; sometimes called "margosa") is a tropical tree related to mahogany that keeps it leaves for most of the year. It grows naturally in India, Burma, and parts of Southeast Asia and is now being propagated worldwide. It is not commonly found in dense forests but is widespread along roadways and around human settlements. Like the pipal, it too seems to be a tree that has flourished through human cultivation. Neem trees can live to up to 200 years and reach a height of ninety feet. I have seen neem trees with trunk diameters of about three feet; the bark on the trunk is dark and rough. The slender, bright green, nonsymmetrical leaves of the neem tree are serrated and shaped like a scimitar. They branch off their stem in either alternate or opposite direction and grow two to three inches long. In the springtime neem trees are glorious, covered with small white flowers that emit a sweet jasmine-like fragrance. Later in the year they develop numerous small olivelike fruits. Like pipal trees, neem trees also provide very good shelter and shade.

Because of its wide range of unusually useful qualities, neem has been propagated in over thirty countries. National researchers in the United States have concluded: "Neem is a fascinating tree...it seems to be one of the most promising of all plants and may eventually benefit every person on the planet.... Indeed, as foreseen by some scientists, this plant may usher in a new era in pest control, provide millions with inexpensive medicines, cut down the rate of human population growth, and perhaps even reduce erosion, deforestation, and even the excessive temperature of an overheated globe."[1] It was introduced into West Africa early in the twentieth century where it grows well and is used for shade and medicine, especially for malaria. It is an excellent tree for ecological reforestation in places like Haiti and because it requires little water it is a leading candidate for helping halt the spread of the Sahara Desert. A Saudi philanthropist planted a grove of 50,000 neems near Mecca to shade and provide comfort for the millions of pilgrims who camp each year on the plains of Arafat.[2] In these and countless other ways the neem tree is proving to be useful worldwide in dealing with a variety of environmental challenges, leading some to claim that it is a tree that promises to solve many global problems.

There is archeological evidence to suggest that, along with the pipal tree, the neem was sacred to the early inhabitants of the Indus Valley and was perhaps even worshiped by them. Neem trees are depicted in reverent ways with accompanying divinities in some of the artwork found on the earthenware shards discovered in the Indus Valley.[3] The neem tree is honored particularly for its healing abilities in early Puranic literature. Neem tree specialist John Conrick recounts a Puranic story that accounts for its remarkable powers: "Indra, the king of the Celestials, was returning to Heaven with a golden pot filled with Ambrosia he had taken from the Demons. Some of the precious Ambrosia spilled from the pot and landed on a neem tree thereby making neem trees blessed with miraculous healing properties for all eternity."[4]

Because of its immense medicinal value the neem is often called the "wonder tree" or "village pharmacy" and has long been used in many health-related situations. It has been called in Sanskrit *arishtha*, a term with a range of meanings including "safeguard against injury," "medicinal plant," and "bandage."[5] It has also been referred to in Sanskrit as *sarva roga nivarini*, "the curer of all ailments," and by Muslims as *shajar-e-mubarak*, "the blessed tree."[6] Conrick reports:

> In the ancient book, *Brihat Samhita*, the neem trees should be planted near the home to ensure good health to those that live there. Villagers with easy access to neem trees have developed many innovative uses for them. It is a common practice for villagers to wash wounds in water boiled with neem leaves. They put fresh leaves under their mattresses and in stored grain to repel insects. They feed their children neem leaves and oil to treat or prevent a variety of ailments including intestinal worms, malaria, encephalitis and meningitis. A paste made from neem leaves is used to treat scabies, external fungi, smallpox and head lice. Adults eat neem leaves to control diabetes, epilepsy, ulcers, headaches and fevers.[7]

I met a man in Banaras sitting at the base of a neem tree he worships daily who collects and eats five freshly fallen neem leaves every day. He told me he does this to receive the blessings of Ma in the form of good health, and assured me that as a result he rarely gets sick. Stout neem twigs are used daily by many in India for dental health; the end of the twigs are first chewed to create bristles and the teeth are then brushed with the subsequent toothbrush. Neem twigs are known to contain natural substances that prevent cavities and gum disease. Patnaik writes: "Renowned for its antiseptic and disinfectant properties, the tree is thought to be particularly protective of women and children. Delivery chambers are fumigated with its burning bark. Dried margosa leaves are burned as a mosquito repellent. Fresh leaves, notorious for their bitterness, are cooked and eaten to gain immunity from malaria."[8] History of the use of neem for medicinal purposes in Ayurveda goes back thousands of years, and neem tree derivatives have been some of the most potent ingredients in many Ayurvedic remedies. Because of the exceptionally effective results of neem in a wide range of medicinal uses, today there is increasing interest in it globally. Conrick, founder and director of the Neem Association, writes in his book, *Neem: The Ultimate Herb*:

> Although neem is one of the most ancient and most widely used herbs on earth, intense scientific investigations of the properties of neem are only

now being undertaken. These studies are quickly verifying the efficacy of its traditional uses and are finding even more uses for neem. This illustrates again that traditional wisdom can guide the efforts of modern science in discovering remedies for human ailments. From almost the very beginning of recorded human history, people have taken advantage of the remarkable neem tree. Even before ancient herbalists discovered the analgesic qualities of the willow tree—from which aspirin is derived—people used branches, fruit and leaves from the neem tree to cure many illnesses.[9]

Conrick provides a vast inventory of the various illnesses and health issues that neem is used to prevent or treat, including: psoriasis, diabetes, AIDS, cancer, heart disease, herpes, periodontal disease, skin disorders, allergies, ulcers, birth control (both men and women), hepatitis, fungi, malaria, external parasites, insect repellent, and insecticide.[10]

Neem has proven to be so successful and potentially lucrative for the pesticide industry that it has been at the center of recent GATT and WTO patent wars between Indian farmers and multinational corporations.[11] For example, in 1994 the European Patent Office granted a patent for an antifungal product to the US Department of Agriculture and the US-based multinational agrochemical corporation, W. R. Grace and Company. The Indian government soon challenged the decision, arguing that the process for which the patent had been granted had been in use in India for over two millennia. In 2000 the European Patent Office ruled in India's favor, but W. R. Grace and Company mounted an appeal on the grounds that the procedure had never been published in a scientific journal, and that the corporation's method represented a genuine innovation in extracting the natural chemicals from neem seeds. This appeal was lost in 2005 and the European Patent Office revoked the neem patent, keeping the tree free of patent restrictions.[12]

Many health and beauty aids are available today worldwide with some neem derivative in them; this is especially true in India, where the neem tree has been furnishing healing products for a long time. As Conrick remarks, "Long revered for its many healing properties, neem came close to providing a cradle-to-grave health care program and was a part of almost every aspect of life in many parts of the Indian subcontinent up to and including the modern era."[13] Historically, the most critical use of the neem tree in traditional Indian medicine was for the treatment of smallpox.

Before the World Health Organization eradicated the disease, derivatives from the neem tree were commonly used to treat smallpox in India. Smallpox patients were made to drink remedies prepared from neem compounds, their bodies were washed in a neem-leaf solution, and boughs from a neem tree were used to fan the patients to keep them cool. Smallpox has long been associated with the goddess Shitala in northern India, and because of her attraction to coolness, Shitala (her name means the "Cool One") has a close connection with the cooling neem tree. The majority of the neem tree worshipers I spoke with in Banaras identified the tree as a form of Shitala. Gupta reports that when someone came down with smallpox, "Neem leaves are strung on the doorway to announce Sitala's presence in the house. She is one of seven sisters, and by her presence is meant that someone is afflicted by smallpox."[14] Crooke noted the connection between neem trees and Shitala in his nineteenth-century study of religion in India: "The special abode of Shitala is the nim [neem] tree, and hence a [smallpox] patient is fanned with its leaves."[15] While smallpox is no longer a threat in India, Shitala maintains a connection with illnesses such as fevers and chicken pox: "With the eradication of smallpox, now bathing in a margosa-leaf infusion, excellent for soothing scabs and clearing away scars, marks the ritual termination of an attack of chicken pox or measles."[16] Although Shitala is still associated with various illnesses, I found her to be much more for her worshipers.

People still worship the neem tree as Shitala for protection from dangerous fevers, but this is not the only reason they worship her, for she is a goddess who offers much protection and life-blessings of all sorts. A man who daily cleans a neem tree shrine located at the top of Bhadaini Ghat in Banaras told me that Shitala is a very compassionate goddess (*daya devi*). I asked him what he meant. He introduced me to his four-year-old son and narrated this story. "My son was born premature and was not healthy. The doctor told us he would surely die, but I prayed to this neem and because of Ma's kindness he lived. As you can see, today he is very healthy. This is due to the blessings of Ma. I come here every day to thank her." He then turned toward two elderly women who had just entered the temple and said: "These women have come here to worship this tree every day for the last thirty years. Because of this they have lived full and happy lives, and their children and husbands have been safe, healthy, and well cared for. The results of worshipping Ma in the form of this neem tree include receiving good food, good health, good family relationships, and overall happiness. Therefore, people also come here to thank Ma for the blessings she brings to their lives. She is particularly fond of red hibiscus flowers. Neema Ma takes good care of us." A woman at this same temple later told me why she worships this neem tree. "We get good health, peace of mind, and we get our desires fulfilled by the goddess. She has been very good to my family, so I worship her here every day." Various members of a family that worship the neem tree in front of the house in which I lived told me that they worship this tree as Shitala for the general well-being of the family and for the "blessings [*ashirbad*] of Mother." I watched a man worship an unadorned neem tree in front of a Shitala temple one morning by offering water, hibiscus flowers, and incense. He told me that people worship this tree "to fulfill whatever desires they have. For example, some women come here to ask for a child, or if they are not married, a good marriage. But people ask for different things. I came here today just to honor [*manta*] Ma."

The anthropologist Susan Wadley confirms all of these views in her study of Shitala in northern India.[17] She maintains that, in addition to being associated with diseases, Shitala is identified as a goddess of good fortune and the granter and protector of children. In support of this contention she notes that Shitala is addressed in a hymn of praise as: "O you who give good fortune and sons to women."[18] Babagrahi Misra, another anthropologist, agrees, "From the position of a disease-deity She has been transformed to a children's deity now."[19] Now as a goddess of good fortune, Shitala is also identified as a caring Mother and savior of the world. In the *Shitala-Chalisa*, she is addressed as "Mother of the World" (*jag ki mata*) and "Preserver of the World" (*jadaddhatri*).[20] Although Shitala has been identified with dreaded diseases such as smallpox and malaria,[21] Wadley notes that Shitala increasingly lacks malevolence and any association with smallpox, especially in the region in and around Banaras. This was certainly the conclusion I came to from the many conversations I had at neem tree shrines with her worshipers, who tended to identify her as a source of a variety of life-blessings.

A man I met at a Durga temple on the pilgrimage circuit that encircles Banaras, in which a neem tree was being worshiped, informed me that the neem is the "goddess-tree" (*devi-vriksha*). While the majority of the neem tree worshipers I spoke with in Banaras identified the goddess of this tree as Shitala, for them Shitala is usually considered to be one of the many forms of the great Goddess Maha Devi, the Mother of Life, who assumes many forms to nourish all aspects of life. She is commonly addressed as Ma, Mata, Mai, or Maiya, all words that mean "Mother" and are used commonly to address a goddess within Hinduism. The identification of a neem tree as Mother is often very personal. A woman who worships a particular neem tree daily told me: "All neem trees are sacred [*pavitra*], but this one is special to our family. This one is *our* Mother." Although everyone I spoke with identified the neem tree as a goddess, there was no exact agreement on which form of the goddess she is. Many simply called her "*nima mai*" or "*nimiya maiya*," which means "Neem Mother." This is a general name used to address the particular goddess of the neem tree; I heard it spoken many times, saw it written on signs at various tree shrines, and heard it in several Bhojpuri songs that celebrate the neem goddess.[22] A popular Bhojpuri song sung in the region of Banaras opens: "Mother [*maiya*] comes and sits on her throne on a branch of the neem tree."[23] The song goes on to identify the mother goddess of the neem tree as the great goddess Durga and petitions her to fulfill the worshiper's desire, in this case a child.

The neem tree has been identified with a great variety of goddesses throughout India. For example, in the south this tree is identified with the goddess Mariamma in Tamil Nadu, with Kali in Kerala, and with Yellama in Karnataka; and in the northwest the neem is associated with the goddess Nagnechia in Rajasthan and with Nimbajadevi in Gujarat.[24] The identification of the neem tree as Shitala, however, is very common in northern India, especially in the northeastern portions of Uttar Pradesh and in the states of Bihar and West Bengal. Moreover, in these latter regions Shitala is commonly identified with Durga. When I was in Bodh Gaya, I talked with two Hindu workers who were in charge of sweeping the temple there. One told me: "For us there are two sacred trees. One is a god [*devata*]; the other is a goddess [*devi*]. The first is the pipal; the second is the neem. The pipal is Vasudeva; the neem tree is Shervahani." The latter name means "She who rides a Tiger" and generally refers to Durga. But when I asked if the neem is also Shitala, this man said, "Yes, they are the same goddess."

Many neem tree worshipers in Banaras identified the neem tree as Durga, the great goddess who takes many forms. There is a neem tree shrine in the Chetganj district of Banaras called Shervali Nima Mai. As Shervali is another name for Durga, here too the goddess of the neem tree is identified as Durga. The simultaneously unified and diverse theology of the Great Goddess in Hinduism is such that Shitala as the goddess of the neem tree is easily identified with the great goddess Durga. The man who had established the neem tree shrine behind his sweet shop explained to me, "This devi is Ma." When I asked, which Ma, he continued: "Shitala or Durga; they are the same. The neem is the body [*sharir*] of Shitala, but you can also say that it is the body of Durga in her form as Shitala." One day I was talking with a priest of a Hanuman temple in Banaras about tree worship. After confirming that the pipal tree is Vasudeva, he asked me what I had found out about neem trees. I mentioned that I had discovered the neem is regarded as Shitala. "Not only Shitala," he informed me, "but all nine forms of Durga. Most people regard the neem as Shitala, but others see it as some other form of the goddess Durga."

March 19, 2007, was a full and busy day in the city of Banaras. Not only was it the day of the Somvati Amavasya Vrat described at the beginning of chapter 3, it was also the start of the new year according to the Hindu calendar, the day of a solar eclipse, and the beginning of Vasant Navaratri, an important spring festival in which the goddess is worshiped for nine days. Navaratri celebrates the defeat of the world-threatening buffalo-demon Mahishasura by the Great Goddess in her powerful form as Durga.[25] A boon guaranteed that Mahishasura could not be killed by any male, so the life-threatening king of demons was able to overthrow all the male gods. It fell upon the Goddess to deal with Mahishasura. She slew the king of demons with strength and grace, and reestablished the order that is necessary for the ongoing nourishment of all life. Two Navaratris are celebrated: (1) the autumn Sharadiya Navaratri, which occurs on the first nine days of the bright fortnight of the lunar month of Ashwin (September-October) and culminates on the tenth-day victory commemoration of Dasara; and (2) the spring Vasant Navaratri, which occurs during the first nine days of the bright fortnight of the month of Chaitra (March-April) and is dedicated to the youthful form of the Great Goddess. Each of the two Navaratris is a very auspicious time for worshipping the Great Goddess in her variety of manifest forms.

Since this season marks a very active time for worship of the Great Goddess in the form of a neem tree, I decided to visit several neem tree shrines I had discovered in the Chetganj district of Banaras, all of which are furnished with clothing and facemasks. I spent most of my time at one particular neem shrine. A round white marble temple of a diameter not much more than eight feet topped with a conical roof now encloses a large old neem tree that stands at the intersection of an alley and a busy street. Four holes in the roof accommodate four massive branches of the tree that stretch upward toward the sky and orange grating at eye level allows one to view the tree without going into the cramped interior of the temple. I was told that this structure is a fairly new addition to the tree shrine, the contribution of the owner of a catering company situated next to it whose mother used to worship this tree daily. When she died her family encased the tree in the marble temple to honor her and insure continuation of the blessings of Nima Mai, for the owner attributes the well-being of the family and his success in business to the blessings of the goddess of this neem tree. The tree has been wrapped with ornate red cloth, and seven metal faces have been attached to its trunk; one of them—Shitala Ma—has been enclosed in a separate tiny white marble shrine built against the trunk of the tree (figures 5.2 and 5.3). On the day that I visited this temple, the seven facemasks were adorned with ornate red cloth and garlanded with hibiscus and marigold flowers. A steady stream of worshipers waited to make offerings at this tree shrine. As she left the temple, one woman identified the tree for me: "She is the Goddess. This is Navaratri so we worship the many forms of the goddess these days, like Durga and Kali." A man standing nearby added: "In Navaratri the main face [*mukh*] is Durga. Every goddess is really Durga, but she has many faces. Shitala Ma is one of the faces of Durga and the neem tree is her residence [*nivas*]." Another woman worshiping at this temple called the neem "Durga Ma" and explained, "all nine forms of the goddess are here in this neem tree, but Shitala is the most important among them."

The neem tree, then, is identified with Shitala, who as an aspect of Durga is commonly regarded as a form of the Great Goddess, the Mother of Life. Three technical and related Sanskrit terms are used generally to express the theology of the great goddess in Hinduism: *maya, shakti,* and *prakriti*.[26] *Maya* is the "creative force" by which the world is manifested. *Shakti* means "power" or "energy"; it is the divine power that is inherent in and animates all life. *Prakriti* connotes "nature" or "matter" and comprises the very physicality of life. Although these

Figure 5.2 Neem tree shrine in the Chetganj district of Banaras

three terms frequently have negative connotations in many of the philosophies informing Hindu ascetic traditions that aim to renounce the world as a dangerous illusion,[27] in the goddess traditions that embrace all life as sacred they are viewed in a positive light. David Kinsley says it well:

> As *sakti*, *prakriti*, and *maya*, the Devi is portrayed as an overwhelming presence that overflows itself, spilling forth into creation, suffusing the world with vitality, energy, and power. When the Devi is identified with these three well-known philosophic ideas, then, a positive point is being made: the Devi creates the world, she is the world, and she enlivens the world with creative power. As *sakti*, *prakriti*, and *maya*, she is not understood so much as binding creatures to finite existence as being the very source and vitality of creatures. She is the source of creatures—their mother—and as such her awesome, vital power is revered.[28]

Figure 5.3 Inside view of neem tree shrine; the white marble enclosure at the bottom is dedicated to the goddess Shitala Ma

In sum, the Great Goddess is that very source of the flourishing of life itself, with which the neem tree is closely identified.

Conceptions of the neem tree replicate the same two views we encountered in the situational theology of the pipal tree; namely, some tree worshipers regard the neem as the residence (*nivas*) of the goddess, while others regard it as the body (*sharir*) or natural form (*svarupa*) of the goddess. A man I spoke with beneath a neem tree that stands before the Shitala temple near the Durga Kund in Banaras informed me: "This is Shitala Ma's neem. She lives in this tree." He pointed to a bed hanging in the tree to make his point. A small bed is often hung from a neem tree for the goddess to sleep in at night. One of the priests attending this temple agreed: "The tree is not Shitala Ma, but rather she resides beneath the neem tree. This tree is special to Ma, so people honor it." When I asked him why people worship it, he replied, "For the same reasons they worship in the temple." Significantly, the same day another man made a quite different point at this very same temple. "This neem tree is a form [*rupa*] of the goddess," he informed me. "There are two forms of the goddess here: the one in the temple and the tree itself." A young woman cleaning the neem temple at Bhadaini Ghat made a similar case: "This tree itself is Shitala Ma" (*Ye per hi Shitala Ma hai*).

There is a temple deep inside the narrow lanes of the Chetganj district of Banaras that well illustrates the widely held notion that the neem tree is the body of Shitala. A small Durga temple, constructed from white marble and red wrought iron cage walls with a pyramidal roof, has been built right up against a large neem tree. Inside the temple is a *murti* of Durga fashioned from white marble. In the wall behind her and slightly to her right is a framed opening that gives access to the neem tree. A facemask has been placed on the tree so that the worshiper who visits the temple has a view of this face (figure 5.4). Although there is a body of

Figure 5.4 Inside of Durga temple in Banaras; the framed face of Shitala in the background is attached to a neem tree

Durga in the temple in the form of artistically crafted stone, the only body there is of Shitala is the tree itself. When I remarked on this to a woman worshiping at this temple, she said, "Yes, the tree itself is the body [*sharir*] of Shitala Ma." Some worshipers seem to hold both views. One woman who worships a neem tree daily for the peace of her household told me "the neem is both the residence [*nivas*] of Shitala Ma and the natural form [*svarupa*] of Shitala Ma." "But," she insisted, "the tree and the devi are one [*ek hi hai*]." I visited another neem tree shrine located near the main road to the Banaras airport. This shrine had a dual focus: the tree itself is adorned with clothing and a facemask, and a small temple standing next to it houses an image of the goddess Shitala. A man who came to worship the neem tree informed me that the temple was constructed only a short time ago, whereas the tree has been worshiped for a long time. He explained that the tree itself is "the main essential form [*khas svarupa*] of Ma."

Among the two conceptions—that the tree is the residence of the goddess or the tree is her embodied form—I found the latter to be by far the most common. A great number of people reported to me that a neem tree is the "*svarupa* of the goddess," even in the case where the tree is left unadorned. The fact that most people regard the neem tree itself as an embodied form of the goddess is especially true for those who report they have a close relationship with a particular neem tree, as intimate relationships with a neem tree are typically associated with the view that the tree is a *svarupa* of the goddess. A woman who worships the neem tree at Bhadaini Ghat everyday told me: "Ma's powerful presence [*shakti*] is in this tree. This tree is her *svarupa*. I worship her here everyday and now have a special relationship [*sambandha*] with this tree."

The term *svarupa* is a technical one with an expedient double meaning. It literally means "own-form" and frequently refers to "the form assumed by a deity."[29] Therefore, from a theological perspective, it means the specific form a deity takes in the world. Divinity within Hinduism is typically understood to be infinite and pervasive, but manifests in particular concrete forms. Accordingly, divinity—although unified at the unmanifest level—can manifest as a multitude of individual beings. A particular tree being, then, is both distinctive and nondifferent from the Supreme Being. The term *svarupa* has another meaning, and that is "one's own form of divinity." God or the Great Goddess is everywhere and everything, but one's *svarupa* is an approachable concrete "portal" into the infinite. That is, among the countless multitude of forms, this is the very particular one to which the worshiper is drawn and develops a special relationship. Neem tree worshipers say, "All trees are sacred, but this one is *my* mother." The nature of human beings is such that we do not have close relationships with the abstract general, but rather with specific, individual beings. The *svarupa* is that particular, individual form of divinity for a particular worshiper. Tree worshipers do not tend to relate to a huge number of trees, but rather a few, or perhaps only one they can connect with as an *individual* and with whom they can establish a close emotional bond. From the devotee's perspective, then, a particular neem tree as a *svarupa* is a particular form of the goddess with whom the worshiper can develop an intimate relationship, often called a *sambandha* in the languages of northern India.

On the back side of Lolar Kund, not far from Tulsi Ghat in Banaras, is an active Kali temple. In the small courtyard of this temple is another temple dedicated to Shitala. Before Shilala's temple stands an unadorned, medium-sized neem tree (figure 5.5). One morning I watched a young man offer this tree water, incense, red hibiscus flowers, and bright red sindur powder; he then circumambulated the tree and bowed his head to it. As he was putting his sandals back on I commented that it seemed to me that people worshiped both the tree and the temple image. "Yes," he said, "both are *svarupas* of the goddess. One is a *murti-rupa*, the other is a *prakriti-rupa*. But both are the goddess, so people worship them both."

Figure 5.5 Intimate interaction with bare neem tree near Lolarkund

The first term that he used—*murti-rupa*—referred to the embodied form of divinity that had been installed in the temple. It was a stone form that had been artistically crafted by human hands, and the divinity had been invited into it by the temple priests via a ritual procedure called the *prana-pratishta* ("establishment of life-breath"). The second term—*prakriti-rupa*—he applied to the tree to designate it a "natural form" of divinity that appears without the aid of any human intervention.

    This man did not feel the need to evaluate these two forms; he merely considered both of them valid "bodies" of the goddess. I met others, however, who gave priority to the tree-form of the goddess. A man worshipping at another Shitala temple explained: "The goddess's power [*shakti*] is not actually in the statue [he used this English word for the *murti*, the embodied form in the temple]; it is in the tree itself. The temple was built after the neem tree was already here. Shitala Ma has been here for a long time as the tree." My friend Nagendra made the same point when we came upon a Kali temple that was built around a neem tree less than a year before our visit. Inside the temple was a mature neem tree wrapped in ornate cloth with a facemask affixed to it. The tree was obviously older than the temple. "See, the tree was here long before the temple," Nagendra said. "First there was the neem tree. Alone, it was worshiped as the goddess. Then some devotees of hers decided to build this temple around it and add some more *murtis*. But the worship of the tree was first and is most important. The neem is the first form of the goddess Shitala." His point was that the worship of the tree is paramount and prior to the worship of any temple image that was added later. Trees appear naturally and are a natural expression of animated life; temples are built by humans and the *murti* has to be established through ritual technique. For many people, recognition of this fact gives precedence to the tree form of a divinity.

    It is not uncommon to find a neem tree being worshiped by itself, independent of any temple form of Shitala, which reinforces the point that the tree is the principal form of the goddess. There seems to be a progression in the development of neem tree shrines in Banaras. First, the trees are worshiped without any ornamentation added to the trunk. The neem tree in the courtyard of the Kali temple on the backside of Lolar Kund is one such tree. I was told that the small nearby shrine used to house a Shiva linga, but due to the popularity of Shitala here, the priests decided to install an image of Shitala in the shrine. If this is true, here is another instance in which the tree preceded the temple. The neem tree at this place is a medium-sized tree that grows out of the slate deck of the courtyard. No apparel has been affixed to the tree, which is enclosed only by a circle of bricks lining the soil at the base of the tree. Yet this tree is regarded as an embodied form of the goddess, and is frequently adorned with garlands of red hibiscus flowers, known as "*devi-phul*," the favored flower of the goddess. One spring morning I sat on the edge of a well watching people come and worship this tree. While some just touched the tree reverently with their right hand, or made a simple water offering, a group of three older women and two young girls performed an elaborate worship that morning for the "health and well-being of the family, and to honor Ma." After approaching the tree, the women set their plastic puja baskets down near its base and took out objects to be used in their ritual. They offered water to the roots of the tree from a copper pot, smeared its trunk with turmeric and sindur paste, and placed fruits, red hibiscus flowers, and sugar crystals near its base. They circumambulated the tree, then ended their worship by holding the tree with both hands and placing their heads reverently to its trunk. Only after finishing this did they walk over to the small Shitala temple in the compound and offer a few flowers. Clearly, the unadorned tree was the primary focus of their worship.

The next stage in the development of a neem tree shrine involves dressing the tree in clothing befitting a goddess. The neem tree standing before my house in Banaras, for example, was wrapped in a red *chunri* with gold tinselly borders (figure 5.6). A *chunri* is a type of red cloth tie-died with ornate designs in other bright colors that is commonly offered to a goddess in Hindu India. Stones from the Ganges were recently added to the shrine as forms of Shiva lingas, and a tulsi plant was placed in the ground at the base of the tree during my residence in Banaras. Every morning a member of a family that lives nearby this tree sat before it and offered it water, incense, and flowers. They also rewrap the tree with new ornate cloth from time to time as needed or as determined by some particular festival, such as Navaratri. Although this tree is primarily the site of the worship of this single family, I saw others stop to worship here too. This neem tree seems well on its way to becoming a neighborhood shrine, and I would not be surprised to see it expand into something more elaborate in the near future.

The final touch in the development of a tree shrine is the addition of a metal facemask (called simply a "face" [*mukha*] by my informants) made of brass, copper, or silver. Very importantly, the facemask must have eyes. When I first discovered a facemask attached to a neem tree near Bhadaini Ghat, I was surprised and thought it was unique, a one-of-a-kind expression of some vision of a particular tree worshiper. My wanderings throughout Banaras, however, soon led me to discover many dozen such shrines, and I have concluded there must be hundreds of these shrines tucked away in the back alleys of the city. This was perhaps the most unexpected discovery in my research; although I had never come across this practice in any literature, adorning neem trees with clothing and a facemask turned out to be rather common. In fact, if a neem tree is worshiped for any length of time and is in any way protected, the norm is for it to be ornately clothed and featuring a facemask with prominent eyes (figure 5.7). The brass facemask on a neem tree that is wrapped with a large

Figure 5.6 Dressed neem tree that stands before the author's house in Banaras

decorative *chunri* and stands tall in a park not far from Gaya Ghat in Banaras has white conch-shell eyes with inlaid black pupils. Some of the facemasks on neem trees are quite human looking.

It was such neem trees I had in mind when I questioned Stewart Guthrie's notion of religion as unconscious anthropomorphism in chapter 1. In the context of neem tree shrines, we encounter a case of intentional anthropomorphism. Guthrie's view of anthropomorphism may help explain "faces in the clouds," which in the end are not really there, but it seems to me that it does not help us to understand the faces on these trees, which are a physical reality, and furthermore, are applied deliberately by human worshipers. Guthrie sees anthropomorphism as an "unconscious perceptual strategy," but here we encounter something quite different. In this instance we encounter a strategy concerned with something other than perception that is pursued consciously; those who apply facemasks to trees certainly recognize them as trees and understand that they do not naturally feature

Figure 5.7 Worshipers making an offering to the face of a neem tree in an enclosed shrine

humanlike faces. If not an unconscious perceptual strategy, what might the strategic aim of attaching facemasks to trees be? What does one get out of placing a facemask on a tree that might not be there if this addition had not been appended? My ethnographic data suggests that this is done to enhance a *relationship* with the tree as a *person*.

I spent more time at the neem tree shrine situated at the top of Bhadaini Ghat in Banaras than at any other. More than fifty times during my year of research I climbed the steep stone steps of Bhadaini Ghat and walked sixty meters into a narrow alley at the top these steps to a modest, pale salmon-colored temple called the Shri Nanghan Bir Baba Mandir. This name refers to a saint who had died an unfortunate death and is now honored at this location. The inside of the temple is rectangular, measuring approximately ten feet by twenty feet, with white tile-covered walls. On the east side of the temple are stone images of the Baba and his companion, which are always smeared with bright orange sindur paste. On the west side stands a large neem tree with a trunk measuring thirty inches in diameter; a large hole has been left in the ceiling to accommodate the huge crown of the tree. A small black stone Shiva linga is situated on the north side of the tree, and a sindur-smeared Hanuman is housed in a niche in the wall to the west of the neem tree. The tree is wrapped with ornate red cloth that is periodically changed, especially during festival seasons. A crowned brass facemask of the goddess has been attached to the tree at eye level. The eyes have been highlighted with a light pinkish paint and black pupils (figure 5.8). A bright red dot of sindur powder is usually applied to the goddess's forehead as a decorative *bindi*, and a tiny ring has been added to her nose. At the base of the tree is a small pair of raised white marble feet. Offerings to the goddess of this neem tree are often placed at her feet, but when worshipers address the tree as "Ma," they typically look into her face.

Figure 5.8 Bhadaini Ghat neem tree shrine; note the tear falling from the goddess's left eye

During one of my visits to this temple, I talked with a young man who cleans the temple every morning as an act of service to the goddess of this neem tree. He disclosed that it was he who had added the facemask to the tree. I asked him why. "Because," he said, "this makes it easier for people to see ['have *darshan* of'] the goddess in the tree and worship [*puja*] her more easily. It helps people develop a stronger relationship [*sambandha*] with this neem." I asked another man who comes to this tree shrine daily why he thought that the face was added. "For worship [*puja*]," he said. I pressed him for further explanation. "Shitala Ma is just like a person [*vyakti*]. That is why people put a face [*mukha*] and clothes on her."

Over the course of my time in Banaras I asked many people who worship at this tree shrine about the face on the tree (figure 5.9). All agreed that it was added "for *puja*." One woman said that it makes *puja* "higher" (*upar*). She and the others meant this in two ways. First, this was done for the goddess herself. The face and ornate clothing were added as a way of honoring with beautiful

Figure 5.9 Bhadaini Ghat neem tree

things the goddess of the neem tree, usually conceived of as Shitala, who as a goddess appreciates fine dress. Several people told me that the ornate clothing and dress make *puja* more beautiful; the adornment (*sringara*) of a deity is certainly a key part of Hindu *puja*.

Second, the clothing and face were added for the benefit of the worshipers. It was done to make *puja* easier for them, as it allowed them to envision the goddess with less effort. Moreover, and perhaps most importantly, the clothing and particularly the face are added to facilitate a "connection" with the goddess of the neem tree. A tea-shop owner who has placed a facemask on a neem tree behind his shop told me "the face helps me connect [*rishta*] to the tree." Several people drew my attention to the eyes of the facemask. "When I look into her eyes I feel very connected to Ma," one man remarked. Many others said that the face made *darshan* more powerful and intimate. *Darshan* is the heart of much Hindu *puja*, and the eyes on the embodied forms of divinity are crucial. The word literally means "seeing" but is best translated as "visual communion," for the seeing works both ways: one sees the deity and is seen by the deity. As Diana Eck writes: "The prominence of eyes of Hindu divine images also reminds us that it is not only the worshipers who sees the deity, but the deity sees the worshiper as well. The contact between the devotee and deity is exchanged through the eyes."[30] The fashioning of a face and placement of eyes on a tree had occasionally been recorded by early European travelers in India:

> We know from *Mythologie des Plants* that 'in the seventeenth century there existed near Surat a sacred banyan tree, supposed to be 3000 years old, which the Hindus would never cut or touch with steel for fear of offending the god concealed in its foliage. They made pilgrimage to it and honored it with religious ceremonies. On its trunk at a little distance from the ground a head had been roughly carved, painted in gay colors, and furnished with gold and silver eyes. The simulacrum was constantly adorned with fresh foliage and flowers, the withered leaves which they replaced being distributed amongst the pilgrims as pious souvenirs.'[31]

The personality of a tree is brought out with the aid of the ornamentation and a face with *eyes*. Interaction and connection through the eyes is a central experience in Hindu worship, thus the eyes on the face of a neem tree facemask are vital.

Alfred Gell includes Hindu *murtis* in his theoretical consideration of the anthropological study of art, "since nowhere are images more obviously treated as human persons than in the context of worship and ceremonies."[32] Noting that *darshan* is a "two-way affair," he is concerned particularly with understanding the kind of intersubjective relationship that can be established and experienced through the eyes: "So far as the Hindu material is concerned, the key to the process of animation seems, initially at least, to depend on the logic of looking and being seen. Imagistic devotion is a visual act (as opposed to prayer, etc.) and it is accomplished entirely by looking. Specifically, it is accomplished by looking into the eyes of the god; union comes from eye contact."[33] For Gell, the eyes and other features added to some nonhuman object—in his case a sphere—are for far more than decoration; they give access to interiority: "Adding features which apparently make the sphere more 'anthropomorphic' (by the addition of eyes, a mouth, etc.) do not just serve the purpose of making the sphere a more realistic 'depiction' of a human being, they render it more spiritual, more inward, by opening up *routes of access* to this inwardness."[34] Looking into the face of the goddess with prominent eyes on a neem tree, then, is an important feature in the establishment of a deep connection with her.

The fields of cognitive, evolutionary, and developmental psychology, and cognitive neuroscience have jointly identified the special nature of face recognition in human beings.[35] Olivier Pascalis and David Kelly argue in a scientific journal article entitled "The Origins of Face Processing in Humans," that there is a consensus in contemporary research which now demonstrates that face processing holds a unique status within the brain, and there is evidence of an innate tendency to pay attention to and connect with faces from birth.[36] Others involved in similar research concur, "The evidence presented here suggests that the infant enters the world with a detailed representation of the human face."[37] Brain researchers assert that face processing played an important role in human development, and that face recognition was crucial to the continuation of a species that depends heavily on establishing strong relationships for survival. In short, we are evolutionarily conditioned to bond with faces; perception of faces is key to establishing strong connections and relationships for human beings. Face recognition and connection, scientists claim, is present in newborns; it is "functional from the very first moments of life." That is, we are programmed at birth for establishing relationships through face recognition. And, of course, the face we connect with most intimately is the human face, with the eyes of utmost importance. Two Canadian psychologists have found: "For newborns, a pair of eyes may have privileged status; they track schematic eyes as far as a complete schematic face. Two-month-olds presented with photographs of faces exhibit visual fixation patterns similar to those of adults, in that they focus more on the eyes than on any other facial feature."[38] Pasclis and Kelly maintain that the face newborn humans connect with most closely is a human (usually female) face with a frontal view in which both eyes are wide open in a direct gaze. This is exactly the kind of face that is placed on neem trees in Banaras. Whether present at birth or learned, human beings connect with and through faces. Indeed, tree worshipers report that the face helps them recognize the goddess of the neem tree and better bond with her: "When I look into the face of the goddess on the tree," one woman explained, "I feel a strong connection [*sambandha*] with this tree." Rather than being the result of primitive and confused thinking (or even an unconscious perceptual strategy à la Guthrie and Hume), the placing of a face on a neem tree might best be seen as an intentional and effective strategy to connect with a nonhuman species.

I had occasion to return several times to the neem tree shrine described at the beginning of this chapter and talk with the owner of the sweetshop located directly in front of it. He told me that he himself dresses the tree and had personally attached the faces to it. I asked him why. "My heart told me to do this, so I did," he responded. I pointed out that not all neem trees being worshiped in Banaras had faces on them and then asked him what advantage there is to adding a face to the tree. "Yes, this tree is the same as those without a face. Ma is present in all neem trees. But it is easier to have *darshan* of Ma when there is a face on the tree. The face also makes *puja* easier, and it makes our relationship [*sambandha*] with her more firm [*mazbut*]. The face helps us remember her and keep her in our hearts." Another man who had come to worship this neem tree added: "The face makes *darshan* of the goddess easier. The tree is the goddess, but it is easier to have a relationship [*nata*] with the goddess if a face is there. It is easier to see the goddess in the tree, or the tree as the goddess with a face on it." One day after Nagendra and I had visited several neem trees with facemasks on them and talked with a fair number of tree worshipers about the faces, he summed up the intention behind the facemasks for me: "First there was simply the neem tree, but then people put a face of the goddess on the tree, thinking: 'If we put a face on the tree it is better for our worship.' The face is what helps them to have a hearty relationship with Ma as the neem tree." The main point that he was making—and this point was confirmed by many others—was that the face made a connection or relationship with the goddess of the neem tree more possible, more powerful, and more intimate. Three Hindi terms were used to in this context: *sambandha*, *nata*, and *rishta*. All three mean "connection" or "relationship" and are usually understood to signify a familial relationship between two sentient beings for the benefit of both. Facemasks are not attached to all neem trees, but when present they serve to enhance further the positive relationships people have with the trees.

The facemask also makes the personhood (*vyaktitva*) of a tree more obvious. A man who worships an adorned neem tree everyday explained: "Shitala Ma is a kind of person [*vyakti*]. That is why people put a face on her and give her clothes." Early in my research on sacred trees in Banaras, I asked people whether the neem tree they were worshiping was a person or had personhood.

The answer I inevitably received was affirmative. Sacred trees in Indian Hindu culture are clearly assumed to be living beings—usually deities; as such, they are powerful "persons" (*vyakti*)—certainly animate, sentient beings with feelings and consciousness with whom one can communicate and establish meaningful, mutually beneficial relationships. Here the human–nonhuman boundary is ontologically fluid. I, therefore, offer the following hypothesis from my ethnographic research for further consideration: the degree to which one sees personhood in some nonhuman being—such as a tree—is a highly significant element in determining whether one develops a close or mutually beneficial relationship with that being.

Among all sacred trees, people in Banaras have the most intimate relationship with neem trees. While pipal trees and even banyan trees, as we will see in the next chapter, have a scary side often associated with ghosts and death, neem trees do not. As a tree worshiper stated: "Everyone wants a neem tree growing near their house because it brings Mother's blessings. But not a pipal tree, because it not only brings blessings but also frightening things." While people are afraid to go to pipal and banyan trees at night, they frequently chose to be close to neem trees. There are many songs addressed to the goddess of the neem tree that express a very affectionate relationship with her. I never heard of any such songs about pipal or banyan trees. The presence of the female neem tree near or even intertwined with the male pipal tree is sometimes believed to placate the more frightening side of a pipal, in very much the same way that the presence of a goddess consort mollifies a fearsome male god. Therefore, people seek to live near neem trees, often planting them in front of their houses or places of business, and work to establish close relationships with them. On the road to the airport in Banaras is a sweetshop with a large neem tree growing right in the middle of the tiny shop, creating very cramped quarters (figure 5.10). This tree is wrapped with ornate red cloth and a metal facemask has been attached to the trunk. The owner of the shop worships the goddess of the neem tree daily. While the tree causes some inconvenience and makes it difficult to move around in the cramped shop, he reports, "Ma blesses our lives and our business. My success in business and the well-being of my family are due to the blessings of this neem goddess. We are happy she is here. If this tree were to be cut I would lose my land and my family would be ruined." Through a variety of culturally defined interactions and ritual processes, then, close relationships with neem trees are both expressed and experienced in the context of tree shrines.

Special relationships with neem trees also include another kind of relationship: they are sometimes married to other trees—most commonly the pipal—and sometimes even to people. Not only does this mean that neem and pipal trees are planted so that they grow together—as in the case of the intertwined neem-pipal

Figure 5.10 Neem tree shrine in middle of shop selling sweets and snacks

trees at Assi crossing in Banaras that "called" me to this project—but also the two are not infrequently regarded as a married couple. I visited a Durga temple on a hilltop near Hampi in southern India where a neem and pipal tree were growing together. The English-speaking local guide accompanying me identified them as "husband and wife trees, because the neem is a goddess and the pipal is a god." Beneath this fertile union was a collection of snakelike naga stones. In her study of sacred plants, Gupta writes: "*Aswattha* [pipal] is regarded as a symbol of the male and ceremoniously married to a Neem tree which is symbolically female. In villages of India, usually these two trees are grown side by side with a platform built round them. On the platform intertwined or coiled snake stones are placed which are symbols of fertility."[39] Although I might remove the word "symbol" from this statement, Gupta describes a rather familiar scene in India. I frequently encountered in my own travels in southern India around Bangalore a village neem-pipal tree shrine in which a line of naga stones had been placed between the two trees. Although less common in northern India, I came upon this kind of tree shrine there too; in all cases the two trees were inevitably a neem and a pipal. Abbot found the same in his early twentieth-century study of sacred trees in India. He reports the most common form of tree marriage is "the marriage by Brahmin and non-Brahmin of the neem (female) to the ashvatha (male); the trees are planted and reared together and if one dies it is replaced. The thread ceremony of the ashvatha is first performed and after this the marriage to the neem."[40] He notes that the combined energy of married neem and pipal trees is particularly powerful.[41] Randhawa too notes: "The pipal and neem trees are commonly grown together in Mysore State [now Karnataka]. The pipal is regarded as symbol of the male and neem as symbol of the female and a ceremonial marriage of these trees is performed."[42] The performance of tree marriage highlights cultural assumptions about the sentience and relationality of a tree.

On June 12, 2007, *The Times of India* reported the marriage of a neem and pipal tree in a grand ceremony in Palakkad, a town located in the mountainous region of the southern Indian state of Kerala.[43] Many years before, the chief section controller of the Southern Railway, T. M. Sreenivasan, had planted a pipal tree near a Ganesha temple and honored it with great love. His family continued to care for the tree after his death and decided to marry it to a neem tree that had grown by chance next to it. After setting the appropriate day with the aid of an astrologer and employing a Hindu priest, the wedding was conducted on May 27th in traditional south Indian style: "In the auspicious *subha muhurat* [favorable moment] between 8:30am and 9:30am, he was married to the neem who is four years younger to him. The bride was wrapped in a traditional Kanchpuram silk sari which cost Rs 20,000, and a gold *mangalsutra* [marriage necklace of a bride]. She looked innocent and elegant as she flushed with tender green leaves. He was in a silk *veshti, angavasthram* and sacred thread made of silver and gold. There was a sumptuous feast for the guests." The newspaper quotes Sreenivasan's son as saying: "Money is irrelevant, if a ritual can integrate man with nature. Astrologer Panickar says that the wedding will bring prosperity and well-being to the people around. But the couple has to be worshipped everyday."

In addition to marrying other trees, trees are sometimes also married to human beings in Indian culture. Like humans, trees are considered to be both male and female so that the tree selected for a mate will be of the opposite sex from the concerned individual. The novelist Bharati Mukherjee published a book entitled *The Tree Bride* that is about a woman who as a young girl was married to a tree because she had been widowed when the boy groom died from a snakebite on his way to the wedding. Her father had her married to a tree so that she would avoid the life-long misfortune of being regarded as a cursed and unmarriageable woman.[44] Her dowry was hence buried at the base of the tree, and from time to time she offered flower garlands and Sanskrit prayers to her tree-husband. Throughout her life the tree bride communed with trees as her relatives. *The Tree Bride* is the sequel to a previous novel in which Mukherjee recounts the moving moment when this young girl, named Tara Lata, met her future husband:

> Then, it's time for the *shubho-drishti*, the rite of auspicious gaze when the bride gets her first glimpse of the face of the man she is marrying.... The bridal veil is lifted. Tara Lata straightens her bowed head, and raises her gaze slowly, very slowly. Her bridegroom is brave and steadfast. He has waited for her all night in the perilous wilderness. He has waited for her alone, unflinching, though deadly snakes slither out of flooded holes at his feet, and leeches crawl across his toes, and crabs scuttle up his shins and predatory beasts gouge his solid stomach. The bridal gaze angles up his strong, slender torso as tall as a ship's mast, and scales up, up, to where the tip of his head disappears in the night-black winter skies. She feels his arms, as strong as tree branches, brush against her, enfold her, shield her from life's potential brutalities. The whispered lamentations were wrong. She is not a woman cursed by a goddess and shunned like an outcaste by her community. She takes her greedy fill of the auspicious glimpse. And now she recognizes her bridegroom. He is the god of Shoondar Bon, the Beautiful Forest, come down to earth as a tree to save her from a lifetime of disgrace and misery.[45]

The result of her salvific marriage to this robust tree led to a strong, independent, and heroic life for Tara Lata.

Marriage to a tree may also be done to avoid the inauspiciousness of a third marriage that is believed to lead to the death of either the bride or bridegroom, or to correct a problematic horoscope.[46] After decorating a tree with the appropriate clothing and ornamentation, Abbot reports that a bridegroom addresses a blossoming tree with this mantra: "I bow to thee, auspicious deity, to thee, the daughter of the sun. Oh goddess, protect me. You have come here as my wife. Oh sun, you have been created by Brahma for the good of all living beings; you are the presiding deity of the trees and the promoter of love among the gods, please destroy forthwith the sin of my third marriage and also death." Hopkins writes: "In India, tree-marriages are common. The wife who otherwise would get the evil result of a third marriage on the part of her husband thus casts the evil on the tree substitute, she herself becoming the fourth wife. This is a modern survival of a more general custom, according to which a tree was actually wedded to a human being, as a similar anthropopathic creature."[47]

Vijaya Nagarajan records her observations of a ritual in which a man was married to a pipal tree because he was not successful in finding an appropriate human bride. During the wedding, garlands were exchanged between the groom and the bride, with a priest helping the tree bride offer her garland to her new husband. After the exchange of the nuptial garlands, the couple was honored by feasting them; a plate was placed before the tree and another before the groom as he sat next to his bride. "Marrying trees," Nagaranjan contends, "is part of the repertoire of solutions offered to families in the throes of suffering.... It is believed that trees have an enormous capacity to absorb suffering, since they have an abundance of auspiciousness, goodwill, and generosity."[48] The ritual interaction between trees and humans, however, demonstrates more than strategies to cope with suffering for Nagarajan: "The ritual of a person marrying a tree is, then, both a symbolic and literal reminder of our 'kinship' with the natural world."[49] Moreover, rituals of marriage to trees are "a way of restoring the earth by establishing relationships with the powerful, creative, and auspicious force of trees."[50] The historian of religions Mircea Eliade concurs, maintaining that the marriage between humans and trees in general "shows the feelings of solidarity between men and plants."[51] Thus, as authentic "persons," trees and humans are related, and trees are legitimate partners with whom humans can enter into significant relationships.

We have seen that neem and pipal trees often have intimate relationships in India; the former is a mighty deity that well displays the ambiguity of power and the latter a therapeutic goddess available for close relationship. It is now time to turn to the other member of the trinity of sacred trees: the potent and everlasting banyan that reveals the association between trees and immortality.

6

Trees of Immortality

> The banyan tree never dies.
> —common saying in Banaras

> I meditate on Bala Mukunda,
> who at the time of the destruction of the world
> lies in the hollow of a banyan leaf holding his lotus-toe
> in his lotus-mouth with his lotus-hand.
> —Bilvamangal, *Balamukundastakam*
> (posted at the site of the Akshya Vata in Gaya)

> Oh banyan tree, thank you for looking after my husband.
> In years to come, may all married women come to see you
> and offer thanks and prayers.
> —Madhur Jaffrey's Savitri story

When the present world-cycle comes to a close and a great deluge brings an end to all life, a single tree will remain standing. This is the Akshaya Vata, the Immortal Banyan, the only individual tree ever designated with a proper noun in Hindu scriptures. The Matsya Purana explains that Shiva assumed the form of the Akshaya Vata banyan tree and eternally protects this immortal tree with his mighty trident.[1] Thus, when the great dissolution of the world occurs, among all life forms this tree alone survives. This particular text also declares that Lord Vishnu stays at the Akshaya Vata during the period in which the universe is in a state of dissolution. The Bhagavata and other Puranas tell how the great ageless sage Markendeya discovers the form in which Vishnu or Krishna resides at this undying tree.[2]

Because of his power of ascetic discipline and great devotion, Markendeya was granted an embodied vision of the end of the world. He suddenly found himself swimming in the vast ocean of pure potentiality after the world had been completely flooded.[3] After flailing about in the frightening dark waves for what seemed like eons, he came upon a young banyan tree (*nyagrodha-pota*) growing on a small island that rose out of the water. In some accounts Markendeya alone survives a fiery destruction of the world and seeks refuge at the place where

Vishnu dwells.⁴ In any case, Markendeya found himself at the eternal banyan tree and sitting safely beneath it witnessed an enormous flood engulf the entire world. High on a branch of this tree he noticed a most amazing sight: a small radiant infant, tucked into the hollow of a leaf, fast asleep. The child was sucking its toe. When Markendeya moved closer to investigate, the baby drew a breath, sucking Markendeya into its tiny body. Markendeya was astonished to see that inside the infant was the entire universe. Eventually the baby breathed out, expelling Markendeya, who fell back into the cosmic ocean. Now he realized that the resplendent child was none other than Vishnu in the form in which he rests while the universe is in its dormant phase prior to the creation of the next cycle of existence.

Although the Akshaya Vata tree that holds the Lord who holds the entire universe within his body is affirmed by all Puranas to be immortal, the location of the eternal tree differs. There are at least three banyan trees that I am aware of in north-central India which people claim to be the Akshaya Vata: one each located in the three famous pilgrimage centers (*tri-sthali*) of Prayag (Allahabad), Varanasi (Banaras), and Gaya.⁵ Several people told me that many believe that all three trees are linked by far-reaching roots. I travelled in search of the elusive Akshaya Vata of Allahabad at the confluence of the Ganges and Yamuna Rivers in the spring of 2007. Unfortunately, access to the tree is restricted, since it is now situated within the walls of the old fort in Allahabad, currently occupied by the Indian army. Pilgrims visiting this famous banyan tree these days have to content themselves with a view of the tree from a boat on the Yamuna River. When we arrived at a spot where we could see the tree, my boatman identified this particular banyan tree as the "Krishna tree" and said that it is the residence (*vas*) of Vishnu. Many people associate this tree with Krishna, and indeed on the pilgrimage maps of Allahabad the torso and head of Krishna appear out of the Akshaya Vata located inside the fort. While in Allahabad I purchased a small Hindi pamphlet that extols the greatness of this ancient religious site. Regarding the famous banyan tree, the author writes:

> The Akshaya Vata stands within the fort near the confluence of the rivers. The religious belief is that at the time of the dissolution of the world [*pralaya*], the Akshaya Vata is not destroyed. At the time of the world's dissolution, Lord Vishnu takes the form of Balamukunda [baby Krishna] and lies on a leaf of this immortal tree. At this time he puts his own lotus-toe into his own mouth and remains in this posture. There is a famous Sanskrit verse about this:
>
> > *I bow my head to Balamukunda, who at the time of destruction*
> > *lies in the hollow of a banyan leaf holding his lotus-toe*
> > *in his lotus-mouth with his lotus hand.*

> It is said that in olden times people who came here desiring liberation [*moksha*] would jump into the confluence from a branch of the Akshaya Vata and obtain liberation by offering up their life, and would not incur the sin of suicide.[6]

Because of the latter practice, access to the tree was also restricted during the period of British colonial rule. Although there are very few days of the year that pilgrims can have direct contact with the Akshaya Vata banyan tree here (the fort is open occasionally for this purpose), they often include a distant viewing of it in their pilgrimage to Allahabad, and a priest at the tree shrine passes out leaves that have dropped from the tree as sacred souvenirs (*prasad*). I was told that many people seek some kind of contact with this tree to achieve *moksha*, the ultimate immortal liberation.

The Brahma Purana advises a devotee to visit the Akshaya Vata banyan tree where Markendeya sought refuge with Vishnu, comparing it to the Kalpa-Vriksha wishing-tree, since it survives throughout all eons (*kalpas*). The pilgrim is instructed to circumambulate this tree three times and worship it with great devotion, reciting the following mantra: "O banyan tree, you are immortal, surviving all through the Kalpa. You are the abode of Vishnu. O banyan tree, dispel my sin. O Kalpa tree, obeisance to you!"[7] This text goes on to enumerate the religious advantages of worshipping the eternal banyan tree: all sins are eliminated and great benefits are obtained. "By visiting Vishnu in the form of the banyan tree that has originated from the body of Krishna and that is a great being consisting of the splendour of Brahman and by bowing to it, the devotee derives a benefit that is superior to the benefit of the Rajasuya and horse-sacrifice. Redeeming the members of his family he goes to the world of Vishnu."[8]

The Akshaya Vata of Banaras is located within the compound of the famous Kashi-Vishvanath temple. Mostly women worship this tree for the health and long life of family members, but it does not seem to be a major attraction for the crowds of pilgrims visiting this popular temple every day. The Akshaya Vata at Gaya is another matter; it is typically included in a visit to this pilgrimage center. The Akshaya Vata at Gaya, moreover, has its own ambiance and set of rituals associated with it. I included visits to the Gaya banyan tree during my excursions to the nearby Bodhi Tree of Bodh Gaya. It is an ancient and marvelous tree (figure 6.1). There is a glass case near the base of the tree with a picture of Krishna lying on a banyan leaf sucking his toe as the texts describe. It has several large gnarled trunks that are all completely covered with bright pieces of red, yellow, and white cloth that have been tied to the tree by pilgrims. A priest who attends this tree shrine and guides pilgrims through the rituals conducted in its shelter told me that people tie the pieces of cloth to this tree to get their wishes fulfilled, often for a child. In this sense too the banyan is a *kalpa-vriksha*, a "wishing-tree." One of the Sanskrit verses

Trees of Immortality

Figure 6.1 The Akshaya Vata banyan tree at Gaya

written on the wall here proclaims: "The Lord makes immortal that place where the Tree of Immortality is praised by priests and food is given to the ancestors." Indeed, pilgrims also come here to perform rituals under the tree for the benefit of their deceased ancestors.

Specifically, Gaya is an important place to perform *shraddha*, the ritual to feed, honor, and aid one's deceased ancestors.[9] In general, *shraddha* rites are performed to help the ancestors enjoy a happy state (*bhukti*) while in the heavenly realms (*pitr-loka*) and finally achieve ultimate liberation (*mukti*).[10] Professor Rana P. B. Singh of Banaras Hindu University, who has been researching *shraddha* rites in Gaya for some time, told me that the ritual is performed to give long life to ancestors in the future, as well as to seek the blessings of long and abundant life from them. Part of the *shraddha* ritual involves *pinda-dan*, the offering of balls of rice to the ancestors. Singh explains that the *pinda-dan* offerings are made on banyan leaves, "for the banyan leaf is an excellent vehicle for offerings concerned with the blessing of long life." In addition, he told me the long and happy life for ancestors and one's self that is accrued from the performance of *shraddha* is also the main fruit of worshiping the Gaya Akshaya Vata banyan tree itself—which according to him is a form of Vishnu. In a section of the text called the Gaya Mahatmya ("Greatness of Gaya"), the Vayu Purana stresses the favorable results of worshiping the banyan tree and making offerings at this auspicious site. "Whatever is given at the Vata tree at Gayatirtha to the Pitrs will be Akshaya (indestructible). By seeing, bowing to and worshipping

Vatesha [Lord of the Banyan] with calm and composed mind, the pilgrim will lead his ancestors to the indestructible and eternal Brahmaloka."[11] The priests attending the Akshaya Vata of Gaya certainly promote this viewpoint. One of them told me: "If you make an offering here and worship this tree your ancestors will be very happy. It will be very good for you too. Many benefits will come from this." The Gaya Mahatmya found in the Narada Purana extols the great benefits of performing *shraddha* with the *pinda* rice balls under the Akshaya Vata: "He who, with special efforts, performs the rite of Shraddha at the Akshaya Vata along with this and visits, salutes, and worships Vatesha (the Lord of the Banyan tree) with concentration and purity of mind shall take his Pitrs [ancestors] to the everlasting and eternal city of Brahma."[12] The Vayu Purana agrees, "If the Shraddha at Akshya Vata is performed with great care and effort the pilgrim will lead his Pitrs [ancestors] to the indestructible and eternal Brahmaloka."[13] Performing the *shraddha* offerings at the Akshaya Vata, then, is thought to lead to the immortality of both the performer and his ancestors. This text too identifies this immortal tree as the eternal residence of Vishnu. "Whatever is offered to the Pitrs... at the Vata at Gaya is Akshaya [immortal]. Obeisance unto that Yogashayin [Vishnu in yogic slumber] who has assumed the form of an infant boy and who sleeps on top of the Vata tree in that vast sheet of cosmic waters."[14] The cultural association of the banyan tree with long life and immortality is clearly expressed in these Puranic stories. Thus, there is no better place to conduct *shraddha* than under the Akshaya Vata, the immortal banyan tree. This tree is closely associated with efforts to influence or control life and death.

The banyan (*Ficus benghalensis*), like its many aerial roots, is known by many names. In Sanskrit it is called the *nyagrodha* ("growing downwards") or *vata* ("surrounded"), and sometimes *bahupada*, an appellation that means "many footed."[15] In Hindi, it is known as the *bargad* or *bar*. The English name banyan was given to this species of tree by early British visitors to India who observed that merchants commonly conducted business, and sometimes even worship, under this arboreal giant. A merchant is called a *bania* (often spelled *banya*) in northern India; thus the name "banyan."[16] The banyan tree inspired the imagination of many Englishmen, including the early nineteenth-century English poet Robert Southey:

> It was a godly sight to see
> The venerable tree
> For o'er the lawn, irregular spread,
> Fifty straight columns propt its lofty head,
> And many a long depending shoot,
> Seeking to strike a root,

> Straight like a plummet grew towards the ground...
> So like a temple did it seem that there
> A pious heart's first impulse would be prayer.[17]

Southey was, of course, referring in this poem to the distinctive feature of the banyan: that it sends down aerial roots, which over the course of time become massive trunks, so that a single tree creates a small forest radiating steadily outward from the original trunk. Perhaps it is for this reason that the banyan tree has become a favored contemporary metaphor for Hinduism—simultaneously singular and vastly divergent—as a world religion. Thus, in addition to spawning new trees through the distribution of its seeds, the banyan tree can reproduce itself and extend itself into time endlessly by creating new and self-supporting trunks. The banyan reaches its fullest glory in open spaces, and like the pipal and neem, historically has benefited from human cultivation. Current circumstances such as crowded urban spaces and pavement now prevent many banyans from developing to their full extent, but historically there are records of huge banyan trees. Monier Williams reports, "A tree of this kind called the Kabir-Var, on the banks of the Narbada near Broach, continued multiplying itself every year by sending down roots from its branches till it became a forest capable of sheltering an army of 7000 men."[18] The botanist Santapau records the size of several large banyan trees, including one from the state of Maharashtra, noting that "in 1882 the tree was 483 meters in circumference, its length from north to south being 181 meters and from east to west 134 meters."[19] He also writes about the banyan tree that was planted by seed in the Royal Botanic Garden in Calcutta in the year 1782. Its dimensions in 1900 were as follows: "The original stem then was 15 meters in girth, the number of aerial roots was 464 in size from a few centimeters to over 3.6 meters in girth; the circumference of the crown of the tree was about 377 meters." In 1965 the number of aerial root trunks of this huge banyan tree numbered 1,044, and although the tree had not been allowed to spread freely, its circumference measured 416 meters. This tree is now recorded in the *Guinness Book of World Records* as the largest banyan tree on the planet. A sign erected in the garden in 2005 claims that there were then 2,880 root trunks (called "proproots" on the sign), and that the tree occupies 1.5 hectares (one hectare is approximately 2.5 acres).[20]

Because the banyan tree grows steadily outward in a circular fashion from its central trunk while planting additional forms of itself with aerial roots, it is sometimes called the "walking tree." The cultural botanist Gupta writes, "The ability of the tree to support its ever growing branches by the development of adventitious roots from its branches, roots which hang down and act as props over an ever widening circle, represents eternal life and that is why the tree is called *Bahupada*, one with many feet, and is a symbol of long life, and associated with divinity."²¹ Over time a banyan tree can spread over much territory, and eyewitness reports make it clear that under ideal conditions the "feet" of the banyan can easily number more than a thousand. As the central shaft of the tree dies out, others take its place, sending out more aerial roots that will become massive trunks themselves, and on and on the process continues. It is often difficult to tell where the "original" tree stands. In this way a banyan tree can go on indefinitely; many people in Banaras told me that it lives forever. As Malla notes, "It is a self-generating plant and does not die."²² In this manner, it is the "immortal banyan," the Akshaya Vata.

Banyan trees can reach a height of about one hundred feet. The trunks have a fairly smooth and light bark with rope-like tentacles frequently creeping down their sides (figure 6.2). The leaves are broadly oval in shape with smooth edges. They grow up to six inches long and are rather stiff and leathery, making them suitable plates for ritual offerings. The small figs of the banyan turn red when ripe and are full of tiny black seeds. Several stories are told in Indian literature about these seeds. The Vishnu Purana compares the miracle of such an enormous and multifaceted tree coming from such a tiny seed to the miracle of the vast universe contracting into and manifesting out of Vishnu, the supreme progenitor of the universe. "As the wide-spreading Nyagrodha tree is compressed in a small seed, so at the time of dissolution, the whole universe is compressed in

Figure 6.2 Large banyan tree at the Rishi Valley School in the southern state of Andhra Pradesh

thee as its germ. As the Nyagrodha germinates from the seed, and becomes first a shoot, and then rises into loftiness, so the created world proceeds from thee, and expands into multitude."[23] In a story found in the Chandogya Upanishad, a wise father uses a seed from a banyan tree to teach his son Shvetaketu about the true nature of the self and the mystery of the manifestation of the entire diverse world from a unified nothingness.[24] The father asks his son to cut open a fruit from an enormous banyan tree and report what he sees. Shvetaketu discovers tiny seeds within the fruit. The father then requests his son to cut open one of the seeds and report what he finds. The son does so and declares that he sees nothing. "From that nothingness, that finest essence that you cannot even perceive, came this huge banyan tree that stands before us," explains the father. "That finest essence is the essence (or "Self" [atman]) of this whole world, and you yourself are essentially that, my son." Because of its ability to teach lessons about the true nature of reality the banyan is often known to be a "tree of knowledge." In a Buddhist context, Kashyapa, the Buddha just prior to Shakyamuni Buddha, is said to have achieved enlightenment beneath a banyan tree.[25] The profound mystery present in the banyan, then, is not only related to ongoing, inexhaustible, and ever-expansive physical renewal but also infinite insight.

The roots of the banyan are said to be both extremely deep and everlasting. On the day of an important banyan tree ritual, an article that extolled the greatness of the banyan tree appeared in a popular Hindi daily newspaper, the *Dainik Jagaran*. The article quotes the views of the head priest of the Kashi Vishvanatha temple, the most famous of all temples in Banaras: "According to philosophical texts, the roots of the banyan tree reach endlessly deep. This depth is a symbol of the infinite and indicator of sacredness [pavitrata]. Therefore, there is a special quality of greatness in the worship of the banyan tree [vata vriksha]."[26] A story is told in Allahabad of the Mughal emperor Aurangzeb's attempt to destroy the Akshaya Vata there by having it burnt to the ground.[27] It is said that new sprouts appeared from the remaining roots and grew into the tree that now stands at the confluence of the Ganges and Yamuna Rivers. Whether this narrative is historically accurate or not, it gives expression to the belief that the banyan tree cannot die, but rather eternally renews itself from the profound and inexhaustible depth of its roots. In his chapter entitled "The Power of Trees," Abbot writes, "The banyan tree's habit of throwing down tendrils which take root, and become massive trunks before the parent tree has even withered, not unnaturally suggests longevity; planting a banyan-tree is one way of attaining long life."[28] It is reported that when a person plants a banyan tree the following prayer is recited: "May I abide in heaven as many years as this tree continues growing on the earth."[29] A man in Banaras told me that the base of a banyan tree is a favorite place to bury the placenta of a newborn for the long life of the child. For these reasons, the banyan tree is also known as a "tree of life."

Not only is a banyan tree, like all sacred trees in India, considered to be a powerful animate being, it is also deeply rooted in the source of all life that humans seek connection with, depend on, and receive blessings from. Trees in general are associated with the very wellspring of life's vitality, and banyan trees in particular are considered to be an embodiment of ever-lasting life that continuously renews itself. The historian of religions Mircea Eliade maintains that a general pattern regarding trees is found in many religions: "The trees signify the universe in endless regeneration; but at the heart of the universe, there is always a tree—the tree of eternal life or of knowledge."[30] According to Eliade, trees such as the banyan are sacred because they are an expression of the inexhaustible nature of life and for this reason are at the center of pursuits pertaining to the achievement of immortality: "the divinity revealed in the cosmos in the form of a tree is at the same time a source of regeneration and 'life without death,' a source to which man turns, for it seems to him to give grounds for his hopes concerning his own immortality."[31] Nathaniel Altman concurs: "Trees are Nature's perfect examples of growth, reproduction, and regeneration. Among early humans, trees were regarded as the primary source of life on Earth. Whether a tree lost its leaves every fall to grow new ones in the spring, or was green throughout the year, it symbolized *the mystery of perpetual generation*."[32] Notions of immortality worldwide, then, are often closely linked with trees. Immortality, or at least longevity, is commonly sought in India at the foot of a tree—and most likely in the shelter of a banyan tree. As we have seen, the *shraddha* death rite that aims to achieve immortality for one's ancestors is frequently performed at the base of a banyan tree, and we will soon see that the virtuous wife Savitri brought her husband back from death under a banyan tree. The ever-renewing banyan tree is then a very good place to deal favorably with both life and death. But just who is the divinity associated with this tree?

For many tree worshipers in northern India, the banyan is a form of Shiva. Gupta notes, "*Nyagrodha* symbolises Shiva and is, therefore, held sacred."[33] Malla concurs, "In Brahmanical Hindu religion, *vata* [banyan] was identified with Shiva."[34] Vateshwar, which means "Lord of the Banyan," is also a common name for Shiva. A Shiva temple that stands under a large banyan tree at Triveni Ghat in Rishikesh is called the Mrityu-Jaya Mahadeva, that is, "the Great God who Conquers Death." A priest of this temple told me that this tree is an appropriate location for the temple, since Shiva can assume the form of a banyan tree, a tree known for its longevity and influence over Yama, god of death. I was discussing tree worship one day with a woman I met under the Assi Ghat pipal tree who told me, "Vasudeva resides in the pipal, Durga Ma in the neem, and Shankara Mahadeva [Shiva] in the banyan." This is a widely held view. Some tree worshipers identify the banyan directly as Shiva, because its tangled aerial roots resemble Shiva's dreadlocks or matted hair (*jata*). A woman I met worshiping a banyan tree said to me: "The banyan is Mahadeva. Look, this tree has his *jata*." Ample textual support for the view that the banyan is an embodied form of Shiva can be found in the Puranas. In the story with which this chapter began, the Matsya Purana identifies the banyan as a form of the mighty Shiva. Near the end of the Kartik Mahatmya of the Padma Purana is a discussion of why the pipal and banyan are the two trees most worthy of worship (*adhik pujane yogya*).[35] The epic narrator Suta says, "The pipal is the form [*rupa*] of Bhagavan Vishnu, and the banyan is the form [*rupa*] of Rudra [Shiva]."[36] The Skanda Purana also identifies the banyan tree (*vata*) as an embodied form (*rupa*) of Shiva.[37]

While the majority of ethnographic and textual accounts affirm that the banyan is Shiva, some regard it as a form of Vishnu. For example, a woman I met who was worshiping a banyan tree for the long life of her husband and the health of her family told me that the banyan is "Lord Vishnu," and the Narada Purana claims that a banyan tree growing at the Vaishnava center of Jagannatha Puri, which is a Kalpa Vriksha tree that obliterates sins and grants great benefits, is "Vishnu in the form of the holy banyan tree."[38] A number of people I spoke with, however, were not inclined to identify the banyan with any particular god or goddess, but instead regarded it as the residence of many gods and goddesses. I had a conversation about sacred trees with a man near a tree shrine consisting of a combination of a pipal, neem, and banyan near Bhelupura in Banaras. He told me, "Vasudeva resides in the pipal, Durga resides in the neem, and all gods and goddesses reside beneath the banyan." There are a few large pipal and banyan trees growing at the old Adi Karmadeshvara temple, the oldest surviving temple in Banaras and the first major stop on the pilgrimage circuit around the city. A priest residing there informed me that the pipal is Vasudeva, "but the banyan [*bargad*] is not really a specific god [*devata*]. Many gods live beneath it." When I asked a man I met under a large banyan tree in the interior of Banaras if he could identify the god of the banyan, he said: "It is no god, but the banyan is a good place to conduct worship. For this reason, there are many gods under a banyan tree." This is exemplified by a huge banyan tree perched atop Gaya Ghat in Banaras: underneath its ample canopy are a collection of small temples dedicated to Kali, Durga, Shitala, Shiva, Hanuman, Ganesha, and Radha-Krishna. Here too is a small shrine for the divine couple Savitri and Satyavan. In such cases, the copious shade and shelter of a banyan tree serves not so much as the body of a deity, but as a natural temple for a multiple of gods. I asked a man in Banaras why people worship beneath a banyan tree. "For the same reason they worship in a temple," he replied. I have seen many small temples nestled beneath the expansive canopy of a banyan tree. It is very common to find stone Shiva lingas beneath a banyan tree, and I noticed during my year of research that the banyan is a favorite place for goddess temples—especially those of the goddess Kali. There is a Kali temple beneath a banyan tree next to the big pipal tree at Assi Ghat, and several Kali temples I visited in Haridvar were located underneath banyan trees. I pressed the priestess of a Kali temple located under a large banyan tree in Chitaranjan Park in Banaras to tell me why Kali is often found beneath banyan trees; she replied simply, "because the shelter of a banyan tree is a peaceful place." As Crooke noted in his nineteenth-century study, "Thus the banyan with its numerous stems may fitly be regarded as the abode of gods or spirits."[39] A habitat crowded with divinities, the abundant shelter of a banyan tree is site of much worshipful activity.

The Sankata Devi temple near Scindhia Ghat in Banaras well illustrates this. The temple houses a metal form of the goddess as Durga, her foot planted victoriously on the body of the buffalo demon Mahisha. One enters the open square courtyard of the temple on the northeast side from a gateway leading off one of the narrow alleys that characterize this section of Banaras. On the far corner of the courtyard is a doorway leading into the goddess's main temple, but in the center of the courtyard stands a remarkable banyan tree. Beneath the tree a multitude of gods and goddesses are housed in eight small temples. The temples have been here for so long that many of them are now enveloped by the tree, seeming to melt into its trunk (figure 6.3). People come to have significant contact with divinity at the base of this banyan. Most of the people I observed here made a clockwise round of the tree, touching the feet of the various gods and goddesses with their right hand and then placing it to their forehead and heart, making a water offering here, a flower offering there. Importantly, they include in their circuit similar reverent and direct interactions with the tree itself.

The trunk of this gnarled tree is about six feet in diameter. It is encased within an octagonal container that measures approximately twenty feet across and is capped with a white marble platform about three feet high. On it are the eight small temples; a few are only about six feet in height, whereas the spires on others reach up twenty feet and are now embedded in the tree. They are all painted beige on the outside with turquoise blue interiors. A red flag with a swastika—the Hindu sign of "well-being"—has been placed in the branches of the tree above them. On the southeast corner of the crowded platform is a temple dedicated to Ganesha, the elephant-headed god who blesses human endeavors. Shiva is very prominent at this shrine. A black stone Shiva linga has been installed in the temple on the south side of the tree, with a white marble form of his consort Parvati beside him. The largest of the temples, which houses five Shiva lingas, is on the west side; the goddess Parvati is here too. On the north side of the tree is another temple sheltering another Shiva linga. An orange sindur-smeared form of Hanuman, as "He Who Takes Away All Troubles," stands in a temple on the northeast side. To the east side of the banyan is a place with easy access to the tree itself, where water, incense, sindur power, wheat paste, and flower offerings are made directly. The tree appears to be treated both as the overarching

Figure 6.3 Banyan tree shrine in the center of the Sankata Devi temple courtyard near Scindhia Ghat in Banaras; the small temple in the center of the photograph is dedicated either to the divine couple Lakshmi and Narayana, or to Savitri and Satyavan

temple for this tree shrine, as well as another divine form to be worshiped in its own right. Next to this opening is a temple that houses a male and female pair. Although from an iconographic perspective they looked to me to be the goddess Lakshmi and god Narayana, several people I spoke with told me that they are Savitri and Satyavan. This is possible, for it is common to find beneath a banyan tree images of this pious couple, who are at the center of a famous story about longevity and conquering death.

Long ago there lived an honorable but childless king and queen who made a pilgrimage to a powerful banyan tree and there worshiped the goddess Savitri Devi, a form of Brahma's consort Sarasvati.[40] She was so pleased with them that she blessed them with a beautiful and virtuous daughter, whom they named Savitri. The people of the kingdom regarded her as a heavenly princess. She led a very devout life, and when it came time for her to marry, her father sent her out with the court minister to find a husband of her own, since he himself could not find one worthy of her. When she returned from her travels she told her father that she had found the man she wanted to marry: a virtuous man who speaks only the truth, appropriately named Satyavan ("Truthful"). She described him to her father while he was sitting next to the knowledgeable sage Narada, who happened to be visiting the royal court, as the son of a righteous king, who because he had become blind, lost his kingdom and had to flee into the forest with his wife and son. Satyavan now lived a humble life in a woodland ashram, gathering food and firewood in the forest and looking after his mother and father. After listening to Savitri's account, Narada turned to the king and confirmed that Satyavan was indeed a very worthy young man, but informed the king that there existed a daunting problem: Satyavan was fated to die exactly one year from this day. The king conveyed this heartbreaking information to Savitri and tried to dissuade her from marrying Satyavan. But her mind was made up; regardless of predictions, Satyavan would be her husband. A celebratory wedding soon followed.

After the wedding Savitri and Satyavan lived together happily in the forest ashram. Savitri was ever mindful of Narada's prediction and kept careful track of the days. One morning she realized that the day Satyavan was destined to die was coming in three days. She immediately began a fast to save his life. The ill-fated day arrived on the new moon in the hot summer lunar month of Jyeshtha.[41] Savitri rose early and bathed; she then worshiped the gods and touched the feet of her parents-in-law. When Satyavan took up his hatchet and headed for the forest, she insisted on going with him. Satyavan began his work of gathering fruits and dry wood. Soon he developed a severe headache, and holding onto a branch of the banyan tree under which Savitri rested, he asked his virtuous wife if she would hold his head on her lap while he took a short nap. Savitri sat on the ground beneath the banyan tree, waiting anxiously as she held her husband. Before long, a being as radiant as the sun appeared; he was dark in color, wearing a crown, and dressed in yellow clothing. The god identified himself as Yama, Lord of Death, and said that he had come to take Satyavan away. Yama ensnared Satyavan's soul with his noose, pulled it from his body, and began to drag it away.

Leaving the body of her husband in the care of the banyan tree, Savitri followed Yama on the path leading to the land of the dead. When he noticed her behind him, Yama turned and told her that since she was still alive she could not follow. But Savitri insisted that a wife's place is with her husband, and so persevered along the terrifying road of death. Finally, Yama was so impressed with Savitri's devotion to her husband that he granted her any boon she wished. She requested the restoration of her father-in-law's eyesight and kingdom, many sons for her own father, as well as many sons for herself. Immediately, without thought, Yama granted her requests. Clever Savitri then pointed out to Yama that since she could only have children with her one and only husband, he must give life back to Satyavan. Yama had no choice but to comply. Savitri returned to the banyan tree and thanked it for looking after the body of her husband while she was away. She rejoined her revived husband; soon sight was restored to her father-in-law who regained his lost kingdom, her own father had many healthy sons, and she and Satyavan lived a long and happy life together, also blessed with many sons.

Every year on the new moon day (*amavasya*) of the hot lunar month of Jyeshtha this story is told under a banyan tree in conjunction with a special ritual in which the tree itself is worshiped. This ritual, called the Vata Savitri Vrat, is another of the women's vrats celebrated in northern India.[42] Small pamphlets based on a section of the Skanda Purana and readily available in Banaras tell the story of Savitri and inform women how to perform this vrat.[43] The text counsels a woman choosing to perform this ritual to fast beginning on the thirteenth day of the lunar month of Jyeshtha (May-June) in preparation for the culminating worship of the goddess Savitri on the fifteenth day of the new moon. When the day scheduled for the worship of Savitri arrives, she should proceed to a banyan tree (called the Savitri Sthala, the "Place of Savitri"). There she is to worship an embodied form of Savitri (identified with the goddess Sarasvati), offering her incense, flowers, and various foods, including fruits, coconuts, and cucumbers while reciting this mantra: "Obeisance to you, O goddess, who hold a lute and a book, and display an *Om*. O mother of Devas, grant me exemption from widowhood." She is also to circumambulate the Savitri Sthalaka banyan tree 108 times (or less if desirable), and while sitting under this tree, to listen attentively to the story of Savitri. A woman is promised great benefits in the Skanda Purana from the performance of the Vata Savitri Vrat ritual, including wealth and prosperity, but primarily a blessed marital state. "There shall never be a widow in the family of a woman who performs this vrat, nor a barren woman, nor an unlucky wretched one."

The new moon day of Jyeshtha fell on May 16th in the year 2007, and I was in Banaras for the occasion. The most popular site in Banaras to celebrate the Vata Savitri Vrat is a place known as Dharma Kup, the "Well of Righteousness," a site connected to Yama, who is sometimes called Dharma Raja, Lord of Righteousness. This is an ancient site. In her book on Banaras, Diana Eck describes Dharma Kup as "the 'Well of Dharma,' surrounded by shrines and shaded by tall banyan trees. There is the Shiva temple of Dharmesha, where the Lord of Death, called Yamaraja or Dharmaraja, received his jurisdiction over the fate of the dead, a power he wields everywhere on earth except in Kashi."[44] One enters the Dharma Kup compound by walking under a triangle-shaped archway off a narrow alley just downstream from the famous Dasashvamedha Ghat.

The archway is painted bright yellow and announces with red and blue lettering that this is the location of two important temples: Shri Dharmeshvara Mahadev Mandir and Shri Vata Savitri Mandir. As one walks into the compound from the east, the Dharmeshvara Mahadev temple is immediately on the left. This Shaivite temple is connected with Yama, lord of death and judge of righteousness (Dharma), since Shiva holds great power over Yama. Singh and Rana write of it, "There is the Shiva temple of Dharmesha, where the Lord of Death, called Yamaraja or Dharmaraja, received his jurisdiction over the fate of the dead."[45] One of the priests of this compound told me that Yama sits here meditating near the Dharma Kup well. All of the structures within the Dharma Kup compound are painted pale yellow, and there is an old and mysterious feel to the place. The octagonal-shaped Dharma Kup well is at the center of the compound and is enclosed by an octagonal wall. An iron gate opens into this enclosure, providing access to a series of Shiva shrines that are built into the sides of the wall. To the east side is an old pipal tree whose roots have engulfed two of the Shiva shrines, framing cavelike openings with its twisted limbs. A Hanuman temple has recently been added to the east side of the pipal tree.

Just south of the Dharma Kup well stands a tall banyan tree with a trunk diameter of about four feet. I was told that this is a remnant of a much larger tree that stood here several years ago. Nestled against the west side of the tree is the other important temple of the compound, the Vata Savitri Mandir. This small red temple houses an embodied form of a goddess. The stone form is about a foot high and stands before a green and white tile background with a bright yellow "OM" (a connection to the Savitri mantra cited above) painted on the red wall above it. A sign above the goddess informs us that this is Savitri Devi, the one whose devotion to her husband was so great that she was able to bring him back to life through the worship of a banyan tree (the goddess Savitri and virtuous wife Savitri merge). Regarding this, the Hindi daily *Dainik Jagaran* announced on the day of the worship of the banyan: "According to the Puranas, Savitri brought her husband Satyavan back to life by the power of worshiping the banyan tree [*vata-vriksha ke pujan ke prabhav se*]."[46] For this reason women come here to worship both the embodied form of Savitri in the temple and the banyan tree itself. Sometimes the two identities coalesce, and the tree too is regarded as an embodied form of Savitri.

This site is normally quiet most days of the year, but on the new moon day of Jyeshtha it is crowded with hundreds of women who come here to worship. I reached the Dharma Kup compound just before sunrise on the morning of the Vata Savitri ritual. The weather was unusually cool and pleasant for mid-May on the plains of northern India; the sky was cloudy and a light rain had just ended. Women were already busy in the dim morning light making their offerings to the goddess in the temple, worshiping the banyan tree, and wrapping it with string.

The temple offerings included ornate red cloth, flowers, coconuts, cucumbers and other vegetables, and a variety of fruits. Offerings to the tree took different forms, but always included a water offering. I watched one woman offer water to the roots of the tree from a brass pot. After setting down her pot, she applied dots of sindur powder to the trunk and offered marigold flowers, incense, uncooked white rice, and a clay *aarati* lamp at the base of the banyan. She then tied a red and yellow string to the tree and wrapped it while going around it clockwise nine times. In conclusion she placed a hand on each side of the tree and bowed her head to its trunk. All the women I observed making their offerings directly to the tree afterwards circumambulated it five, seven, or nine times, wrapping it with red and yellow string. By the end of the day it was ornately clad with string (figure 6.4).

Figure 6.4 Worshiper wrapping the Dharma Kup banyan tree; note the tree offerings in the foreground

The worship of the tree went on throughout the day, ending sometime in the mid-afternoon. Hundreds of women came to break their fast here and worship the banyan. The majority were wearing bright red saris; in fact, many were dressed in lavish red wedding saris and wore their auspicious wedding jewelry. I was told that any woman who was married within a year of the last Vata Savitri day comes here in her wedding outfit and worships the banyan for the long life of her husband, but I also noticed older women decked out in wedding garments. While the style of this colorful worship varied, all of the women made offerings at both the temple and the trunk of the tree, and wrapped the tree with colorful string. I observed a group of women offer the tree water, insert sticks of lit incense in the ground beneath it, and then lay out an orange-cloth altar at the base of the tree. They placed flowers, fruits, uncooked white rice, sweets, and balls of cooked whole-wheat flour on the cloth altar. After worshiping the tree in this fashion, they got up and wrapped the tree with string while circumambulating it seven times (figure 6.5). They ended their circuit by touching the tree affectionately and putting their heads to its trunk. They laughed together and seemed in high spirits after finishing their offerings. One of the women then took out a booklet and proceeded to read the story of Savitri to a small group of women as they all sat beneath the tree. Another assembly of women were seated nearby as an elderly woman told the story of Savitri. One woman from this group laid out a green cloth for her altar and offered red bangles, white sugar crystals, and a packet of red bindis to the tree, all items appropriate for a goddess. A woman accompanied by her husband showed me what she had in her puja basket: water from the Ganges, turmeric paste, cooked chickpeas, sweets, puffed bread, balls of cooked whole-wheat flour, marigold flowers, a jasmine garland, and red sindur powder. She also had two tender fig buds from a banyan tree that she intended to eat to break her fast right after she finished her worship. I encountered four women who had taken small pieces of a leaf from the banyan tree, rolled them up and tied them with the red and yellow string, and inserted them into their nose rings. They told me that this was a way of carrying the blessings (*ashirbad*) of the banyan tree home with them. Another woman showed me two leaves that had fallen from the tree that she was taking with her to place on her home altar.

I visited eight banyan trees on the day women concluded the Vata Savitri Vrat. But there was no separate temple for Savitri at any of the other trees I visited, as the tree itself served as both the temple and the divine form being worshiped. I observed a group of three women worship a large banyan tree in Chitaranjan Park. They used matted grass fans as an altar on which they offered turmeric paste, packets of decorative red bindis, uncooked white rice, balls of cooked whole-wheat flour, sugar crystals, and rupee coins. On the ground at the base of the tree they poured water and inserted sticks of lit incense. They could not circumambulate the tree because a Kali temple built beneath it

Figure 6.5 Group of women worshiping the Dharma Kup banyan tree on the occasion of the Vata Savitri Vrat

blocked their path, so they improvised by wrapping the red and yellow string and placing garlands of jasmine and marigold flowers around a large knot that protruded from the trunk. They finished their worship by bowing their heads to the trunk of the tree. A small banyan tree growing in a white marble planter on the other side of the park was so completely wrapped with red and yellow string and covered with marigold garlands that its trunk was no longer visible (figure 6.6). Women attending this tree jostled with one another to give it a drink of water from copper pots. I worked my way along the Sonarpur Road leading from Dasashvamedha to Assi Ghat, visiting banyan tree shrines along the way. I came upon a group of six women worshiping a large banyan tree that grows in front of a police station located on this road. They made their offerings to the tree on several large banyan leaves, and inserted burning sticks of incense in apples and guavas before placing them at the base of the tree.

Figure 6.6 Women worshiping a banyan tree in Chitaranjan Park in Banaras for the Vata Savitri Vrat

They adorned the tree with garlands of marigold flowers, dabbed the tree with bright spots of red sindur power, and wrapped it with red and yellow string by walking around it clockwise. They too ended their worship of the banyan by touching their heads reverently to its trunk.

When I arrived at the banyan tree growing at Assi Ghat, worship was well under way and the tree was clothed with a great deal of red and yellow string. The priest of the Kali temple that is situated beneath this tree was on hand to assist the women in their worship. He supplied leaves from the tree for their offering plates by plucking them from high branches with a long bamboo stick. When he found out why I was there, he sat me down and told me the entire Savitri story. He finished his rendition of the story by declaring: "It was by the power gained from worshiping a banyan tree that Savitri herself was able to bring her husband back to life. Therefore, these women too worship the long-living banyan tree in order to get the blessings of this tree for the long life of their husbands. They also do this for their own happiness and the well-being of their families." On the road to the airport in Banaras, there is a large banyan tree whose aerial roots have been allowed to dig into the ground; it now has dozens of rooted trunks. As I passed by it, I noticed that several of the trunks were wrapped with red and yellow string and decorated with flower garlands. Although I did not see this tree on the morning of the Vata Savitri worship, rings of women clad in red wedding saris simultaneously circling the multiple stems of this banyan must have been a magnificent sight.

An article appeared in the Banaras edition of the *Dainik Jagaran* the day before the worship of the banyan trees explaining the great benefits of the Vata Savitri Vrat. Its author, Bhagavatisharan Mishra, said, "This vrat is performed by auspicious women for the purpose of keeping their marital auspiciousness [*saubhagya*] firm."[47] Most women I spoke with generally agreed with Mishra. They told me that they performed this vrat for *suhag*, a Hindi version of the Sanskrit word *saubhagya*, which means a happily married state, or for the long life (*lambi ayu*) of their husbands. Although women worship banyan trees for a good marriage any day of the year, this particular day is deemed to the most potent for this purpose.[48] I observed a few younger girls worship the banyan tree at Dharma Kup, and their mothers told me that they were doing this for a "future happy marriage." One woman I spoke with reported: "The god of the banyan [*vata-devata*] has much power [*shakti*] to give the blessing [*ashirbad*] of a happy marriage. That is why on this one day of the year I bring my daughter here so that we both can worship this tree together. It is very old and has a lot of power. This is a very good place for this puja." A happy married state for a woman depends upon her husband's long life, and the banyan tree is understood to have the ability to grant this blessing. While many women simply said they worship the banyan tree because this was the tree Savitri worshiped, others further explained that they worship the banyan tree "because it has the power of long life." Mishra puts it this way: "The banyan tree [*vata vriksha*] has a very long life; therefore, the ritual is concluded in the shelter of a banyan tree and the tree is worshiped and wrapped seven times with raw string. The story of Savitri is heard beneath the banyan tree while wearing leaves from the tree. According to the Puranas, the Vata Savitri Vrat gives marital happiness [*saubhagya*] to the women who perform it. Those who listen to the story of Savitri here with devotion will have all their wishes fulfilled, all their sorrows taken away, and they will be filled with happiness."[49] Women growing up in India are encouraged from an early age to practice vrats such as this one to ensure the well-being of themselves and their families. In addition to daily worship, these vrats constitute a major part of women's religious activity. Worship of a banyan tree on this occasion obviously promises much, and women's expectations are high; however, immediate results are not anticipated. One woman remarked, "Only time will tell how successful we have been today."

Who is the banyan tree in the eyes of these particular tree worshipers? As in the case of other sacred trees, there is no exact agreement; different interpretations often seem to be passed down from mother to daughter. One woman told me simply that the divinity of the banyan is *"bargad ka Bhagavan"* (Lord of the banyan). The day before the Vata Savitri worship, a priest of a nearby Shiva temple told me that the banyan is the form of a man (*admi ka rupa*) for women. This confirmed the view of a woman I met worshiping the Dharma Kup banyan tree in January for the long life and good health of her husband. When I asked her about the tree, she said: "It is very sacred [*pavitra*]. It is the husband of Savitri." The mother of one of my friends in Banaras told me that she regards the banyan as Brahma, "the husband of the goddess Savitri."[50] She first offers a sacred thread (*janeu*) to the banyan and then takes it home for her husband to wear. She also offers food to the tree and then takes it home for her husband to eat as special *prasad*, in this way ensuring his long life. The view of the banyan tree as Brahma or Satyavan, however, was not common among the women performing the Vata Savitri Vrata. One woman I spoke with the day of this worship identified the divinity of the tree in general terms as "the god of the banyan [*vata devata*] who protected Savitri and Satyavan and had the power [*shakti*] to help Savitri secure her wish." Most, however, were more specific. A woman worshiping the Dharma Kup banyan, who had just returned from a trip to London to visit her son, told me that the banyan is "Vishnu Bhagavan." I heard this from several others. A man who was standing near the tree watching the worship said, "The banyan is Vishnu in the form of this tree who gives the blessing [*ashirbad*] of the happily married state [*suhag*] to these women, just as he did to Savitri, who resides beneath this tree." Most of the women I talked with who were performing the Vata Savitri Vrat, however, identified the tree as a goddess.

Although a couple of women told me that the banyan at Dharma Kup was simply a banyan goddess (*vata devi*), the great majority identified it specifically as a tree form of the goddess Savitri Devi herself. When I first heard this from a group of three women, I was a bit surprised, and so pressed them, asking, "You mean that the banyan tree itself is Savitri Devi?" "Yes, the tree is Savitri Devi," they all confirmed with bobbing heads. Many of the women worshiping at the Dharma Kup tree on the day of the Vata Savitri Vrat told me the banyan tree was Savitri Devi. This was also true at the other banyan trees I visited that day. "This banyan is Vata Savitri Devi," said a woman at the banyan in front of the police station on the Sonarpur Road. "We worship her in the form of this tree for a long and happy marriage." Later in the day I returned to the Dharma Kup banyan tree with a friend who had grown up in Banaras. When I explained to him that most of the women had told me that the tree itself is Savitri, he was incredulous, informing me that he had always heard that the banyan was a male divinity. He himself asked several more women gathered here about the identity of the divinity of the banyan, and they too repeated that it is Savitri Devi. Still perplexed, my friend went home and spoke about this with his mother, who had performed the Vata Savitri Vrat for decades. She said that for her the banyan is a male divinity, but that Savitri, Satyavan, and Yama are all invoked in the tree for the purpose of this ritual, so in the context of the ritual the tree may indeed be seen as Savitri. There seem to be two major views operative here. One, that the tree itself is Savitri, and the other, that the tree is a male divinity—often identified as either Vishnu or Shiva—under which Savitri resides. When I spoke with the priest of the Kali temple beneath the banyan tree at Assi about the fact that most of the women I met who had conducted the Vata Savitri Vrat identified the banyan as Savitri Devi, he said, "The banyan is Rudra [another name of Shiva] and it is the residence [*nivas*] of Savitri. But, no matter. God is one and all gods and goddesses reside in the banyan tree, so if they choose to see it that way it can be Savitri Devi too." Here is concrete expression of that central Hindu concept that whereas ultimate divinity is one, she or he can be conceived of in a great variety of ways that depend on the disposition of the individual worshiper who is embedded in a particular social network. In either view, this sacred tree is understood to have the power to conquer death and grant the blessing of a long and healthy life. Here is clear testament to the role trees play in human efforts to influence or control death, or as is illustrated in the Savitri story, even trick the god of death to get a long life.

The Skanda Purana and other early Sanskrit texts that prescribe the Vata Savitri Vrat say very little about worship of the banyan tree. Savitri's story in the Matsya Purana does not even identify the tree as a banyan. Puranic accounts say Savitri was able to bring Satyavan back to life and insure a blessed life for her family by the power of her own wifely virtue and devotion to her husband. But the living ritual story of Savitri is different from the Sanskritic textual stories. Scholars, priests, and tree worshipers in Banaras today report it was the power of Savitri's worship of the banyan tree itself (*vata-vriksha ke pujan ke prabhav se*) that restored her husband to life. The banyan tree—long known for its endless life and control over death—is now the central feature of the Vata Savitri Vrat. It is difficult to determine how this change came about, but perhaps it attests to ascending notions of the concrete presence of transformative power in the form of a banyan tree as compared with the more intangible influence resulting from women's virtue. The banyan tree is not only regarded as a powerful being who has the ability to bless the worshipper and her family members with long and happy lives, but is ritually available for worshipful influence.

The Vata Savitri Vrat also illustrates the way in which trees mediate ideal gender and family roles in northern Indian culture, in some social contexts leading women to become quite intimate with trees. A man I became acquainted with during my stay in Banaras told me about an experience he had with his own mother regarding the Vata Savitri Vrat. That morning she did what she had done every year on this day for the last several decades; she worshiped a banyan tree for the health and long life of her husband and three adult sons. For the last twelve years she has kept a banyan tree in a large pot in her backyard and performs the Vata Savitri worship every year to this small tree. Two other women joined her in the worship of the banyan, and her elderly husband and youngest son, now in his fifties, were present. Her son reported to me that when she had finished worshipping the tree and had circumambulating it eight times, wrapping it with red string, she looked at it somberly for a while. She then glanced around at her family members and burst into tears saying: "I don't take very good care of this tree. Sometimes I even forget to water him. (Turning to the tree:) I'm so sorry. (Now looking appreciatively at her husband and son:) But even though I neglect him look how he continues to bless my life. (Back to the tree:) Thank you!" What, we might ask, is disclosed by such intimate worship and tender relationships with a tree?

7

Arboreal Reflections

> What I want to emphasize here is the fact that trees
> have always been treated as living human beings.
> —K. D. Upadhyaya, "Indian Botanical Folklore"

> We would never cut this tree; it is a goddess.
> If we honor her she treats us well.
> By harming her we would bring harm on ourselves.
> —tree worshiper in Banaras

> What is the epistemological status of a world within which
> speaking to trees would appear as an appropriate behavior?
> —Erazim Kohak, "Speaking to Trees"

One of the joys and challenges of living in another culture for an extended period of time is finding oneself among others who view the world quite differently. It is possible in this situation to catch a glimpse of how the world might look beyond the depiction fashioned by one's own culture. Time with the millions of people in India who assume trees to be of a different nature than do the great majority of those in American culture gave me many opportunities to reflect on trees in a new way. What did I learn while sitting in the shade of the sacred trees of India? What is the expression of reality that bursts forth from the tips of the long and numerous branches of tree worship in India? What possibilities exist within a worldview in which trees are conceived of and honored as special sentient beings with whom one can establish mutually beneficial relationships? Before addressing these questions, it might be useful to review briefly a few of the common features that are encountered in the religious attitudes and activities of Indian tree worship.

Sacred trees in India are known to have important practical values. Pipal, neem, and banyan trees all provide abundant shade and shelter in an environment that can produce trying weather, ranging from the intense sunshine and heat of the summer months to the torrential rains of the monsoon season. For this reason, the spaces under the canopies of these trees are recognized as inviting and protective refuges, and as such have for a long time been commonly regarded in Indian folklore and literature as suitable sanctuaries for either conducting routine business or engaging in religious activities; the ever-expansive banyan tree in particular is capable of providing sufficient cover for a small village. Belonging to the family of fig trees, both pipal and banyan trees yield an edible and useful fruit; and the neem tree is so beneficial for dealing with health issues that it is often known as the "village pharmacy." In fact, all sacred trees in India are prized for their medicinal potency and have long been used to prevent and treat a variety of diseases in traditional Ayurvedic medicine. But as we have seen sacred trees are valued for far more than their practical utility.

Although tree worshipers in India conceive of sacred trees in numerous ways, they tend to agree that the tree is either the abode (*nivas*) of a god or goddess, or—more commonly—an embodied form (*rupa*) of a god or goddess, a view well supported by Puranic scriptures. The pipal tree is most typically considered to be an embodied form of Vishnu, but also, for example, the residence of Lakshmi or Shani. The neem tree is characteristically regarded as some natural form (*svarupa*) of the great goddess Durga, usually Shitala, but is also believed to be a favorite shelter for the seven divine sisters. The banyan is normally viewed as Shiva, but many of the women performing the Vata Savitri Vrat see it as the goddess Savitri; it is also commonly regarded as a favored dwelling place for all gods and goddesses. This is also true for other sacred trees: the amala is conceived of as a sylvan form of Mother Earth; the bel tree is associated with Shiva but is sometimes considered to be a residence for the goddess Lakshmi; and the kadamba tree is regarded as an embodied form of Krishna by women performing Kartik rituals at Assi Ghat in Banaras.

Trees are, therefore, regularly thought to be embodied forms of divinities who have a strong physical and relevant presence in the world. The most common response to an awareness of the divinity in or as a tree is worship. Similar acts of worship may have different intentions. Sometimes gifts are offered to a tree out of a motiveless sense of love and appreciation, simply honoring the tree while not seeking anything specific in return. One woman, for example, told me that she worships trees "because trees give us so much. Our lives would not be possible without them. We do this *puja* just to honor God as this tree." In this case, worship is an expression of gratitude; it is a gesture of appreciation for that upon which life depends. Perhaps more generally, however, trees are worshiped to obtain certain results by establishing a positive relationship with them. Ritual gift giving is frequently a process of mutual exchange: something is given with the hope of a reciprocal return. Another tree worshiper informed me: "I make offerings to trees so that my life and family might be blessed in return with good health and happiness." The man I met who was worshipping a tree to secure a good job further underscores this point. Whatever the motive, most

Hindus acknowledge the source of transformative power to be some aspect of God (Bhagavan, Ishvara, or Devi), and in this context God is encountered in the concrete and particular form of a tree that is the focus of a variety of worshipful acts.

Water offerings are a standard feature—one might even say the essential element—of tree worship in India. As a favored offering to an honored guest, water is recognized as a vital ingredient of all life. This is particularly true for trees; as huge storehouses of water, trees require plenty of it. Many people told me that water is a tree's greatest need and preferred gift. Water is given to a tree to nurture, honor, and care for it; it is an expression of affection and appreciation for the tree. I once talked with a temple priest in Banaras who was watering a pipal tree with a garden hose, a seemingly mundane task. I asked him what he was doing. "I am doing *jal-seva* [service or worship by offering water]," he replied. "I do this because this tree gives me shade. This makes me happy, so I honor [*manta*] this tree by giving it water." Water may also be offered to a tree as a present with some kind of expectation attached to it. Tree worshipers in India offer water and other gifts—such as flowers, sweets, incense, and fruits—to sacred trees as a way of showing gratitude to a tree, but they also do so in the pursuit of the "good life" that includes domestic happiness, success in business, excellent health, long life, and material abundance. Moreover, a tree is often approached with offerings in quest of spiritual accomplishments; sacred trees are known to be good locations for receiving rewards of supreme value, such as enlightenment or admission into a heavenly abode. Verbal prayers typically accompany all of these requests. Tree worshipers in India clearly assume that they are in the presence of a discerning being who can hear their praises and petitions, be moved by their offerings, and is capable of having a significant impact on their lives.

Wrapping sacred trees with cotton string—sometime white, but usually multicolored red and yellow—is another common feature of tree worship in India. Although any tree might be wrapped by anyone any day of the year, this is done especially by groups of women on specific festival days. Pipal trees are wrapped for a happy marriage on a Somvati Amavasya, the day a new moon falls on a Monday.[1] Considered to be significant forms of the Earth Goddess, amala trees are wrapped on Akshaya Navmi in the auspicious month of Kartik.[2] A kadamba tree is wrapped and celebrated as the "Krishna tree" by women at Assi Ghat in Banaras on Margashirsha Panchami, the fifth day after the end of Kartik.[3] And banyan trees are wrapped for the long life of the husband on the new moon of the hot summer month of Jyeshtha.[4] Wrapping a tree is a grand finale that intentionally produces a beautiful effect. Dressing and ornamenting a tree with colorful string—considered to be a form of suitable clothing—is understood to be a way of honoring it. It is also a way of engaging in mutual protection.[5] As in the case of the familial tradition of Raksha Bandhan, in which a woman ties a string around her brother's wrist to bless and protect him, as well as seek his blessings and protection, so too worshipers wrap tree beings both to care for them and to seek their blessings and protection. Here is another physical expression of the dynamic reciprocal relationships people have with trees in India.

Tree worshipers in northern India honor trees in additional ways. They remove their shoes in the proximity of sacred trees. They build protective structures around them and place other deities beneath them. They circumambulate them, keeping the right side of their bodies toward the tree—a well-established means of showing honor to a respected being in Indian culture. They smear a special sindur paste on their trunks and wave honorific aarati lamps before them, two more ways of expressing reverence for venerable beings. They chant Sanskrit mantras and sing songs of praise to trees. These are all ways of pleasing and revering an important person. Tree worshipers also interact with sacred trees tactilely, making physical contact with them in intimate ways. They hug them, massage them, touch their heads to them, and on occasion, even kiss them. Although I observed it often, I never failed to be moved by the sight of a person embracing a tree. A couple of days after Diwali of 2008, for example, I visited a magnificent neem tree shrine that is part of the Kalu Bir Baba Mandir in Banaras. I entered the temple slowly to let my eyes become accustomed to the dim light, and as I did I encountered a very touching scene. A woman was bent over with her head pressed against the base of the neem tree, clasping both sides of it with her hands. She was crying and repeatedly calling upon "Ma" to come to her assistance. I felt that I was witnessing a profound emotional exchange. She clearly regarded this tree to be an influential presence whom she could communicate with intimately.

What are the assumptions and implications embedded in such intimate acts? First and foremost, trees are considered to be sentient beings; they are animate life forms endowed with feelings and consciousness. We read in the *Laws of Manu*, a text that dates back some two thousand years: "All trees and plants are full of consciousness within themselves and are endowed with the feeling of pleasure and pain."[6] It is common to find people in India today who treat trees as special sentient beings. Jagannath Poddar, the director of Friends of Vrindaban, for example, explained to me that his organization has long been involved in the religious activity of protecting and planting trees in the region of Braj to nurture the sacred groves and love bowers of that area. He recalled an incident that he thought well illustrated a widely shared view of trees in Braj: "I remember once I was trying to tie a banner in a tree at Tatiasthan, I was not allowed to do so as they said the tree would get hurt. The trees of Braj-Vrindavan are considered to be saints and they are meditating. This is our feeling for the trees."[7] Current acts of tree worship, however, are perhaps the strongest ethnographic confirmation that beliefs about the sentience of trees that go back thousands of years are still very much alive and functional in India.

Moreover, a number of tree worshipers I spoke with claimed that it is possible to communicate with trees. The many prayers addressed to trees certainly depend upon the assumption that trees can hear and respond to human petitions, but the further assertion is made that sensitive humans can also hear trees. I met a swami in the Himalayas who reported: "Trees are very sensitive beings who can tell which persons mean them harm and which persons are friendly towards them. The trees respond and act differently depending on the nature of the person interacting with them. Sensitive people can sense the being of the tree rather easily. They can also communicate with trees. Sensitive people can hear trees speak in a way." Ranchor Prime tells of the experience with a tree that led Balbir Mathura, founder of the organization Trees for Life that has planted thousands of trees in India, to do the work he does:

> Influenced by this religious sensitivity to trees, and by his inner affinity, Balbir in his childhood had actually experienced a close relationship with a tree. It was the lemon tree that grew in his garden. Each day he would get a fresh lemon from this tree for his tea. He used to say to this tree, "You have provided me with so much nourishment and love, one day when I am rich I will plant thousands of lemon trees." One day he felt as though the tree spoke to him. He never forgot that tree. "All during those years in America this lemon tree friend kept coming back to remind me of my promise, 'When are you going to do it?'"[8]

In her book *Plant Lives: Borderline Beings in Indian Traditions*, Ellison Findly records an interview in which one of the workers for Trees for Life recounts his own experience with the sentience of trees and subsequent communication with them: "Having been brought up in a rural environment during younger days I was told by my grandparents that plants and trees could respond to us and they had feelings too. And so, I used to spend some time with my grandparents in the village each day and learn how to speak to trees. I started to talk to trees and plants! Every time I used to visit the trees and plants in the farm, I used to feel that they were welcoming my presence. I used to ask them how their day went and tell them what I did the whole day."[9] I spoke with several tree worshipers who reported that they had regular communications with the tree they were worshiping. Trees, in short, are influential persons not radically separate from the human world; on the contrary, trees and humans share enough characteristics in common to make significant interaction and relationship possible.[10] The marriage of trees and humans is even recognized and conducted in India.

Beyond being sentient, the activities described above reveal that sacred trees are assumed to be powerful beings who have the capability to influence human lives in tremendously potent ways. They can also be exemplarily noble. As we saw in the context of the Buddhist Jataka stories, trees are not only sentient but also might be quite gracious: they may be bodhisattvas preaching compassionate nonviolence to all beings and sometimes even sacrifice their own life for the sake of others. Even more important, trees have an unusually beneficial presence; they can be embodied forms of divinities who cure humans of many types of illness and bless their lives with countless modes of abundance. We thus come again to a deliberation on the cultural construction of nature, and a consideration of animism, personhood, and anthropomorphism introduced in the first chapter, but now as viewed from the specific vantage point of the sacred trees of India rather than through the progressive agenda of late nineteenth and early twentieth-century anthropologists.

Why are trees viewed the way they are in much of Indian society? In short, the answer might simply be "because they are," and we return to that "common sense" realm of the socially constructed nature of nature. I asked an acquaintance in Banaras whose family is quite involved in tree worship why they worship sacred trees. "We do this because our ancestors did it," he told me. Although he used different words, he was saying something similar to what I heard from others when I asked them this same question. A common response frequently involved the Hindi word *manna*. The word *manna* is best understood to mean simultaneously "to perceive, to believe, to accept, to regard, to honor, and to worship." When people answered me, for example, with "*Ham aisa mante hai*," they were saying, "We see or regard the matter like this, and honor and worship in this way." This simple sentence conveys much. In effect, the people I questioned were stating: this is the way we (family members and peers who surround us) perceive the world and act in it. Reality in general is present for most human beings in an unexamined manner; most are unaware of the historical processes that have shaped their worldview, or even that their worldview is shaped by particular historical processes at all. A parallel response to the question "Why don't you worship trees?" put to the average American would most likely be: "Because we don't. Because my parents didn't. Because the people I spend my time with don't."

While in theory human beings are open to a wide range of possible views of reality, we do not usually find people living in such an open and undetermined state, for their cultural view of reality is assumed in the process of socialization. The definition and application of the concept of animism is as much a cultural construct as is the cultural phenomena identified by this term. People raised within the dominant Christian society of the contemporary United States have been taught since birth to regard trees as inanimate things;[11] whereas, people within the dominant Hindu society of contemporary India have been taught since birth to regard trees as animate beings. Those who say *ham aisa mante hai*, reveal a view of the world that determines the perception of, experience with, and behavior toward say a tree. All cultural lenses are not the same, however; they can lead to very different experiences of the world. Change the lens and a completely new world opens up. This too seems to be acknowledged in the common statement *mano to dev, nahi to patthar* ("If you regard it as such it is a god, otherwise it is just a stone."). That is, if you see or honor it as such, then a natural form like a stone or a tree is a divinity, otherwise it is something quite "ordinary" (another cultural construction). Seen through the cultural lens I encountered in northern India, a tree is present as a sentient being with whom one can develop a mutually beneficial relationship.

The impression one gets from reading much of the early scholarly literature on tree worship is that it is a remnant of "primitive religion" performed only by "primitive peoples." The conclusion I drew from my conversations with hundreds of people residing in northern India about tree worship is that a wide variety of the majority of people in India worship trees at least occasionally—some through specific acts, others by general veneration—and many do so daily. Tree worship is readily accepted as a meaningful feature of the religious landscape of India. It would be extremely difficult to argue that India is a primitive country. India today is very much plugged into the globalized world, even leading the world in many areas of information technologies, computer programming, engineering, medical training, and high-tech commercial outsourcing.[12] As mentioned in chapter 3, I saw evidence of pipal tree worship right in the most westernized commercial area of Khan Market in the nation's capital of New Delhi, and observed tree worship in the leading technological centers of Bombay and Bangalore. In my travels around India, I have encountered every kind of human person worshiping sacred trees: men and women, rich and poor, young and old, educated and uneducated, computer programmers and housewives, Hindus and Buddhists (even an occasional Muslim and Christian), and a multitude of castes and occupations. Among the tree worshipers I interviewed were several professors who teach at Banaras Hindu University in such subjects as chemistry, business, medicine, and biology, including a professor who received a Ph.D. in physics from an American university. All of them were quite open about the fact that they worshiped trees and were not hesitant to articulate why they did so. Although tree worship does seem to be on the rise in North America and Europe, it is still for the most part performed privately and on the periphery of society. In contrast, India tree worship is conducted openly in a variety of public spaces. Rather than dismissing tree worship as a childish form of human activity, it is perhaps best to view it as another potential mode for human experience and reflect on what is possible within this cultural viewpoint that is not possible without it.

Tree worship, I would argue, is a matter of cultural "difference," not an encounter with "the primitive mind." Instead of employing the culturally loaded concept of progress to evaluate other cultures, it would be better to acknowledge difference without hierarchy and explore the possibilities within different cultural worldviews with regard to nature, ever mindful of biological feedback loops. If we do not want to slip back into the prejudiced colonial agenda of previous scholarship and its concomitant interpretation of "animism," then we must be open to an understanding that the Indian view of trees encountered among tree worshipers is just as valid as the dominant American view—or perhaps going even further, that this worldview has something to offer us. What all worshipers of sacred trees in India share is the notion that a tree is not only a conscious, animate being but also a powerful person with whom one can establish a mutually beneficial relationship. Indian tree worship, then, invites us to reconsider that aspect of animism that not only regards human life as sentient and imbued with spirit, but acknowledges that humans share these characteristics with nonhuman beings.

The primary focus of this study has been the conception of trees in the context of the tree shrines of northern India. Cross-cultural studies make it clear that views of nature are far from universal; everything gets filtered through a particular interpretive cultural lens, and different lenses result in different perceptions of and experiences in the world. As we saw in the first chapter, such concepts as animism and anthropomorphism are implicated in a modern Western cultural construction of nature that sets a firm boundary between the human and nonhuman. The cultural construction of nature in Indian society has resulted in much greater continuity between the human and nonhuman, which are both regarded as parts of the same whole. As a Western academic concept, the presence of animism—the belief that spirit is present in nonhuman life forms—has been used to mark a society as "primitive" and to distance it from "civilized" societies, which maintain the radical uniqueness of human beings while vigilantly defending the boundary between the human and nonhuman. In exemplary fashion, Tylor contended that animism is the very basis of a "primitive religion" that characterizes the confused mental state of the very lowest of human development. Since tree worship was a prime example of primitive animistic religion for Tylor, many agreeing with him regarded the interaction with and worship of a tree as a sign of childishness or even madness. The accusation of madness, however, is reversed in India; to ask a person worshiping a tree if that tree is sentient makes the questioner susceptible to suspicions of idiocy.

From the perspective operative at the tree shrines of northern India, the inquiry this book began with—"Who is a tree?"—makes complete sense. I asked many people on numerous occasions this question (most simply in Hindi: "*Ye vriksh kaun hai?*") and received a variety of answers without any hesitation or indication that it was an odd question. Whereas the human-nonhuman divide has characterized much modern Western thought, which insists that personhood applies only to human beings, here we encounter an application of the concept of personhood that includes more than human beings, extending even to trees. Many tree worshipers informed me, "Trees are persons just like you and me."

However it may be conceived, a sacred tree in India is commonly regarded as an animate being with sentience not radically unlike other animate beings, including humans. This is true for many people from all walks of life in India today, even in the major urban centers. Unless we wish somehow to label the new global information technology centers such as Bangalore, Bombay, and Delhi—all places I observed professionals worshipping trees—as "primitive," we need to challenge any representation of animism as indicative of a primitive understanding of the world. As discussed in chapter 1, many developments in contemporary biology have brought into question the sharp boundary between human and other life forms, while recognizing characteristics shared by different species. Although this division was maintained as the very mark of "civilized" thought for many early "modern" anthropologists, perhaps animistic thinking in part is simply a way of recognizing the groundless nature of such boundaries and acknowledging the significant connections between different life forms. Some contemporary anthropologists, including Philippe Descola and colleagues, maintain that the nature-human dichotomy often does not fit the ethnographic case.[13] This is clearly true in the instance of the "people trees" of India. Tree worshipers in India assume that trees can in some fashion communicate with, feel the touch of, and respond to human beings who approach them with offerings, petitions, and affectionate care. Here the tree-human divide is not considered immensely wide or unbridgeable, and the practice of appending facemasks to trees serves to further erode any perceived distance that remains. Such assumptions and acts have been labeled "anthropomorphic" by those who resist acknowledging that nonhuman beings share anything significant with humans.

Anthropomorphism too has typically been used to identify and pigeonhole certain forms of human activity as confused, childish, or primitive. We saw in chapter 1 that many early scholars of religion viewed anthropomorphic activity as the result of mistaken perception. But in the case of Indian tree worship, might we glimpse another possible way of regarding anthropomorphic activity? The ornamentation and placement of faces on neem trees in Banaras is a clear case of anthropomorphic activity, but one that is quite deliberate and performed with clear purpose. Neem tree worshipers know that a tree is a tree, but report that they affix a humanlike face to it to enhance their *relationship* with the tree as a form of the goddess. Many testified, "We do this to more easily *connect* with Nima Mai [the goddess of the neem tree]." This inclination seems to find support in modern psychological brain research that concludes the human brain is hard-wired to recognize and connect with human faces, particularly those with eyes wide open. This is the type of face that is attached to neem trees and interacted with through the ritual gaze of *darshan*.

Tree worshipers tell us that the face helps them better to recognize the goddess of the neem tree and connect with her. One woman explained to me, "When I look into the face of the goddess on the tree I feel a strong connection [*sambandha*] with this tree." Rather than the result of primitive and confused thinking (or even an unconscious perceptual strategy as Guthrie argues), this anthropomorphic practice may be seen as a deliberate and effective strategy to connect with and facilitate a vigorous relationship with a tree. Recognition of this opens up an understanding of anthropomorphic strategies as ways of connecting with the larger than human world. In contrast to Guthrie's contention that religion as anthropomorphism is a cognitive strategy for coping with an ultimately unknowable world, this data supports Robert Orsi's notion that religion is "a network of *relationships*" between human and sacred beings, and that it "offers its practitioners opportunities *to form deep ties*" with divine beings.[14] In this case, the opportunities for deep ties are enhanced by placing a humanlike facemask on a tree. A relationship is possible with trees without facemasks, but those who attach them to trees report that the faces augment the relationship, thereby making the connection more powerful. In sum, rather than demeaning this as a kind of primitive mistake, such anthropomorphic action is best viewed as an intentional strategy to nurture a relational connection with a nonhuman species.

One of the major ideas to emerge from my ethnographic research on tree worship in India is the concept of mutually beneficial relationships. By offering water to a tree, for example, a tree worshiper is doing something favorable for that tree. In return, the tree gives common things such as shade, shelter, clean air, and fruit, and also special things such as good health, domestic happiness, long life, and spiritual enhancement. Almost all of the tree worshipers I spoke with made reference to this mutual relationship. A woman who worships trees in Banaras said simply: "If we honor them, they take care of us." A man in Rishikesh explained: "If you respect me, I will treat you well. If you don't, I won't. It is the same with a tree." A neem tree worshiper told me, "If you treat her well, she will treat you well." Many people informed me that they honor trees because of the wonderful services and blessings that trees provide all living beings. For some the mutually beneficial relationship with a tree can take the loving form of a friendship. A man I met in Banaras who narrated a life-long relationship with a particular pipal tree, testifying that over the years he had developed a deep friendship with this tree, taking it frequent gifts of water and hugging it with affection. When he is in a depressed mood, he goes to this tree and reports that his spirits are lifted while embracing and being embraced by the tree. "I get great comfort from this dear friend of mine," he reported. "I have been loving this pipal tree for a long time; I do what I can for him, and he blesses my life in so many ways." The mutually beneficial relationship can also take a protective form. This harkens back to early texts, such as the *Manu Dharma Shastra* which states, "A tree protects as it is protected [*vrikso raksati raksatah*]."[15] As noted particularly in chapter 4, some people establish close bonds with trees by caring for them and giving them supportive gifts with the expectation that the tree divinity will defend them from threatening forces. Some tree worshipers approach pipal trees with offerings on Saturday, for example, with the understanding that this potent embodied form of the mighty Vasudeva will shield them from the negative influences of Shani, the planetary god Saturn. Whether the relationship is motivated by love or fear, the idea held in common by all tree worshipers is that the positive treatment of trees benefits both parties. Malla underscores this point, "The idea was that if properly cultivated and nourished, a tree has the capacity to fulfill all the desires of mankind."[16]

There is something wonderfully circular about the connection between physical acts of worship and loving relationships with trees. By caring for, making offerings to, and interacting with trees in intimate ways, many tree worshipers explain that they come to see trees in a new way; through these physical acts they better perceive the special nature or divinity of a tree. Once this begins to occur they become more profoundly attached to the tree, feel greater emotional affection for the tree, and concomitantly more committed to honoring the tree in caring ways. The physical acts of love generate increased love and the increased love further motivates more loving acts, and on and on this loving dynamic goes in an ever-expanding fashion. "The key to all mutually beneficial relationships," a Hindu priest I spoke with about this told me, "is love." In the end it comes down to what kind of relationship we humans chose to have with nonhuman beings; the world one perceives is the world one inhabits. And the world may turn out to be more "peopled" than we ever imagined.

Attention to three terms that arise in the context of tree worship in India is very useful for understanding the worshipful interaction with embodied forms of divinity. The three terms are *svarupa*, *seva*, and *sambandha*. The *svarupa* is a specific form of divinity to which one is particularly drawn. In the context of tree worship, the *svarupa* is a particular tree that one regards as an appealing manifest form of a god or goddess and visits on a regular basis for the purpose of worshipful expression. This worship takes the form of *seva*, ritual acts of "loving service" to the tree in the form of water offerings, and so forth. This loving interaction with the tree results in a connected relationship, or *sambandha*. The goal of much tree worship is to establish an intimate relational bond with a certain tree for a variety of reasons, ranging from the acquisition of some specified benefit to a significant appreciative connection with the very source of life. Some tree worshipers express the aim of achieving through *seva* to a particular individual tree the perception of and connection with divinity everywhere. This grander goal introduces an additional possibility and a fourth term, *sarvatma-bhava*: the realization of the divinity of everything. (Often expressed as "Seeing God as everything and everything as God.")

Although trees are regarded as powerful beings, they are also paradoxically vulnerable. It is obvious to anyone living in the increasingly deforested world of today that trees are extremely susceptible to the logger's axe, chainsaw, and bulldozer. Some people I encountered in my research on sacred trees in northern India told me that one of the reasons certain species of trees became sacred is that since they were known to be exceptionally valuable for the welfare of human and other beings, the great sages declared them sacred and established their worship as a way of protecting them. This was commonly cited as an example of environmental consciousness within Hinduism. One woman told me beneath the pipal tree she was worshiping that "the sages [*rishis*] marked these trees as sacred [*pavitra*] to protect them for the benefit of the environment." A man in Dalhousie insisted: "Trees like the pipal used to provide good shade. For this reason the ancient sages marked them as worthy of worship so people would not cut them down. Now people just see them as religious. As a god, or something like that." Many Indian scholars today agree with this increasingly popular environmental explanation, suggesting that this may be the foremost reason trees are worshiped. The botanist Gupta, for example, writes: "The worship of trees in India is understandable as the trees not only provided shade in the hot scorching summers, food, medicine and fuel but the forests meant rain which was essential for a purely agricultural economy. The trees being beneficial to humanity, to protect them became a religion and were converted into the abode of tree spirits or *vanadevatas*."[17] The art historian Malla concurs, "In order to save these trees from being cut by the wood hunters, these trees were associated with certain religious beliefs."[18] Malla moves beyond this assertion, however, to promote an ecological explanation now quite fashionable among certain intellectuals who consider tree worship in India today.

> The main idea of our ancestors was to maintain the ecological balance in the environment. They appear to have been seriously concerned about this natural problem and its consequences.... Our ancient Indians were not only concerned about the medicinal qualities of trees but were equally aware about the atmospheric changes, pollution and ecological balances. They, therefore, tried their best to save trees, particularly those which were held useful for the survival of humanity. Just to save these trees from various damaging agencies, trees were identified with gods and goddesses. Thus by showing different kinds of gains, merits, etc., our ancestors encouraged people to protect the trees, to organize pleasure gardens and to save the forests. On the other hand, by prescribing various kinds of punishments, which include a life in hell, attempts were made to protect the trees and forests.[19]

These statements promote an intriguing expression of eco-piety. Although tree worship certainly contributes to the protection of trees and the prohibition of cutting them, this argument strikes me as problematic. It is a bit too Machiavellian in suggesting that a few elites decided the religious consciousness of the majority toward trees, it is dependent on a modern view of ecology not present in ancient texts, and it regards religious sentiment as an epiphenomenon of environmental concerns. This explanation has it that first appeared an eco-consciousness that was over time transformed into the religion of the masses. Perhaps a bit uncomfortable with tree worship on the world stage, certain intellectuals are happy to latch on to an explanation that privileges environmental consciousness, an idea with increasing global purchase. Their position, however, seems to be contradicted by a historical record that indicates trees have been worshiped as forms of divinity for a very long time in India. In fact, evidence of tree worship is found throughout history worldwide, long before concerns over large-scale deforestation or atmospheric alteration and pollution arose. It seems more likely that the relationship is the reverse of Malla's position: the view of a tree as a divine "person" has been in place for centuries and has in all probability contributed—whether deliberate or not—toward protecting trees that are considered sacred, whether regarded as the abode or body of a god or goddess.

Poul Pedersen reminds us: "No Buddhist, Hindu, or Islamic scripture contains concepts like 'environmental crisis,' 'ecosystems,' or 'sustainable development,' or concepts corresponding to them. To insist that they do is to deny the immense cultural distance that separates traditional religious concepts of the environment from modern ecological knowledge."[20] More recently Emma Tomalin has argued for a distinction between what she calls bio-divinity and environmental concerns. Bio-divinity refers to the notion that nature is infused with divinity. This is an idea that has been around in India for a long time; the environmental crisis, however, is relatively new, as are the concerns related to it. Tomalin insists, therefore, that "there is an immense difference between the priorities and concerns of the modern environmentalist and the world-views of much earlier Hindu sages, poets, and philosophers."[21] Regarding sacred groves in India, Tomalin argues that "any protection of biodiversity was coincidental rather than intentional and that sacred groves were protected out of respect for the deity rather than because of an innate belief in the intrinsic value of nature."[22] Acknowledging that Hinduism is not intrinsically "eco-friendly," however, does not mean that aspects of Hinduism cannot be interpreted to support contemporary environmental thinking. As Tomalin recognizes, "Religious traditions constantly re-invent themselves precisely through making claims about the past in order to accommodate new ideas."[23] Sacred views of trees in India might indeed now be very useful as a resource to promote the protection and care of trees and forests, but we need to recognize that ecological concerns were not historically primary in Indian tree worship.

There are genuine religious beliefs associated with sacred trees that do contribute to their protection and the prohibition against cutting them. Some have even argued that the idea of divinity in trees and religious sanctions against destruction of them is perhaps "the most successful method of conserving and preserving them."[24] In chapter 3, we saw that the pipal tree is regarded as either the abode of Vishnu or more frequently as an embodied form of Vishnu. Because of the tremendous respect Hindus have for the supreme God Vishnu, the pipal tree is not cut. In the words of one pipal tree worshiper: "I love this tree. He gives us so much. For this we are thankful. Why would we ever want to harm him?" Here we observe the presence of a positive ethic motivated by affection and appreciation. In chapter 4, however, we encountered a more repelling ethic motivated by fear. Stories about very bad things happening to people who cut or abuse a sacred tree abound in northern India. By harming a sacred tree, one risks provoking the wrath of a very powerful divinity who can cause great misfortune for the perpetrator of the assault. "If we would have cut down this pipal tree during the construction of the hotel, then our business would have been ruined," a hotel managed informed me. A man who had just worshiped a neem tree in Banaras told me: "All neem trees are sacred [*pavitra*]. People should never cut them because they give us many things. Ma blesses us in this form with good life [*accha jivan*]. If we cut them, Ma will punish us and harmful pollution [*pradushan*] will be caused." Abbot puts it this way: "Cutting a tree is a form of *himsa* [violence] and all *himsa* destroys *barkat* [life blessings].... trees are preserved from destruction by a reverence in many cases based on the fear of consequences."[25] Regardless of our understanding of the causes, there has indeed been a prohibition operative for a long time in India against cutting trees deemed sacred. There does seem to be some kind of ethic operating in the case of sacred trees, but it is most likely an implicit "environmental ethic," rather than an explicit one. Whether one calls this an environmental ethic or not, it must surely be acknowledged that trees which are considered sacred fare far better in the hands of humans than trees without this characterization.

But what about the rest of the trees? How valuable is an ethic that singles out particular species and ignores others in its ethical concerns? Although sacred trees enjoy certain protections, other trees have been and continue to be destroyed in India. Deforestation is as rampant in India as it is elsewhere. Despite this, I want to highlight tree worship as a resource within Hinduism that opens up the possibility of a more universal ethic. As we are pressed more and more to consider our relationship with the nonhuman world, this is a resource that is already in place and accessible to the vast number of humans living within Hindu religious culture. Moreover, there are people inhabiting this culture who even now express this universal ethic in word and deed. The religious environmentalist and Chipko spokesman Sunderlal Bahuguna, for example, is well-know for teaching that a central idea of India's ancient forest culture is the understanding of the entirety of nature—including all trees—as sacred and therefore worthy of worship and protective respect.[26] But a more universal ethic with regard specifically to trees was also suggested by several of the ordinary tree worshipers with whom I spoke. A man who worships a neem tree behind his sweet shop said to me one day: "I worship this particular neem tree as the goddess, but all neem trees are the goddess. In fact, all trees are the goddess." A woman I spoke with beneath the large pipal tree at Assi Ghat remarked, "For me not only this tree is sacred [*pavitra*], but all trees are sacred." Such attitudes show the possibility of moving from the care of a particular tree to the care for all trees. This more universal view was expressed to me by another tree worshiper in Banaras, "God is in all trees, because God can come in any life form: human, animal, or tree." I spoke one day with the priest of a Hanuman temple that includes a pipal tree shrine. He told me: "All trees are sacred [*pavitra*]. Therefore we Hindus here never cut them. When a tree dies, or a branch dries out, we might cut it, but we never cut a living [*hara* ("green")] tree." Sitting in his forested ashram in Vrindaban, one man told me, "Yes I worship trees, all trees are sacred beings and should not be harmed." Similarly, a baba I met in the Chitaranjan Park of Banaras as we both watched a woman worship a banyan tree on the day of the Vata Savitri worship said to me: "All life is a manifestation of God, so if a person sees God in a tree this is good. Let her worship that tree as God, knowing that God is in all beings. We should see all trees in this way and treat them with care." All of these views contain within them the basis for an ethic that includes all trees (even all beings) in its circle of concern. This became most apparent to me, however, in another conversation under another sacred tree.

One day I visited the large pipal tree that stands atop Chauki Ghat in Banaras. There I met a woman who was a *sadhvi*, a female practitioner who had renounced ordinary domestic life to devote herself to spiritual pursuits. I talked to her about my research and at one point in our conversation she explained what she thought was the real value of worshiping a tree. "From the heartfelt worship [*hardik pujan*] of a single tree one can see the divinity [*daiva*] in that tree and feel love [*bhava*] for it. After some time, with knowledge [*jnana*] one can then see the divinity in all trees. Really, in all life. All life is sacred [*daivik*] because God is everywhere and in everything. This tree is a *svarupa* of Vasudeva. As it says in the Bhagavad Gita, from devotion to a *svarupa* [one's own particular form of God] comes awareness of the *vishvarupa* [universal form of God]." In brief, this knowledgeable woman was expressing something deeply significant: worship of a particular can open up a more reverent attitude toward the universal. Regarding trees, her point was that the worship of a particular tree could lead to the realization of the sacrality of all trees—and by extension, of all life. This philosophical perspective is readily available through exposure to the basic teachings of the Bhagavad Gita and other Vedantic texts. Although it would be difficult to say exactly how such notions affect everyday behavior, this woman's views would not be alien to most tree worshipers in India.

We have already encountered the term *svarupa* in other statements made by tree worshipers. It denotes an individual form of God, in this context embodied as a particular tree. The term *vishvarupa*, on the other hand, means "taking on, or existing in, all forms,"[27] and refers to the universal or all-pervasive form of God. Specifically, it is a reference to the cosmic form of Krishna in the Bhagavad Gita.[28] In this popular text, we meet the hero Arjuna, who has a close devotional relationship with Krishna in the particular form of his charioteer. Because of this intimate relationship, Krishna reveals to Arjuna his *vishvarupa*, his universal form that includes everything. From this revelation Arjuna comes to understand that the particular form (*svarupa*) of Krishna with which he has developed a close relationship is ultimately nondifferent from the totality of reality (*vishvarupa*). Knowledge, or *jnana*, for the Bhagavad Gita means specifically the realization that all of reality is radically interconnected and fully divine (*Brahman*). Significantly, the Gita does not conclude with this infinite perspective, for intimate relationships are possible only with finite embodied forms, but importantly, intimate relationships with finite forms that are recognized to be nondifferent from the infinite. Krishna returns to the finite form of Arjuna's charioteer, but Arjuna's perception of him is now augmented by his knowledge that this particular form of Krishna is not different from the infinite totality of reality. As related to trees, the point the *sadhvi* seemed to be making with her reference to the Bhagavad Gita is that while intimate, emotional relationships with trees occur with individual sacred trees, with sufficient wisdom all trees are to be regarded as interconnected within the single divine reality. Worship of an individual tree can lead to an emotional relationship with that tree, which can lead to the realization of the divine nature of that tree, which can lead to a deep understanding of the interconnectedness of that tree with all other trees, and beyond this, with all life forms. A related point was made in the Chandogya Upanishad banyan seed story told in the last chapter. Shvetaketu learns that the individual seed of a single banyan tree is ultimately not different from everything else. The other banyan seed story has it that the whole world is present in the banyan seed. That is, the whole is present in the part; an individual tree is not radically separate from other trees, or from other life forms for that matter. The possibility of a grand ethic, then, emerges from the worship of sacred trees that unites the heart (love of an individual tree) with the head (knowledge that all trees are part of a non-dual, interconnected, divine reality). To the degree one recognizes this, worship of an individual tree can be a doorway into a reverential attitude toward all trees, perhaps even all life.

We will never know for certain about the nature of a tree—it seems the human lot is always to view the world through the glass darkly of some particular cultural lens, not to see directly. The more pertinent question, then, is "What might life be like if we took the "personhood" of trees and other life forms seriously?" Such inquiry may be in line with recent developments in botany. Might contemporary science serve as an aid in altering our cultural perspective of trees? The Swiss Federal Ethics Committee on Non-Human Biotechnology, for example, was recently assigned the task of developing a position on the ethical consideration toward plants, and in response published a statement entitled: "The Dignity of Living Beings with Regard to Plants."[29] Committee members argued in this document that plants should be incorporated into the realm of ethical consideration. An editorial in the journal *Nature* appeared shortly after calling this position "downright silly."[30] In response to this skeptical reaction, the UK-based botanist Matthew Hall wrote an article titled: "Plant Autonomy and Human-Plant Ethics."[31] Hall draws upon contemporary research in plant science for support and argues that plants are living beings that do indeed warrant ethical consideration. "With particular relevance to claims that plant ethics are 'silly,' I assert that the ethical consideration of plants is the *most appropriate* stance for humans to take toward plants."[32] He maintains that the treatment of trees and other plants in the Western world is based on *a priori* cultural assumptions, not investigative knowledge. "Contemporary scientific *knowledge* of plants recognizes them as autonomous beings, but as yet, contemporary Western *action* toward plants does not acknowledge their sentient, intelligent, autonomous status."[33] Hall's argument centers on two scientific claims: plants are autonomous and intelligent. Resisting a limited and human-centered definition of autonomy, he identifies the essence of autonomy as "the capacity for ruling one's self" and characterizes autonomous beings as those who "run their own existences and maintain their own identity."[34] He asserts, "Using definitions of autonomy that are not centered on the human, it is relatively simple to construct an argument that plants are autonomous beings."[35] His claim rests on an understanding of plant growth and adaptive responses as active and self-directed processes.

Although there is a difference in time scales—humans respond in seconds while plants respond in days, weeks, or months—plants still are observed to adapt their behavior in directional ways that benefits their survival, growth, and reproduction. This requires a clear perception and ongoing assessment of the environment; plant survival strategies involve learning and making decisions. Recognizing this, scientists consider plants as "autonomous beings in the sense that they are sensitive, active, self-governing organisms."[36] This leads Hall to consider plant intelligence with the assistance of the research of the plant physiologist Anthony Trewavas, who studies the adaptability and internal memory of plants.[37] Based on a definition of intelligence as "adaptively variable behavior within the lifetime of the individual," Trewavas makes a strong case for regarding plants as intelligent. "Since all plants exhibit adaptive plasticity within the lifetime of the individual, they must all exhibit intelligent behaviour."[38]

In summary, Hall argues for a more ethical attitude toward plants with the support of contemporary science through a shift in the culturally assumed views of plants, since it is "our everyday, ingrained, and backgrounded behavior toward plants that more directly violates autonomy and threatens many species of plants, and the animals that live among them, with extinction.... Constructed as radically *other* to the human, nature has been systematically denied the possession of many of the criteria that have come to define moral consideration, such as sentience, consciousness, awareness, volition and rationality."[39] He argues for the need to move beyond an anthropocentric view that regards trees merely in terms of their utilitarian value to humans, which he considers an act of intellectual violence. "By regarding plants purely as passive instruments for human use, we are treating them *as less than they are*."[40] Hall asserts that we face a choice today in our relationship with the nonhuman world between treating such beings as trees as mere resource materials or treating them with the respect due an animate being. The first will lead to further extinction of species and planetary destruction, whereas the second will help establish the long-term relationships of care that are necessary for life to flourish. "Although there are many complex drivers of habitat loss and environmental degradation, I contend that regarding plants purely as resource objects, as materials, is of great significance. From an ecological perspective, purely instrumental human-plant relationships are inappropriate because they pave the way to the destruction of individuals, species, populations, and the connectivities of respect, responsibility and care."[41] An approach to trees and other plants that would be more in line with scientific knowledge and ethical sensitivity would involve a relational attitude toward plants: "In an ecological context, if we wish for health and well-being, then appropriate ways of relating to other beings are those that increase connectivity."[42] Although motivated by an entirely different perspective, this is precisely the kind of behavior we observe at the interactive tree shrines of northern Indian, seen perhaps most clearly at the neem tree shrines in which a humanlike face has been appended to the tree for the purpose of establishing a better connection (*sambandha*) with the tree.

In his recent book *Plants as Persons: A Philosophical Botany*, Matthew Hall contends that the moral consideration of plants is rare in the West and asserts: "a study of different cultural-philosophical perceptions of the plant kingdom is crucial for developing more ethical relationships with the plant kingdom."[43] Although as a scientist he emphasizes that the "increasing body of evidence in contemporary plant science is beginning to demonstrate convincingly that plants share many capacities and capabilities with human beings,"[44] much of the effort he expends in his book involves a survey of different cultural attitudes and behaviors toward plants, a survey that includes India. "Buried within contemporary plant science literature is a growing awareness that plant behavior has many of the hallmarks of mentality. Such pioneering scientific work in many ways echoes the recognition of the attributes of *sentience* and *personhood* that have long been pinpointed in Indian religious literature."[45] The emerging field of Religion and Ecology entails the examination of a range of religious worldviews to understand how they affect human perception and experience of the world and behavior in the world. The differences among worldviews matter greatly, however, for they lead to distinctive human presences on the planet. The particular religious worldviews and cultural lens through which we see nonhuman life make all the difference in the world. Hall again stresses that a crucial choice lies before us: "Within the context of an anthropogenic ecological crisis, the choice between different modes of perception and action is an important one."[46] We saw in chapter 1 that much of the modern Western attitude toward trees came out of a worldview that regarded tree-worship as a prime example of primitive mentality. The march toward civilized modern progress entailed a movement away from the belief that trees were sentient or animated in any significant way. In other words, progress meant silencing the voices of the trees. This calamitous move must be reversed according to Hall, who argues for "the recognition of plants as *other-than-human persons*," and advocates a "dialogical engagement" with trees that would "form the social relationships which are the root of moral consideration and moral action.... Therefore, from a human point of view, human-plant dialogues must be based upon allowing plant 'voices' to be heard and plant presence to be felt."[47] In short, he calls for a return to talking with trees.

This call has been taken up by the philosopher Erazim Kohak, who begins his essay titled "Speaking to Trees" with the question: "What is the epistemological status of a world within which speaking to trees would appear as an appropriate behavior?"[48] Speaking, for Kohak, ideally involves respectful transactions. He claims that speaking to trees would entail "a recognition of nonhuman beings as our autonomous kin, worthy of respect. In Martin Buber's idiom, it is a matter of recognizing such beings as 'Thou'—not as a mute 'it' but as a fellow being in a community of discourse.... Speaking to trees is then entirely appropriate as an expression of respect."[49] This, of course, would mean regarding trees as "persons," which is exactly what Kohak does, arguing that "*person* is a technical term. It is not simply a synonym for a member of the species *Homo sapiens sapiens* but rather a designation of a particular mode of being.... To speak of a being as a person means to recognize it as a being with its own life, its own agenda, its own intrinsic worth and worthy of respect as such."[50] For Kohak, a tree indeed is such a person with whom communication is possible, taking into account (as do tree worshipers in India) that trees do not speak in the same way as humans. "Thus it is quite appropriate to speak to a tree even though the tree will not respond with words but in the way appropriate to its own kind."[51] Consideration of our relationship with trees is not really about truth claims for Kohak, but rather a matter that brings us to the threshold of a crucial choice between living in a world in which we recognize the sentience of trees (and thus the possibility of "speaking to trees" respectfully) or one in which we regard trees simply as raw materials: "When, though, we opt for one or the other, we are not choosing between truth and falsehood. We are, rather, choosing between two modes of speaking, one that heals and sustains, the other that hurts and destroys ourselves and our world alike."[52] Much is at stake here. The silencing of the trees brought about by the modern progressive attitudes shaped by post-Renaissance science and colonial scholarship has lead to highly unfavorable results. "The acts and attitudes shaped by the laconic metaphor of trees as mute and impersonal biomechanisms has brought us to the verge of an environmental catastrophe."[53] Attention to the manner in which we "speak," however, opens up new possibilities: "There remains the reality that some manners of speaking create and heal, others harm and destroy. Our manners of speaking shape both our modes of perceiving and our modes of acting."[54] The conception of trees in the context of the tree shrines of northern India has much to offer our consideration of this pressing human challenge.

What besides a less destructive ecological presence on the planet might be the result of a greater acknowledgment of arboreal sentiency? What else is possible when trees are regarded as "people"? Might taking such a conception seriously aid in enabling us to step out of the perspective of modern thought that boxes humans into an isolated world? Would awareness of the personhood of trees allow us to realize that we are not as alone as we thought, and that many more relationships and significant encounters are possible than ordinarily assumed? Perhaps we live in a world more peopled than we have imagined. As many have noted, the current environmental crisis is in part a religious crisis.[55] This is often attributed to the fact that human beings are increasingly cut off and alienated from the rest of nature because of religious orientations that privilege the human at the expense of other life forms. Acknowledging this means that in addition to exploring new scientific technologies we need to explore worldviews that will get us out of our detrimentally diminished relationship with nature. Opening ourselves to ways of being that expand our awareness to more and more sentient life around us may hold some of the answers. Anthropologists such as Philippe Descola and Gisli Palsson lament that little attention has been given to how non-Western cultures conceptualize and relate to the nonhuman world.[56] The psychologist Ralph Metzner has argued, "Recognizing and respecting worldviews and spiritual practices different from our own is probably the best antidote to the West's fixation in the life-destroying dissociation between spirit and nature."[57]

Indian tree worship offers both a worldview and practice for connecting with the nonhuman world. Taking its implications seriously may help lead to a human presence in the world where nonhuman beings such as trees are treated more favorably and are perceived not only in a fashion that allows them to remain standing to flourish as valuable relatives, but that celebrates the very specialness of their unique being and power. The acts of loving service (*seva*) performed at a tree shrine express deep respect for tree beings, and can engender an ever-expanding love that nurtures a greater sense of care and wonder. Tree worshipers report profound relationships with trees that result in an intimate connection with the very source of life itself. Perhaps the greatest possible lesson consideration of tree worship in India has to teach, then, is a more inclusive worldview and a deep reverence for and strong connectedness with all life.

GLOSSARY

ALAKSHMI (also DARIDRA or JYESHTHA): Goddess of bad luck and ill fortune. The elder sister and opposite of the goddess Lakshmi.
AMALA: A type of myrobalan tree sometimes called the Indian Gooseberry. It is commonly included in the Panchavati list of five sacred trees and has long been worshiped for its nourishing fruit and promise of spiritual blessings.
ARATI: A form of worship in which an honorific lamp is waved clockwise in circles before a divinity, person, or sacred object.
ASHVATTHA: Sanskrit name for a pipal tree.
ATMA: The true "Self"; often understood as nondifferent from Brahman.
AYURVEDA: The traditional Indian system of health and medicine.
BABA: "Father"; common name for a respected male religious figure.
BANARAS: An ancient temple town, destination for pilgrims, and center for the arts and learning located on the bank of the Ganges River. Also known as Kashi, but today commonly called Varanasi.
BANYAN: Common name for the *vata, bargad,* or *bar* tree; a tree easily recognized by its numerous aerial roots. Over time these roots become additional trunks that give this tree an undying quality and allow it to move outward into an ever-expanding circle. It is always included in the Panchavati list of five sacred trees.
BEL: A tree sacred to Shiva and also called the *bilva*. This sacred tree is known by the English name wood apple. It is usually included in the Panchavati list of five sacred trees.
BHAGAVAN: Personal form of divinity.
BINDI: A decorative dot worn between the eyebrows by women. It is often offered in worship to a goddess.
BODH GAYA: Pilgrimage destination for Buddhists and others who wish to visit the Maha-Bodhi pipal tree under which the Buddha achieved enlightenment.
BODHI TREE: Preferred Buddhist name for a pipal tree.
BRAHMA: God of creation.
BRAHMAN: Ultimate reality. The unmanifest unified ground of being from which all diverse forms arise.
BRAJ: A cultural area associated with Krishna that is located about ninety miles south of Delhi on the Yamuna River.
DARSHAN: Sight of or visual communion with a divinity.
DEVATA: A god.
DEVI: Either a goddess or the Great Goddess.
DURGA: A popular form of the Great Goddess. Supreme divinity for Shakta Hindus.
GANESHA: The elephant-headed god of beginnings who removes all obstacles and blesses human endeavors with success.
GANGA: Ganges River and goddess.

GAYA: A pilgrimage town near Bodh Gaya long associated with the performance of *shraddha*, death rites that aim to assist one's deceased ancestors.

GHAT: Stone steps leading down into a body of water. These are often quite wide so as to accommodate gatherings of people.

HANUMAN: The heroic monkey god known for his loyal service and devotion to Rama, a popular incarnation of Vasudeva or Vishnu.

KADAMBA: A species of tree closely associated with Krishna that is well-known for its fragrant spherical flowers.

KALAVA: A red and yellow cotton string used for wrapping and thereby honoring a tree.

KALI: A fierce form of the Great Goddess associated with Durga.

KALPA-VRIKSHA: A mythological "wishing tree" that yields great bounty, insures fertile offspring, and fulfills all manner of desires, including spiritual enlightenment.

KRISHNA: A popular form of the supreme God Vishnu; flute playing beloved of the cowherd women of the pastoral forests of Braj.

LAKSHMI: Goddess of abundance, prosperity, and good fortune; consort of Vishnu.

LINGA: Aniconic form of Shiva.

MA (also MATA, MAI, MAIYA): "Mother"; common address for Great Goddess.

MURTI: Embodied form of divinity.

NAVA GRAHA: The nine heavenly bodies that influence a person's life according to Indian astrology. Shani is said to be king of the nine.

NEEM: A sacred tree also known as the margosa. Its medicinal value is so great that it is commonly referred to as the "village pharmacy." It is usually included in the Panchavati list of five sacred trees.

PIPAL: Perhaps the most sacred of all the trees in India. It is also known by the Sanskrit name Ashvattha, and by Buddhists as the Bodhi tree. It is commonly referred to as the "holy fig tree" and is always included in the Panchavati list of five sacred trees.

PRAKRITI: Nature; natural world; creative life force.

PRASAD: The gracefilled "leftover" of an offering that is given back to the worshiper from the deity.

PUJA: The distinctive form of Hindu "worship" in which worshippers show their appreciation to a divinity through offerings of such things as food, flowers, clothing, incense, and honorific hymns.

PURANA: A term that literally means "ancient," it refers to an important genre of Hindu scripture that dates back early in the first millennium. These fluid texts were compiled by a multiple of authors over long periods of time and give expression to much of the religious thought and practices that make up the living traditions of Hinduism today.

RAMA: A popular form of the supreme God Vishnu; hero of the Ramayana.

RUPA: Form; body; appearance.

SAMBANDHA: Relationship or connection.

SARASVATI: Goddess of the refined aspects of culture, especially learning, music, and poetry.

SATYAVAN: Husband of Savitri.

SAUBHAGYA (also SUHAG): A fortunate or blessed state. Typically refers to the auspicious state of a happily married woman.

SAVITRI: Virtuous woman who brought her husband back to life through her wifely devotion and worship of a banyan tree.

SEVA: "Loving service." It often refers to acts of worship, particularly those done out of appreciation for a divinity and that are not motivated by personal gain.

SHAIVA: "Related to Shiva." This term refers to those who worship Shiva as the highest divinity or ultimate, all-inclusive reality.

SHAKTI: The divine "power" or "energy" that is inherent in and animates all life. It is usually identified as an aspect of the Goddess.

SHANI: The planetary god Saturn.

SHARIR: Body.

SHITALA: Goddess associated with neem trees. Considered to be an aspect of the Great Goddess, she is often identified with smallpox, but is also seen as a goddess of good fortune and the granter and protector of children.

SHIVA (also MAHADEVA): Great God. Supreme divinity for Shaivite Hindus.
SHRADDHA: A ritual to feed, honor, and aid one's deceased ancestors.
SINDUR: Vermilion powder or paste.
SITA: Divine consort of Lord Rama.
STUPA: A relic mound or memorial of the Buddha.
SVARUPA: Literally "own form"; intrinsic form of a divinity.
TRIMURTI: A conception of divinity that includes a tripartite manifestation of Brahma the creator, Vishnu the preserver, and Shiva the destroyer.
VAISHNAVA: "Related to Vishnu." This term refers to those who worship some form of Vishnu as the highest divinity or ultimate, all-inclusive reality.
VASUDEVA: A common name for the all-encompassing Vishnu or Krishna.
VISHNU: All-inclusive God. Supreme divinity for Vaishnavite Hindus.
VRAT: A votive ritual conducted for the welfare of oneself or another. It is typically performed by women, and almost always involves fasting and the devotional worship of some deity.
VRINDABAN: The forest in which Krishna makes love with his cowherdess lovers; a temple town and pilgrimage destination located on the bank of the Yamuna River.
YAMA: God of death.
YAMUNA: River in northern India and goddess of love.

NOTES

Introduction

1. J. H. Philpot, *The Sacred Tree; or, The Tree in Religion and Myth* (London: Macmillan and Co., 1897), p. 4.
2. Ibid., pp. iv–v.
3. Ibid., pp. 1–4.
4. Although these theories have to a large degree been abandoned today, and with them attention to trees, nevertheless they still shape the field of religious studies, which still privileges texts and ideas over practices and emotions.
5. Sir Edward Burnett Tylor, *Religion in Primitive Culture* (New York: Harper and Brothers Publications, 1958; first published in 1871), p. 63.
6. For a good cautionary tale on Frazer's *The Golden Bough*, see Jonathan Z. Smith, "When the Bough Breaks," *History of Religions* 12, no. 4 (May 1973): 342–71.
7. See Kailash Malhotra, Yogesh Gokale, and Ketaki Das, *Sacred Groves of India: An Annotated Bibliography* (New Delhi: Development Alliance, 2001).
8. Although the spellings of each of these three trees involves a very different approach—"pipal" maintains the "i" for this long vowel in Hindi, "neem" uses the "ee" to represent this same vowel, and banyan is an English word—I maintain these popular spellings, since these three trees are most commonly recognized by these names.

Chapter 1

1. The degree to which this distinction is made in our current language became clear to me as I was writing this book on my Mac Powerbook. When I referred to a tree with the pronoun "who," the grammar check in my Microsoft Word program suggested that I use "that" instead, since it was an inanimate nonhuman thing. I resisted this suggestion and followed the cultural paradigm in my ethnography, which referred to trees as persons.
2. Sir Edward Burnett Tylor, *Religion in Primitive Culture* (New York: Harper and Brothers Publications, 1958; first published in 1871), p. 53. Emphasis added.
3. Ibid., p. 10.
4. Ibid., p. 61. Emphasis added.
5. Sir James George Frazer, *The Worship of Nature* (New York: MacMillan Company, 1926), p. 6.
6. The field of Religion and Ecology took a momentous leap forward with a series of ten remarkable conferences on the major religions of the world and ecology that were organized by Mary Evelyn Tucker and John Grim and held at the Center for the Study of World Religions at Harvard University from 1996 through 1998. These conferences brought together more than eight hundred scholars representing a great variety of disciplines from numerous countries to explore the important role religions play in environmental issues. Harvard University

Press has published ten volumes resulting from these conferences in a series titled Religions of the World and Ecology. The conferences also led to the formation of an ongoing academic organization called the Forum on Religion and Ecology, now based at the School of Forestry and Environmental Studies at Yale University. Also noteworthy in this emerging field is the International Society for the Study of Religion, Nature and Culture, an academic organization dedicated to the study of the complex relationships between human beings, their religious beliefs and practices, and their earthly habitats.

7. Lynn White, "The Historical Roots of Our Ecologic Crisis," *Science* 155, no. 3767 (March 1967): 1205–6. Perhaps most famous of the demolition of tree shrines by Christians was the destruction of a great oak by Boniface: "Many European and Asian trees were cut down by zealous Christians over 1000 years ago. At Geismar, in Hesse, Pope Boniface destroyed the 'great Oak of Jupiter, and used the timber to build a chapel to St. Peter'" (Charles Alldritt, *Tree Worship with Incidental Myths and Legends* [Auckland: Strong and Ready Ltd., 1965], pp. 73–74).

8. To be fair, White highlights the life and thought of Saint Francis of Assisi, whose humble religion promoted "the equality of all creatures," as an example of other possibilities within Christianity (1207).

9. This is a phrase from Thomas Berry, author of *Dream of the Earth* (San Francisco: Sierra Club Books, 1990). One could mention many Christian theologians who share White's concerns, but these would certainly include such figures as Rosemary Ruether, author of *Gaia and God: An Ecofeminist Theology of Earth Healing* (San Francisco: Harper, 1992), Sallie McFague, author of *The Body of God: An Ecological Theology* (Minneapolis: Fortress Press, 1993), Charles Cummings, author of *Eco-Spirituality* (New York: Paulist Press, 1991), Matthew Fox, author of *Original Blessings* (Santa Fe: Bear and Company, 1983), and Mark Wallace, author of *God in the Singing River: Christianity in an Ecological Age* (Minneapolis: Fortress Press, 2005).

10. McFague, *The Body of God*, p. 133. Emphasis added.

11. In my mind, Peter Berger and Thomas Luckmann, *The Social Construction of Reality* (New York: Doubleday & Co., 1966) remains a classic in presenting this feature of human experience.

12. I want to be very clear that by claiming that nature is culturally constructed I refer to our differing conceptions of nature and not to the actual ontological status of the nonhuman world.

13. Neil Evernden, *The Social Creation of Nature* (Baltimore: Johns Hopkins University Press, 1992), p. xii.

14. Introduction in *Uncommon Ground: Toward Reinventing Nature*, ed. by William Cronen (New York: W. W. Norton & Co., 1995), p. 25.

15. *In Nature and Society: An Anthropological Perspective*, ed. by Philippe Descola and Gisli Palsson (London: Routledge, 1996), pp. 82–102.

16. Ibid., p. 82.

17. White, "Historical Roots of Our Ecologic Crisis," p. 1205.

18. Thomas Berry, *The Dream of the Earth* (San Francisco: Sierra Club Books, 1988), pp. 125–27.

19. Evernden, *The Social Creation of Nature*, p. 41.

20. Ibid., p. 41.

21. Ibid., p. 49.

22. Ibid., p. 40.

23. Ibid., p. 49.

24. Ibid., p. 57.

25. Ibid., p. 53.

26. Ibid., p. 123.

27. Interestingly, we humans share over 50 percent of our DNA with some types of trees; with certain oak trees the figure is nearer 70 percent.

28. Ibid., p. 93.

29. Ibid.

30. Sir Edward Burnett Tylor, *The Origins of Culture* (New York: Harper and Brothers Publications, 1958; first published in 1871), p. 21.

31. Ibid., p. 26.

32. Ibid., p. 35.

33. Tylor, *Religion in Primitive Culture*, pp. 8–9.

34. Ibid., p. 29.

35. Ibid., p. 61.
36. Ibid., pp. 300–301.
37. Ibid., p. 84.
38. Ibid., p. 255. For Tylor, Hinduism is a prime exemplar of idolatry; see pp. 254 and 256.
39. Ibid., pp. 61–62.
40. David Hume, *The Natural History of Religion* (New York: Macmillan Publishing Company, 1992; first published in 1757), p. 4.
41. Ibid., p. 25.
42. Ibid., p. 16.
43. Ibid., p. 29.
44. Tylor, *Religion in Primitive Culture*, pp. 62–63.
45. Auguste Comte, *The Positive Philosophy* (1875), p. 2.
46. W. Robertson Smith, *The Religion of the Semites: The Fundamental Institution* (1972 [1889]), p. 1.
47. Ibid., p. 84.
48. Ibid., pp. 85 and 89.
49. Ibid., p. 87.
50. Ibid., pp. 90–91.
51. Ibid., pp. 160 and 166.
52. Frazer, *The Worship of Nature*, pp. 14–15.
53. Ibid., p. 17.
54. Sir James George Frazer, *The Golden Bough* (1922/1890), p. 109.
55. Ibid., p. 111. Emphasis added.
56. Although they shared much, cultural anthropologists like Tylor, who looked forward to the day when religion was left behind in a social world determined by modern scientific thought, differed from Christian missionaries, who promoted Christianity as the supreme form of religion for the civilized world.
57. William Ward, *History, Literature, and Mythology of the Hindoos*, 3rd edn. (Delhi: Low Price Publications, 1990 [1820]), vol. III, pp. 261–63.
58. Introduction in *Nature and Society*, pp. 2–3.
59. Ibid., p. 3.
60. Ibid., p. 2.
61. Ibid., p. 7.
62. Ibid., p. 7. Emphasis added.
63. Nurit Bird-David, "'Animism' Revisited," in *Current Anthropology*, vol. 40, Supplement (Feb. 1999): S67–91.
64. Ibid., p. S71.
65. A. Irving Hallowell, "Ojibwa Ontology, Behavior, and World View," in *Culture in History: Essays in Honor of Paul Radin* (New York: Octagon Books, 1960), p. 43.
66. Philippe Descola, "Societies of Nature and the Nature of Society," in *Conceptualizing Society*, ed. by Adam Kuper (London: Routledge, 1992), p. 114. Emphasis added.
67. Ibid. Emphasis added.
68. Hume, *The Natural History of Religion*, p. 12.
69. Ibid.
70. Stewart Guthrie, *Faces in the Clouds: A New Theory of Religion* (New York: Oxford University Press, 1993). The following quotations are drawn from pp. 65–67.
71. Ibid., p. 67.
72. Ibid., p. 64.
73. Ibid., p. 179.
74. Ibid., p. 35. Emphasis added.
75. Ibid., p. 189.
76. Ibid., p. 193.
77. This is particularly true of viruses, those tiny biologically active agents near the boundary between nonliving chemical systems and living cells. On this subject see Lynn Margulis and Dorian Sagan, *What is Life?* (New York: Simon & Schuster, 1995).
78. Guthrie, *Faces in the Clouds*, cited p. 53.

79. Ibid., p. 40.
80. Ibid., pp. 53–54.
81. Ibid., p. 89.
82. Ibid., p. 194.
83. Ibid., p. 38.
84. Ibid., p. 90.
85. Ibid., p. 64.
86. Ibid., p. 89.
87. Ibid., p. 183.
88. Ibid., p. 204.
89. Ibid.
90. Ibid., pp. 3 and 62.
91. Ibid., p. 187.
92. Peter Brown, *The Cult of Saints* (Chicago: University of Chicago Press, 1981), p. 12.
93. Ibid., p. 14.
94. Ibid., p. 12.
95. Ibid., p. 5.
96. William Ward, *History, Literature, and Mythology of the Hindoos*, 3rd edn. (Delhi: Low Price Publications, 1990), vol. I, p. xx.
97. Ibid., vol. I, p. xviii.
98. Ibid., vol. I, p. xxxvii.
99. Ibid., vol. III, pp. 261–63.
100. Abbe J. A. Dubois, *Hindu Manners, Customs and Ceremonies* (New Delhi: Book Faith India, 1999; first published in 1897), p. 655.
101. John Kennedy, *The New Anthropomorphism* (Cambridge: Cambridge University Press, 1992), p. 9.
102. Ibid., pp. 1 and 5.
103. Ibid., p. 9.
104. Jeffrey Moussaieff Masson and Susan McCarthy, *When Elephants Weep: The Emotional Lives of Animals* (New York: Delacorte Press, 1995), p. 30.
105. Ibid., p. 32.
106. Ibid., p. xxiii.
107. See Jane Goodall, *In the Shadow of Man* (New York: Houghton Mifflin Company, 1988).
108. Jane Goodall, "Primate Spirituality," in *Encyclopedia of Religion and Nature,* ed. Bron Taylor (New York: Continuum International, 2005), p. 1303.
109. Marc Bekoff, *Minding Animals: Awareness, Emotions, and Heart* (New York: Oxford University Press, 2002), p. 36.
110. Ibid., p. 50.
111. See Jane Goodall, *Reason for Hope* (New York: Warren Books, 1999), p. 80; and Marc Bekoff, *Emotional Lives of Animals* (Novato, CA: New World Library, 2007), p. 50.
112. Interestingly, Jane Goodall extends her sense of personhood and sentience to trees. She reports that while living in the forest she "became intensely aware of the being-ness of trees." In his book *Dark Green Religion*, Bron Taylor records an interview he conducted with Goodall in which he asked her if she felt "'the energy of the individual trees that seem to be wanting to communicate?' She answered emphatically, 'But I felt that all the time'" (Bron Taylor, *Dark Green Religion: Nature Spirituality and the Planetary Future* [Berkeley: University of California Press, 2010], p. 28). He cites the previous quotation by Goodall on p. 27.
113. Louis de Bernieres, *Birds Without Wings* (New York: Vintage International, 2005), p. 249.
114. Recognizing a similar point, the science writer Connie Barlow raises the issue of using the pronoun "who" in reference to plants: "Animals are enough like people to be awarded this implicit recognition of personhood. But *who* is not tolerated for plants; *which* or *that* is de rigueur" (*The Ghosts of Evolution* [New York: Basic Books, 2000], p. 40).
115. Marie Mauze, "Northwest Coast Trees: From Metaphors in Culture to Symbols for Culture," in *The Social Life of Trees: Anthropological Perspectives on Tree Symbolism*, ed. by Laura Rival (Oxford: Berg, 1998), p. 238. Emphasis added.

116. Stephanie Kaza, *The Attentive Heart: Conversations with Trees* (Boston: Shambala Publications, 1993).
117. Julia Butterfly Hill, *The Legacy of Luna* (San Francisco: Harper Collins Publishers, 2000).
118. Scott Russell Sanders, *Meeting Trees* (Washington, D.C.: National Geographic Society, 1997).
119. I thank Sarah Pike, Professor of Religious Studies at California State University-Chico, for suggesting this connection.

Chapter 2

1. J. H. Philpot identifies tree worship as "the earliest form of divine ritual." See *The Sacred Tree; or, The Tree in Religion and Myth* (London: Macmillan and Co., 1897), p. 16. W. Robertson Smith argues in *The Religion of the Semites* that the sacred tree "holds the first place in acts of worship" (p. 167). Monier Williams writes, "Pliny asserts that the earliest form of temple or church was a tree" (*Religious Thought and Life in India* [Delhi: Great Publications, 1992; first published in 1883], p. 330). Many Indian scholars concur. M. S. Randhawa, for example, declares, "Tree worship was possibly the earliest and most prevalent form of religion" (*The Cult of Trees and Tree-Worship in Buddhist-Hindu Sculpture* [New Delhi: All India Fine Arts & Crafts Society, 1964], p. 1.).
2. Edward Washburn Hopkins, *Origin and Evolution of Religion* (New Haven, CT: Yale University Press, 1923), p. 22.
3. Max Muller, *Natural Religion* (London: Longman, Green, and Co., 1889), pp. 150–51.
4. Philpot, *The Sacred Tree*, p. 1.
5. Nathaniel Altman, *Sacred Trees* (New York: Sterling Publishing Co., 2000), p. 15.
6. David Carrasco, *Religions of Mesoamerica* (San Francisco: Harper & Row, 1990), pp. 100–101.
7. H. D. Elis Davidson, *Scandinavian Mythology* (London: Hamlyn Publishing, 1975), pp. 110–13.
8. Carrasco, *Religions of Mesoamerica*, p. 101.
9. Philpot, *The Sacred Tree*, pp. 110–11.
10. See, for example, John G. Neihardt, *Black Elk Speaks* (New York: Pocket Book, 1975), pp. 29–33.
11. Mircea Eliade, *Patterns in Comparative Religion* (New York: Meridian Books, 1963), p. 267.
12. Laura Rival, "Trees: From Symbols of Life and Regeneration to Political Artifacts," in *The Social Life of Trees: Anthropological Perspectives on Tree Symbolism*, ed. Laura Rival (Oxford: Berg, 1998), p. 7.
13. See, for example, Neihardt, *Black Elk Speaks*, pp. 29 and 178.
14. Eliade, *Patterns in Comparative Religion*, pp. 309–26.
15. "Now in Asia the sacred pole or tree symbolizes the Cosmic Tree, the *axis mundi*, and they are supposed to stand at the center of the world; by climbing his tree, the shaman ascends to Heaven" (Mircea Eliade, *Rites and Symbols of Initiation: The Mysteries of Birth and Rebirth* [New York: Harper Torchbooks, 1975], pp. 77–78).
16. Douglas H. Johnson, *Nuer Prophets: A History of Prophecy from the Upper Nile: The Nineteenth and Twentieth Centuries* (Oxford: Clarendon Press, 1991), p. 50.
17. I had an opportunity to speak about this in 2003 with a few men from a tribe that inhabits Kruger National Park in northern South Africa.
18. James Fergusson, *Tree and Serpent Worship; or, Illustrations of Mythology and Art in India in the First and Fourth Centuries after Christ from the Sculptures of the Buddhist Topes at Sanchi and Amravati* (New Delhi: Asian Educational Services, 2004; first published in 1868), p. 1.
19. E. B. Tylor reports: "With Christianity comes a crusade against the holy trees and groves. Boniface hews down in the presence of the priest the huge oak of the Hessian Heaven-god, and builds of the timber a chapel to St. Peter" (*Religion in Primitive Culture*, p. 314).
20. Hopkins, *Origin and Evolution of Religion*, p. 26.
21. Philpot, *The Sacred Tree*, p. 17.
22. James Frazer, *The Golden Bough: A History of Myth and Religion* (London: Chancellor Press, 1994; abridged volume first published in 1922), p. 109.

23. Ibid., p. 110.
24. Ibid., p. 113.
25. Ibid., p. 114.
26. Ibid., p. 119.
27. Philpot, *The Sacred Tree*, p. 19.
28. Ibid., p. 35.
29. Frazer, *The Golden Bough*, pp. 159 and 665.
30. See ibid., pp. 160 and 659.
31. Ibid., p. 8.
32. Cited by Philpot, *The Sacred Tree*, p. 33.
33. Ibid., p. 39.
34. W. Robertson Smith, *The Religion of the Semites: The Fundamental Institutions* (New York: Schocken Books, 1972; first published 1889), p. 185.
35. Ibid., p. 195. Emphasis added.
36. Smith, *The Religion of the Semites*, p. 132.
37. Ibid., pp. 186–87.
38. Amots Dafni, "Why Are Rags Tied to the Sacred Trees of the Holy Land?" *Economic Botany* 56, no. 4 (2002): 325.
39. Philpot, *The Sacred Tree*, p. 9.
40. Ibid., p. 25.
41. Frazer, *The Worship of Nature*, pp. 248 and 259; citing C. W. Hobley, *Bantu Beliefs and Magic* (London, 1922).
42. Ibid., p. 294; citing J. H. Driberg, *The Lango, a Nilotic Tribe of Uganda* (London, 1923).
43. Altman, *Sacred Trees*, p. 54.
44. Johnson, *Nuer Prophets*, pp. 298–99.
45. Descola and Palsson, *Nature and Society*, p. 7.
46. Y. T. Hosoi, "The Sacred Tree in Japanese Prehistory," *History of Religions* 16, no. 2 (Nov. 1976): 95–119. Hosoi observes that "the indigenous religion of Japan, whether Shinto or folk religion, will cease its function without things which nature richly furnishes, especially trees" (p. 95).
47. See Pipob Udomittipong, "Thailand's Ecology Monks," in *Dharma Rain: Sources of Buddhist Environmentalism*, ed. by Stephanie Kaza and Kenneth Kraft (Boston: Shambala, 2000), pp. 192–94. The abbot of Wat Bodharma in northern Thailand, Phrakhru Manas Natheepitak, is usually credited with being the one who began this practice to santify trees. In 1992, he reported: "If a tree is wrapped in saffron robes, no one would dare cut it down. So I thought that perhaps this idea could be used to discourage logging, and I began performing ceremonies on trees in the forest near the temple" (p.193).
48. Duncan Williams, "Introduction," in *Buddhism and Ecology*, ed. by Mary Evelyn Tucker and Duncan Ryuken Williams (Cambridge, MA: Harvard University Press, 1997), p. xxxv.
49. Marie Mauze, "Northwest Coast Trees: From Metaphors in Culture to Symbols for Culture," in *The Social Life of Trees: Anthropological Perspectives on Tree Symbolism*, ed. Laura Rival (Oxford: Berg, 1998), p. 240.
50. Altman, *Sacred Trees*, p. 59.
51. Arthur Amiotte, "The Lakota Sun Dance: Historical and Contemporary Perspectives," in *Sioux Indian Religion*, ed. Raymond J. DeMallie and Douglas R. Parks (Norman: University of Oklahoma Press, 1987), p. 81.
52. Forrest Carter, *The Education of Little Tree* (Albuquerque: University of New Mexico Press, 1976).
53. See George H. Stankey, "Beyond the Campfire's Light: Historical Roots of the Wilderness Concept," *Natural Resources Journal* 29 (Winter 1989): 18.
54. Ralph Waldo Emerson, "Woodnotes."
55. Henry David Thoreau, *Walden*.
56. Cited in Taylor, *Dark Green Religion*, p. 234.
57. T. Gifford, ed., *John Muir: His Life and Letters and Other Writings* (London: Baton Wicks, 1996), p. 139.
58. See Margot Adler, *Drawing Down the Moon: Witches, Druids, Goddess Worshippers and Other Pagans in America* (New York: Penguin Books, 1986); Starhawk, *The Spiral Dance* (San

Francisco: Harper, 1999); and Graham Harvey, *Listening People, Speaking Earth: Contemporary Paganism* (London: Hurst & Co., 1997). Involvement in tree worship is also evident in the numerous websites on neopaganism.

59. This is particularly true of Deep Ecological forest protection activists such as those associated with Earth First(!). See Bron Taylor, "Earth and Nature-Based Spirituality: From Earth First! And Bioregionalism to Scientific Paganism and the New Age," *Religion* 31, no. 3 (2001): 225–45.
60. Altman, *Sacred Trees*, p. 6.
61. Ibid., p. 9. Emphasis added.
62. Ibid., p. 22.
63. Ibid., pp. 41–42.
64. K. D. Upadhyaya, "Indian Botanical Folklore," in *Tree Symbol Worship in India: A New Survey of a Pattern of Folk-Religion*, ed. Sankar Sen Gupta (Calcutta: Indian Publications, 1965), p. 2.
65. Shakti M. Gupta, *Plant Myths and Traditions in India* (New Delhi: Munshriram Manoharlal Publishers, 2001, first published in 1971 by E. J. Brill), p. ix.
66. Madhav Gadgil and Ramachandra Guha, *This Fissured Land: An Ecological History of India* (New Delhi: Oxford University Press, 1992).
67. Introduction by Gupta in *Tree Symbol Worship in India: A New Survey of a Pattern of Folk-Religion*, p. xv.
68. Descola, "Construction Natures," p. 86.
69. Bansi Lal Malla, *Trees in Indian Art Mythology and Folklore* (New Delhi: Aryan Books International, 2000), p. 25. Monier Williams corroborates this view with a direct reference to trees: "In India, all life is sacred. It might even be affirmed that the Hindus were the first believers in the law of continuity.... In fact, according to the Hindu theory of metempsychosis all trees are conscious beings, having distinct personalities and souls of their own as gods, demons, men, and animals" (*Religious Thought and Life in India*, pp. 330–31).
70. For a good translation of this hymn, the Purusha Sukta of Rig Veda 10.90, see Wendy Doniger (O'Flaherty), *The Rig Veda* (Middlesex, England: Penguin Books, 1981), pp. 29–31. I would suggest un-translating the term "Man" back to the original Purusha when reading the translation of this hymn.
71. Brihadaranyaka Upanishad 2.5.15. See *Upanisads*, trans. Patrick Olivelle (New York: Oxford University Press, 1996), p. 32.
72. See Brihadaranyaka Upanishad 2.3.
73. Bhagavad Gita 15.16.
74. See Brihadaranyaka Upanishad 1.4.
75. Bhagavata Purana 2.1. 32-33. This seems to be a continuation of notions found in the Upanishads. Brihadaranyaka Upanishad (1.1.1) identifies trees as the hairs on the body of the cosmic sacrificial horse from which the whole world originates, and Aitareya Upanishad (1.4) identifies trees as the hairs on the body of the cosmic person Purusha.
76. See Devi-Bhagavata Purana 7.33.21-41.
77. Mohandas K. Gandhi, *The Bhagavad Gita, According to Gandhi*, ed. John Strohmeier (Berkeley: Berkeley Hills Books, 2000), p. 17.
78. Mohandas K. Gandhi, *All Men Are Brothers* (Lausanne: United Nations Educational, Scientific, and Cultural Organization, 1958), p. 119.
79. Bahuguna expressed this to me personally in an interview that took place on June 10, 2000, in Tehri, a town now submerged beneath the huge lake created by damming the Ganges River in the Garhwali region of the Himalaya Mountains.
80. Sunderlal Bahuguna, *The Message of Aranya Culture and Tradition: A Continual Renewal* (Terhi-Garhwal: Chipko Information Centre, n.d.), p. 1.
81. Diana L. Eck, *Darsan: Seeing the Divine Image in Indi*, 3rd ed. (New York: Columbia University Press, 1998), p. 28, citing Kramrisch, *The Hindu Temple*, p. 298.
82. Eck, *Darsan*, p. 38.
83. James Preston, "Creation of the Sacred Image" in *Gods of Flesh, Gods of Stone*, ed. Joanne Waghorne and Norman Cutler (Chambersburg, PA: Anima Publications, 1985), p. 9.
84. Vasudha Narayanan, "Arcavatara: On Earth as He is in Heaven," in *Gods of Flesh, Gods of Stone: The Embodiment of Divinity in India*, ed. Joanne Punzo Waghorne and Norman Cutler (Chambersburg, PA: Anima Publications, 1985), p. 54.

85. Albertina Nugteren, *Belief, Bounty and Beauty: Rituals around Sacred Trees in India* (Leiden: Brill, 2005), p. 53.
86. John H. Marshall, *Mohenjo-daro and the Indus Civilization*, Vol. I (London, 1931), pp. 63–65.
87. E. J. H. Mackay, *Further Excavations at Mohenjo-daro*, Vol. I (New Delhi, 1938), p. 341.
88. K. N. Sastri, *New Light on the Indus Civilization*, Vol. I (Delhi, 1957), pp. 15–18.
89. Benjamin Rowland, *The Pelican History of Art: The Art and Architecture of India* (New York: Penguin Books, 1981), p. 38.
90. Malla, *Trees in Indian Art Mythology and Folklore*, pp. 17–18.
91. Rig Veda 10.97. *The Rig Veda*, trans. Wendy Doniger (O'Flaherty) (Harmondsworth, England: Penguin Books, 1981), p. 285.
92. See, for example, Rig Veda 7.35.5: "To us may Herbs and Forest-Trees be gracious" (*The Hymns of the Rgveda*, trans. Ralph T. H. Griffith [Delhi: Motilal Banarsidass, 1973], p. 353).
93. Malla, *Trees in Indian Art Mythology and Folklore*, p. 27.
94. Brihadaranyaka Upanishad 1.1.1 (p. 7 in Olivelle's translation), and Aitareya Upanishad 1.1.3 (p. 195 in Olivelle's translation).
95. Chandogya Upanishad 6.11 (p. 153 in Olivelle's translation) and 12 (p. 154 in Olivelle's translation).
96. Shvetashvatara Upanishad 2.16-17 (p. 256 in Olivelle's translation).
97. Quoted by Malla, *Trees in Indian Art Mythology and Folklore*, p. 30.
98. N. Venkata Ramanayya, *An Essay on the Origin of the South Indian Temple* (New Delhi: Asian Educational Services, 1985), pp. 4–5.
99. Ludo Rocher, *The Puranas, The History of Indian Literature*, no. 2, ed. Jan Gonda (Weisbaden: Otto Harrassowitz, 1986), pp. 12–13.
100. Skanda Purana 152: 1.
101. See the Skanda Purana 257:44, trans. G. V. Tagare (Delhi: Motilal Banarasidass Publishers, 2003), p. 1061.
102. See the Padma Purana 1.58.24-25, trans. N. A. Deshpande (Delhi: Motilal Banarsidass Publishers, 1989), part 2, p. 764.
103. Matsya Purana 154.506-12. Cited by Vasudha Narayanan (1997).
104. Padma Purana 1.28.32. Translation from Sanskrit in *Shri Padma Mahapuranam*, ed. with introduction by Carudeva Shastri (Delhi: Nag Publishers, 1984), vol. I, p. 85. For an English translation of this text, see *The Padma Purana*, ed. N. A. Dehpande (Delhi: Motilal Banarsidass, 1988), part 1, p. 362.
105. Padma Purana 1.58.11. Sanskrit: p. 171; English: part 2, p. 763.
106. Matsya Purana 59.17-20. See *Matsya Mahapurana*, Vol. I, Sanskrit with English translation, ed. K. L. Joshi (Delhi: Parimal Publications, 2007), p. 232.
107. Padma Purana 1.58.26-28. Sanskrit: p. 172; English: part 2, p. 765.
108. For the first, see Gokulnath, *Chaurasi Baithak Charitra*, ed. Niranjandev Sharma (Mathura: Shri Govardhan Granthmala Karyalay, 1967), p. 8; this is available in translation by Shyamdas, *Chaurasi Baithak: Eighty Four Seats of Shri Vallabhacharya* (Baroda: Shri Vallabha Publications, 1985), p. 21. A tree with Krishna appearing out of every leaf is painted on the wall of a Pushti Marg *baithak* temple in Vrindaban near Bansi Bat to commemorate this event. For the second, the tenth verse of the Giriraj Chalisa, a poem of forty verses that praises the sacred mountain of Govardhana, states that some of the gods took the form of trees (*vriksha-rupa*) in order to witness the manifestation of Krishna in the form of this mountain in Braj. Devakinandana Kumheriya, *Shri Giriraj Chalisa* (Mathura: Giriraj Pustak Bhandar, n.d.), p. 5. I have translated this text in "Forty Verses in Praise of 'The King of Mountains,'" *Journal of Vishnava Studies* 12, no. 1 (Fall 2003): 11.
109. See, for example, an account of why certain trees were left standing in the construction of the Radhakunda ponds in my *Journey through the Twelve Forests: An Encounter with Krishna* (New York: Oxford University Press, 1994), p. 102.
110. See Thomas Weber, *Hugging the Trees: The Story of the Chipko Movement* (New Delhi: Viking, Penguin Books, 1988), pp. 91–94. For more information on the ecological ideas and practices of the Bishnois, see chapter 4 of Pankaj Jain, *Dharma and Ecology of Hindu Commnities: Sustenance and Sustainability* (Farnham, England: Ashgate Publishing,

2011). Jain demonstrates that many of the Bishnoi practices are the legacy of their fifteenth-century guru Jambhesvara, who had a meditative vision that led him to conclude "that humans will have to sustain the environment around them in order for nature to sustain humans" (p. 57), and therefore among other conservation rules prohibited the cutting of any type of green tree.
111. Ibid., p. 92.
112. See Randhawa, *The Cult of Trees and Tree-Worship in Buddhist-Hindu Sculpture*, pp. 7 and 10.
113. Ibid., p. 24.
114. Nugteren, *Belief, Bounty and Beauty: Rituals around Sacred Trees in India*, p. 41.
115. Ibid., p. 42.
116. Naveen Patnaik, *The Garden of Life: An Introduction to the Healing Plants of India* (New Delhi: Aquarian, 1993), p. 62.
117. Tracy Pintchman, *Guests at God's Wedding: Celebrating Kartik among the Women of Benares* (Albany: State University of New York Press, 2005), p. 75.
118. See interview with Ram Narayan Dvivedi in the Varanasi edition of the daily newspaper *Dainik Jagra*, October 31, 2006.
119. Maneka Gandhi notes a connection between the goddess Kali and the banana tree: "The Banana plant is considered sacred to the nine forms of the Hindu goddess Kali" (*Brahma's Hair: The Mythology of Indian Plants*, [New Delhi: Rupa & Co., 2007], p. 47).
120. Tracy Pintchman has recorded these Kartik activities in her book *Guests at God's Wedding: Celebrating Kartik among the Women of Benares*. For some reason, Pintchman does not cover the culminating ritual of worshiping a kadamba tree for the Kartik celebration of the Assi Ghat women.
121. The worship of the kadamba trees occurred on November 10th in 2006 and on November 17th in 2008.
122. These two stories are found in Bhagavata Purana 10.22 and 10.29. The second is usually understood to be the culmination of the first. Although this text clearly states that Krishna stole the clothes of the cowherd women and climbed with them into a kadamba tree, the location from which he sounded the irresistible notes from his flute is not specified. Women's folklore in Banaras, however, identifies the latter location as a kadamba tree. The conflation of these two episodes is also expressed physically in the Chir Ghat kadamba tree shrine in Vrindaban: an image of Krishna playing his flute has been placed in this kadamba tree and pilgrims attach colorful cloth to the tree to commemorate the occasion on which Krishna stole the clothes of the gopis.

Chapter 3

1. In her insightful study of vrats in northern India, Anne Mackenzie Pearson writes: "*Vratas* become a recommended way of expressing faith and devotion to one's chosen deity, as well as a way of soliciting blessings and favors from a god" (*"Because it Gives Me Peace of Mind": Ritual Fasts in the Religious Lives of Hindu Women* [Albany: State University of New York Press, 1996], p. 62).
2. All of the following interviews were conducted in Banaras (Varanasi) on either November 20, 2006, or March 19, 2007.
3. One might legitimately wonder about the gender politics in women's domestic responsibilities and the performance of *vrats*. Although consideration of the gender roles that are perpetuated in women's *vrats* is a complicated affair, I quote Pearson's conclusion regarding the concomitant issue of empowerment: "In sum, insofar as the regular performance of *vrats* gives women opportunities to develop control of their minds and bodies and to take charge of their spiritual destinies, *vrats* are sources of empowerment to Hindu women" (*"Because it Gives Me Peace of Mind,"* p. 217).
4. *Somvati Vrat Katha*, ed. with a Hindi trans. by Daulataram Gaur Vedacharya (Varanasi: Shri Thakur Prasad Pustak Bhandar, n.d.). A version of this story also appears in B. A. Gupte, *Hindu Holidays and Ceremonials* (Calcutta: Thacker, Spink & Co., 1919), pp. 159–65.
5. Ibid., pp. 21–22.

6. Shakti M. Gupta, *Plant Myths and Traditions in India* (New Delhi: Munshiram Manoharlal Publishers, 2001; first published by E. J. Brill (Leiden) in 1971), p. 33.
7. In one of the Buddhist Jataka stories, the future Buddha embodied as a tree spirit expresses fear of a bird that has landed on it because the bird can pass pipal seeds onto it through its droppings, thus suffocating it. See *The Jataka or Stories of the Buddha's Former Births*, trans. by a group of scholars under the editorship of E. B. Cowell (Oxford: The Pali Text Society, 1990; first published in 1895 by Cambridge University Press), Jataka No. 412, Book VII, p. 240.
8. Malla, *Trees in Indian Art Mythology and Folklore*, p. 85.
9. See Vaidya Mahavir Singh, *Pairh-Paudhon ke Tantrik Prakashan* (Hardwar: Randhir Prakashan, 2005), pp. 9 and 11.
10. Ibid., pp. 9–10.
11. See Ganapati Singh Varma, *Pipal Guna-Vidhan* (New Delhi: Rasayan Pharmacy, 1980).
12. Williams, *Religious Thought and Life in India*, p. 336.
13. H. Santapau, *Common Trees* (New Delhi: National Book Trust, 2001), p. 47.
14. K. D. Upadhyaya, "Indian Botanical Folklore," in *Tree Symbol Worship in India: A New Survey of a Pattern of Folk-Religion*, ed. by Sankar Sen Gupta (Calcutta: Indian Publications, 1965), p. 3.
15. Gupta, *Plant Myths and Traditions in India*, p. 31.
16. Ibid., p. xxv. Gupta's dating of the Indus Valley Civilization is off by a millennium; most historians today date its core as occurring in the second to third millennium B.C.E. Naveen Patnaik mentions Indus Valley seals "depicting the sacred fig circled by worshippers" (*The Garden of Life: An Introduction to the Healing Plants of India* [New Delhi: Aquarian, 1993], p. 37).
17. Malla, *Trees in Indian Art Mythology and Folklore*, pp. 15–16. Malla cites the scholar K. N. Sastri's *New Light on the Indus Civilization*, pp. 15–18.
18. A reference to this can be found in the Brihadaranyaka Upanishad 6.3.13. See also Arthur A. Macdonell, *Vedic Mythology* (Strassburg: Karl J. Trubner, 1897), p. 95.
19. Patnaik, *The Garden of Life*, p. 37.
20. Gupta, *Plant Myths and Traditions in India*, p. 33.
21. See ibid., p. 65.
22. Ibid., p. 32.
23. Malla, *Trees in Indian Art Mythology and Folklore*, p. 27.
24. Ibid., p. 27.
25. See Rig Veda IX.5.10.
26. Malla, *Trees in Indian Art Mythology and Folklore*, p. 27.
27. Maitri Upanishad 6.4.
28. Katha Upanishad 6.1.
29. Bhagavad Gita 15.1-2.
30. Patnaik, *The Garden of Life*, p. 37.
31. Gupta, *Plant Myths and Traditions in India*, p. 32. Cites *Mahabharata*, Anusasana Parva.
32. Bhagavad Gita 10.26.
33. Padma Purana 1.58.5. Translation from Sanskrit in *Shri Padma Mahapuranam*, ed. with introduction by Carudeva Shastri (Delhi: Nag Publishers, 1984), vol. I, p. 171. For an English translation of this text, see *The Padma Purana*, ed. N. A. Deshpande (Delhi: Motilal Banarsidass, 1988), part 2, p. 763.
34. Padma Purana 1.58.24-25. Sanskrit: p. 171; English: part 2, p. 764.
35. These are listed in Padma Purana 1.58.14-26.
36. Skanda Purana 6.247.39. Sanskrit: vol. III, p. 202; English Tagare, part 18, p. 1061. For the Sanskrit text, see *Skanda Mahapuranam*, ed. by Nag Sharan Singh (Delhi: Nag Publishers, 1984). For an English translation of this text, see *The Skanda Purana*, trans. G. V. Tagare (Delhi: Motilal Banarsidass, 2002).
37. Skanda Purana 2.4.38 and 47. Sanskrit: vol. I, p. 90; English: Tagare, part 6, pp. 62–63.
38. Ann Grodzins Gold, "If You Cut a Branch You Cut My Finger," in *Hinduism and Ecology: The Intersection of Earth, Sky, and Water*, ed. Christopher Key Chapple and Mary Evelyn Tucker (Cambridge, MA: Harvard University Press, 2000), p. 328.
39. Cited in Singh, *Pairh-Paudhon ke Tantrik Prakashan*, p. 116.
40. This and the following mantra are both written with engraved black lettering on white marble within the pipal tree shrine at Chauki Ghat, Banaras.

41. Rana P. B. Singh and Pravin S. Rana, *Banaras Region: A Spiritual and Cultural Guide* (New Delhi: Indica Books, 2006), pp. 61–62. The Agni Purana citation is 53.3.5.
42. Gupta, *Plant Myths and Traditions in India*, p. 32.
43. Skanda Purana 6.59.9. Sanskrit: vol. III, p. 48. English: Tagare, part 16, p. 245.
44. Skanda Purana 6.247.44. Sanskrit: vol. III, p. 202; English: part 18, p. 1061.
45. Ibid., 6.247.41-42. Keshava, Narayana, Hari, and Achyuta are all names of Vishnu.
46. See Vayu Purana 49.34. For an English translation of this text, see *The Vayu Purana*, 2 parts, trans. by G. V. Tagare (Delhi: Motilal Banarsidass, 1988), p. 958.
47. This popular text is available many places, including Padma Purana 6.71.281.
48. See Padma Purana 5.98.13-16.
49. Shivadatta Mishra, *Kartik Mahatmya* (Varanasi: Shri Thakur Prasad Pustak Bhandar, 2001), p. 98.
50. BBC News, South Asia website, February 15, 2006.
51. The statement: "Vasudeva is everything" (*vasudevah sarvam*), for example, is made in the seventh chapter of the Gita (7.19).
52. See Bhagavad Gita 12.5.
53. Dubois, *Hindu Manners, Customs and Ceremonies*, p. 659.
54. Santapau, *Common Trees*, pp. 47–48.
55. I was in Vrindaban not long after a Somvati Amavasya that occurred on November 16, 2009, and observed several pipal trees along the Yamuna River still wrapped in colorful string.
56. Skanda Purana 6.252.3. Sanskrit: vol. III, p. 204; English: part 18, p. 1069.
57. R. S. McGregor, *The Oxford Hindi-English Dictionary* (New Delhi: Oxford University Press, 1993/2004), p. 849.
58. Nagrendra Mishra, November 9, 2006, Varanasi.
59. I found a third reason for wrapping pipal trees in a Hindi book on the Tantrik uses of trees. The author of this book explains that pipal trees are wrapped with string to hold in and protect the fiery life-giving energy that comes into them from the sun. See Vaidya Mahavir Singh, *Per-Paudho ke Tantrik Prayog aur Chamatkari Prabhav* (Hardwar: Randhir Prakashan, 2005), p. 10. An acquaintance of mine who lives in Banaras compared this to the way a tea cozy holds in and concentrates the heat of the teapot.
60. The practice of honoring a tree by wrapping it with cloth is mentioned in Matsya Purana 59.5. See *Matsya Mahapurana*, Sanskrit with English translation, ed. K. L. Joshi (Delhi: Parimal Publications, 2007), pp. 230–31.
61. I note in passing another rather strange explanation for wrapping trees with string I encountered in one book J. Abbot's *Indian Ritual and Belief*. Abbot claims that the string is wrapped around a tree because "the thread annoys the *shakti* of the tree and coerces it to grant the relief or boon asked for" (p. 327). According to Abbot, the string is removed after the boon has been granted. I never once heard this explanation in the numerous conversations I had with tree worshipers about the wrappings, and when I ran this explanation by tree worshipers they told me it was very mistaken and insisted that the string had to do with honoring and protecting a tree.
62. See the discussion of the Chipko Movement in chapter 2.
63. Ramananda Prasad's commentary in *The Bhagavad-Gita* (Delhi: Motilal Banarsidass Publishers, 1996), p. 200.
64. The worship of pipal tree these days is closely linked to Shani, the planetary god Saturn, who rules over and is best approached on Saturdays. Shani's connection with pipal trees is discussed in the following chapter.
65. This story was told to me by a man who frequents the wrestling Akhara at Tulsi Ghat and worships the pipal tree at Assi Ghat every day. A similar story is told in connection with the famous Sankat Mochan temple in Banaras. See Philip Lutgendorf, *Hanuman's Tale: The Messages of a Divine Monkey* (New York: Oxford University Press, 2007), pp. 260–61. I tell the story in this context, however, because of the popularity of the Assi Ghat pipal tree.
66. *Mahabodhi Mahavihara: A World Heritage Site* (Gaya, Bihar: Bodhgaya Temple Management Committee, 2005), p. 10.
67. David Snellgrove et al., *The Image of the Buddha* (Kodansha: UNESCO, 1978), p. 140.
68. Interestingly, wrapping trees in this manner has become a strategy for protecting them from commercial logging in Thailand. See Pipob Udomittipong, "Thailand's Ecology Monks," in

Dharma Rain: Sources of Buddhist Environmentalism, ed. Stephanie Kaza and Kenneth Kraft (Boston: Shambala, 2000), pp. 191–97.
69. Leaves from the Bodhi tree are often used to represent the Buddha. The official Indian postage stamp commemorating the birthday celebration of Buddha Jayanti depicted a pipal leaf. Some art historians claim that the pipal leaf is the basis of much Buddhist architecture. See, for example, Madhukar Pipalayan, *Vandami Bodhi-Vriksham* (Delhi: Samyak Prakashan, 2006), pp. 106ff.
70. Madhukar Pipalayan, *Vandami Bodhi-Vriksham* (Delhi: Samyak Prakashan, 2006). I thank my friend Professor Andrew Rotman for finding this book for me in the Maha-Bodhi Bookstore while we were touring the temple together.
71. Ibid., pp. 6 and 8.
72. Snellgrove et al., *The Image of the Buddha*, p. 43.
73. Randhawa, *The Cult of Trees and Tree-Worship in Buddhist—Hindu Sculpture*, p. 7.
74. Klemens Karlsson, *Face to Face with the Absent Buddha: The Formation of Buddhist Aniconic Art* (Uppsala: Uppsala University, 2000), pp. 158–59.
75. Ibid., p. 33. See chapter 4, titled "Tree-God Bodhisattvas in the Jataka Stories," for his examination of the Jataka Stories and the former lives of the Buddha as a tree god.
76. Ibid., p. 32.
77. See *The Jataka or Stories of the Buddha's Former Births*, trans. by a group of scholars under the editorship of E. B. Cowell (Oxford: The Pali Text Society, 1990; first published in 1895 by Cambridge University Press), Jataka No. 18, Book I, pp. 51–53.
78. Ibid., Jataka No. 109, Book I, pp. 253–54.
79. Ibid., Jataka No. 307, Book IV, pp. 15–16.
80. Ibid., Jataka No. 465, Book XII, pp. 91–98.
81. Relatedly, one of the Jataka stories recounts that Sujata offered the bowl of rice pudding to the future Buddha, thinking that he was an anthropomorphic form of a banyan tree god she had earlier prayed to successfully for a happy and fruitful marriage. See Henry Clarke Warren, *Buddhism in Translations* (New York: Atheneum, 1974), pp. 71–74.
82. Pipalayan, *Vandami Bodhi-Vriksha*, pp. 118 and 140.
83. Ibid., pp. 71–75.
84. See also, for example, Malla, *Trees in Indian Art Mythology and Folklore*, pp. 95–99.
85. Ibid., p. 28.
86. Pipalayan, *Vandami Bodhi-Vriksha*, p. 118.
87. Kanoko Tanaka, *Absence of the Buddha Image in Early Buddhist Art* (New Delhi: D. K. Printworld, 1998), p. 80.
88. Pipalayan, *Vandami Bodhi-Vriksha*, p. 8.
89. Tanaka, *Absence of the Buddha Image*, p. 80.
90. Ibid.
91. See Vayu Purana 49.34. For an English translation of this text, see *The Vayu Purana*, trans. Tagare, p. 958. *Bodhidruma* here means the Bodhi Tree under which the Buddha attained enlightenment.
92. M. Williams, *Religious Thought and Life in India*, p. 336.

Chapter 4

1. Rudolf Otto, *The Idea of the Holy* (New York: Oxford University Press, 1968), especially chapters 4 and 6.
2. J. Abbot, *Indian Ritual and Belief: The Keys of Power* (New Delhi: Manohar Publishers, 2000, first published in 1932), p. 315.
3. W. Crooke, *An Introduction to the Popular Religion and Folklore of Northern India* (New Delhi: Asian Educational Services, 1994; first published in 1894 by Government Press, North-Western Provinces and Oudh), p. 238.
4. Abbot, *Indian Ritual and Belief*, p. 315.
5. "*Om Shri Krishna Govinda Hare Murare, He Natha Narayana Vasudevaya Namah.*"
6. The *nava graha* are described in Matsya Purana 94. See *Matsya Mahapurana*, Vol. I, Sanskrit with English translation, ed. K. L. Joshi (Delhi: Parimal Publications, 2007), pp. 318–19.

7. Brahma Purana verse 28. See *Brahma Purana*, trans. G. P. Bhatt (Delhi: Motilal Banarsidass, 1986), part 4, p. 956.
8. Brahma Purana, verses 30-33 (p. 956).
9. Skanda Purana 5.1.56.54. See *The Skanda Purana*, trans. G. V. Tagare (Delhi: Motilal Banarsidass, 1997), part 12, p. 223.
10. The Skanda Purana, for example, lists the trees associated with each of the *nava graha*. Moreover, it states that all trees are occupied by a particular god, but that worship of the pipal tree is tantamount to worshiping all the trees (verses 6.252.43 and 49).
11. Much of the information that follows on the various aspects of the *nava graha* is drawn from Robert Svoboda, *The Greatness of Saturn* (New Delhi: Rupa & Co., 1998).
12. See Stephen Markel, *Origins of the Indian Planetary Deities* (Lewiston, NY: Edwin Mellen Press, 1995), pp. 19-20.
13. Markel writes: "Shani is often considered to be the most influential planetary deity next to Surya. Contrary to the Sun God, however, Shani is regarded as malevolent and his astrological influence can cause catastrophic results" (ibid., p. 50). My ethnographic data, suggests, however, that in terms of worshipful interaction, Shani may be in the process of surpassing Surya in the contemporary world. Markel tells another story of the dangerous glance of Shani and how he came to be known as the king of the planets that involves Parvati's son Ganesha. See ibid., pp. 50-52.
14. This story is told in Markandeya Purana 103. See *The Markandeya Mahapuranam*, Sanskrit with English translation by Manmatha Nath Dutt, ed. Pushpendra Kumar (Delhi: Eastern Books, 2005), pp. 385-90. It also appears in Matsya Purana 11. See *Matsya Mahapurana*, Vol. I, Sanskrit with English translation, ed. K. L. Joshi (Delhi: Parimal Publications, 2007), pp. 35-40.
15. Those interested in learning more about the goddess Yamuna can consult my book *River of Love in an Age of Pollution: The Yamuna River of Northern India* (Berkeley: University of California Press, 2006).
16. Svoboda, *The Greatness of Saturn*, p. 166.
17. Ibid., pp. 105-51.
18. Ibid., p. 157.
19. For more on the goddess Yamuna, see my *River of Love in an Age of Pollution*.
20. I purchased two of these: Shivadatta Mishra, *Shanivar Vrat Katha* (Varanasi: Shri Thakur Prasad Pustak Bhandar, 1999), and *Sri Sanivar Vrat Katha* (Delhi: Haridarshan Prakashan Mandir, n.d.).
21. Ibid., pp. 5-6.
22. See also Shivadatta Mishra, *Shani Stotram* (Varanasi: Shri Thakur Prasad Pustak Bhandar, 1998), p. 30.
23. Atul Tandan, "Sukarma aur Samyama ki Shiksha De Shani," in *Dainik Jagaran*, May 15, 2007.
24. These are all names of Vishnu (or Krishna).
25. This story was told to me by many different people in Banaras, a town known for its devotion to Hanuman. See also Lutgendorf, *Hanuman's Tale* (pp. 140-42), for a different version of this story.
26. The following account is taken from Mishra, *Shanivar Vrat Katha*, pp. 4-11.
27. See Mishra, *Shani Stotram*, p. 30.
28. Tandan, "Sukarma aur Samyama ki Shiksha De Shani."
29. Singh, *Per-Paudho ke Tantrik Prayog aur Chamakari Prabhav*, p. 10.
30. Frazer, *The Golden Bough*, p. 115.
31. Rig Veda 10.135. For an English translation, see Griffiths, *The Rig Veda*, p. 636.
32. Matsya Purana 18.7. See *Matsya Mahapurana*, Sanskrit text with English translation by K. L. Joshi (Delhi: Parimal Publications, 2007), p. 67.
33. Jonathan P. Parry, *Death in Banaras* (Cambridge: Cambridge University Press, 1994), p. 191.
34. Ibid., p. 197.
35. Tarun Kumar Vahi, *Pipal ka Per* (Delhi: Raja Pocket Books, 2006). This graphic novelette is part of the Raj Comic Book series and was illustrated by Naresh Kumar.
36. Ibid., p. 2.
37. Ibid., p. 13.

38. For more on Jyeshtha, see Julie Leslie, "Shri and Jyeshtha: Ambivalent Role Models for Women," in *Roles and Rituals for Hindu Women*, ed. Julie Leslie (Delhi: Motilal Banasidass, 1992), pp. 107–27.
39. This account is derived from a Hindi version of the Kartik Mahatmya of the Padma Purana by Shivadatta Mishra, *Kartik Mahatmya* (Varanasi: Shri Thakur Prasad Pustak Bhandar, 2001), pp. 98–101; and another Hindi version based on the Kartik Mahatmya of the *Sanatkumar Samhita* by Balaram Pandey, "Jyeshtha Devi (Daridra Devi) ka Avataran," *Kalyan* 81, no. 3 (March 2007): 582–84. An English translation of the story of Alakshmi can also be read in *The Padma Purana*, trans. N. A. Deshpande (Delhi: Motilal Banarsidass, 1991), pp. 2115–17.
40. Skanda Purana 2.4.48. For an English translation, see Tagare, part 4, p. 63. The Padma Purana mentions that one should not touch an Ashvattha/pipal tree on any day but Saturdays because of Shani's association with Vishnu (Padma Purana 6.115.29).

Chapter 5

1. Eugene B. Shultz et al., *NEEM: A Tree for Solving Global Problems* (Washington, D.C.: National Academy Press, 1992), p. v.
2. Ibid., p. 1.
3. See Malla, *Trees in Indian Art Mythology and Folklore*, pp. 14–20.
4. John Conrick, *Neem: The Ultimate Herb* (Twin Lakes, WI: Lotus Press, 2001; Indian reprint: Varanasi: Pilgrims Book House, 2001), p. 1.
5. Monier Monier-Williams, *A Sanskrit-English Dictionary* (Delhi: Motilal Banarsidass, 1981), p. 88.
6. Vandana Shiva and Radha Holla-Bhar, "Piracy by Patent: The Case of the Neem Tree," in *The Case Against the Global Economy*, ed. Jerry Mander and Edward Goldsmith (San Francisco: Sierra Club Books, 1997), p. 149.
7. Conrick, *Neem*, pp. 3–4.
8. Patnaik, *The Garden of Life*, pp. 40–42.
9. Ibid., p. x.
10. Ibid., pp. x-xi.
11. See Vandana Shiva and Radha Holla-Bhar, "Piracy by Patent: The Case of the Neem Tree," in *The Case Against the Global Economy*, edited by Jerry Mander and Edward Goldsmith (San Francisco: Sierra Club Books, 1997), pp. 146–59.
12. Reported by BBC News (Science/Nature), March 9, 2005. For further details on this case, see Linda Bullard, "Freeing the Free Tree: A Briefing Paper on the First Legal Defeat of a Biopiracy Patent: The Neem Case" (New Delhi: Research Foundation for Science, Technology and Ecology, 2005).
13. Ibid., p. 3.
14. Gupta, *Plant Myths and Traditions in India*, p. 88.
15. Crooke, *An Introduction to the Popular Religion and Folklore of Northern India*, p. 81.
16. Patnaik, *The Garden of Life*, p. 40.
17. Susan S. Wadley, "Shitala: The Cool One," *Asian Folklore Studies* 39, no. 1 (1980): 33–62.
18. *Shrivrataraja*, cited ibid., p. 48.
19. Babagrahi Misra, "Shitala: The Small-Pox Goddess of India," *Asian Folklore Studies* 28, no. 2 (1969): 142.
20. Cited by Wadley, "Shitala," p. 54.
21. See Edward C. Dimock, "A Theology of the Repulsive: The Myth of the Goddess Shitala," in *The Divine Consort: Radha and the Goddesses of India*, ed. by John S. Hawley and Donna M. Wulff (Delhi: Motilal Banarsidass, 1984), pp. 184–203.
22. See, for example, the first song recorded on the VCD titled *Saato Re Bahiniya*. Sung in Bhojpuri by Bharat Sharma "Byas" (New Delhi: Super Cassettes Industries, 2006). I thank Vinay Kumar Sharma of Banaras for finding this CD for me and helping me translate it. The goddess is addressed as *nimiya maiya* in this particular song.
23. I thank Krishna Kantha Shukla of Banaras for collecting this song from his mother and providing a rough translation of it for me.

24. See Avinash Khaire, "Neem: Spatio-Temporal Use in ITK and Contemporary Relevance." Paper presented at the XV Annual Conference of the Bombay Geographical Association, University of Mumbai, February 27, 2009.
25. This story is told in Markendeya Purana 79–80. For the Sanskrit text with English translation, see *The Markendeya Mahapuranam*, ed. Pushpendra Kumar with English trans. by Manmatha Nath Dutt (Delhi: Eastern Book Linkers, 2005), pp. 319–26. See also Thomas B. Coburn, *Encountering the Goddess: A Translation of the* Devi-Mahatmya *and a Study of Its Interpretation* (Albany: State University of New York Press, 1991).
26. See Tracy Pintchman, *The Rise of the Goddess in the Hindu Tradition* (Albany: State University of New York Press, 1994), particularly chapter 2. The classic text of the goddess tradition is the *Devi Mahatmya*; the goddess is identified as the mother of the world in this text. For a readable translation of this text, see Thomas B. Coburn, *Encountering the Goddess: A Translation of the Devi Mahatmya and a Study of Its Interpretation* (Albany: State University of New York Press, 1991).
27. For example, in the *Crest-Jewel of Discrimination* (*Viveka Chudamani*) attributed to Shankara, the world is compared to a scorching forest fire and *maya*, which creates the world, is compared to a dangerous and illusory snake (*Shankara's Crest-Jewel of Discrimination*, trans. by Swami Prabhavananda and Christopher Isherwood [Hollywood: Vedanta Press, 1947], pp. 38 and 49).
28. David Kinsley, *Hindu Goddesses: Visions of the Divine Feminine in Hindu Religious Traditions* (Berkeley: University of California Press, 1986), p. 136.
29. R. S. McGregor, *The Oxford Hindi-English Dictionary* (New Delhi: Oxford University Press, 1993, 15th impression, 2004), p. 1050.
30. Diana L. Eck, *Darsan: Seeing the Divine Image in India* (New York: Columbia University Press, 1998), pp. 6–7.
31. Sankar Sen Gupta, "Introduction," in *Tree Symbol Worship in India: A New Survey of a Pattern of Folk-Religion*, ed. by Sankar Sen Gupta (Calcutta: Indian Publications, 1965), p. xv. I find myself wondering if the face was not carved, but rather a facemask attached to the tree.
32. Alfred Gell, *Art and Agency: An Anthropological Theory* (Oxford: Clarendon Press, 1998), p. 96.
33. Ibid., p. 118.
34. Ibid., p. 132.
35. C. Nelson, "The Development and Neural Bases of Face Recognition," *Infant and Child Development* 10, nos. 1-2 (2001): 3–18.
36. Olivier Pascalis and David Kelly, "The Origins of Face Processing in Humans: Phylogeny and Ontogeny," *Perspectives on Psychological Science* 4, no. 2 (2009): 200–209.
37. Paul Quinn and Alan Slater, "Face Perception at Birth and Beyond," in *The Development of Face Processing in Infancy and Early Childhood: Current Perspectives*, ed. Oliver Pascalis and Alan Slater (New York: Nova Science Publishers, 2003), p. 9. This entire volume is an excellent sourcebook for state-of-the-art research in this area.
38. Laura Smith and Darwin Muir, "Infant Perception of Dynamic Faces: Emotion, Inversion and Eye Direction Effects," in ibid., p. 126.
39. Gupta, *Plant Myths and Traditions in India*, p. 33.
40. Abbot, *Indian Ritual and Belief*, p. 335.
41. Ibid., p. 317.
42. Randhawa, *The Cult of Trees and Tree-Worship in Buddhist-Hindu Sculpture*, p. 61.
43. "When a Neem Tree Married a Peepal Tree," *The Times of India*, New Delhi, June 12, 2007, p. 6.
44. Bharati Mukherjee, *The Tree Bride* (New York: Hyperion, 2004).
45. Bharati Mukherjee, *Desirable Daughters* (New York: Hyperion, 2002), p. 16.
46. See Abbot for a variety of reasons one might marry a tree (*Indian Ritual and Belief*, pp. 287–93).
47. Hopkins, *Origin and Evolution of Religion*, p. 23.
48. Vijaya Nagarajan, "Rituals of Embedded Ecologies: Drawing Kolams, Marrying Trees, and Generating Auspiciousness," in *Hinduism and Ecology*, ed. Christopher Key Chapple and Mary Evelyn Tucker (Cambridge, MA: Harvard University Press, 2000), pp. 458–59.
49. Ibid., p. 458.

50. Ibid., p. 454.
51. Mircea Eliade, *Patterns in Comparative Religion*, trans. Rosemary Sheed (New York: Meridian Books, 1958), p. 308.

Chapter 6

1. This incident is found in the Prayaga Mahatmya ("Greatness of Prayaga") section of Matsya Purana 104.12, 106.12, and 111.10. See *Matsya Mahapurana*, Sanskrit text with English translation by K. L. Joshi (Delhi: Parimal Publications, 2007), pp. 347–48, 351–52, and 364.
2. This story is told in Bhagavata Purana 12.9; Narada Purana 47.6-8 mentions the Akshaya Vata in which Vishnu sleeps at the end of time on the leaf of this immortal banyan tree.
3. Matsya Purana (167.31-67) explains that Markendeya once slipped from the mouth of Vishnu, and while swimming in the cosmic ocean of pure potentiality, beheld the miraculous body of God as a boy sleeping on the leaf of the Akshaya Vata.
4. Brahma Purana 49-53. See J. L. Shastri, *Brahma Purana* (Delhi: Motilal Banarsidass, 1985), pp. 291–308.
5. Narada Purana 52.66-67 claims that the banyan tree that survives the destruction of the world is located in Jagannatha Puri. See Tagare, *The Narada Purana*, p. 1856. This tree is called a "*kalpa-vriksha*," since it remains at the close of the current age (*kalpa*). This adds another meaning to the Kalpa-Vriksha "Wishing Tree."
6. Ramji Sharma, *Prayaraj Kumbha-Mahaparva Mahatmya* (Allahabad: Shri Durga Pustak Bhandar, n.d.), pp. 42–43. A verse in the Matsya Purana claims that anyone who dies under the Akshya Vata (*vata-mula*) goes to the abode of Shiva (106.11).
7. Brahma Purana 54.14. Shastri, *Brahma Purana*, p. 309.
8. Brahma Purana 54.17-18. Shastri, *Brahma Purana*, p. 310.
9. See Jonathan Parry, *Death in Banaras* (Cambridge: Cambridge University Press, 1994), especially chapter 6.
10. Matsya Purana 17.1, for example, identifies these two goals (*bhukti* and *mukti*) as the "fruit" of the *shraddha* rituals.
11. Vayu Purana 49.96-97. See *The Vayu Purana*, trans. G. P. Bhatt (Delhi: Motilal Banarsidass, 1988), part 2, p. 964.
12. Narada Purana, Uttarabhaga 47.3-4. *The Narada Purana*, trans. Ganesh Vasudeo Tagare (Delhi: Motilal Banarsidass, 1982), part 5, p. 1815.
13. Vayu Purana 49.93. See, Bhatt, *The Vayu Purana*, p. 964.
14. Vayu Purana 49.98-99. For a similar reference, see Narada Purana 47.7.
15. In addition to these Sanskrit names, Narada Purana 56.280 adds: Vateshvara (Lord Banyan), Shanta ("Peaceful"), and Purana Purusha ("Ancient Person"). See Tagare, *The Narada Purana*, p. 1891.
16. See Patnaik, *The Garden of Life*, p. 20; and H. Santapau, *Common Trees* (New Delhi: National Book Trust, 1966), p. 39.
17. Ibid., p. 40. I believe in Southey's original, the word in the first line is "goodly," rather than "godly." Santapau's version seems more appropriate to this context, however, so I have quoted it.
18. Monier-Williams, *Religious Thought and Life in India*, p. 337.
19. Santapau, *Common Trees*, p. 42.
20. Available on various websites.
21. Gupta, *Plant Myths and Traditions in India*, pp. 35–36.
22. Malla, *Trees in Indian Art Mythology and Folklore*, p. 80.
23. *Vishnu Purana*, trans. by H. H. Wilson (Delhi: Nag Publishers, 1980), p. 137.
24. Chandogya Upanishad 6.12. For an English translation of this text, see Patrick Olivelle, *Upanisads* (New York: Oxford University Press, 1996), p. 154.
25. Pipalayan, *Vandami Bodhivriksha*, p. 27.
26. *Dainik Jagaran*, Varanasi edition, May 16, 2007.
27. I heard this story from several people when I traveled to Allahabad in 2007 to view the Akshaya Vata there from a boat on the Yamuna River.
28. Abbot, *Indian Ritual and Belief*, p. 333.

29. See Malla, *Trees in Indian Art, Mythology and Folklore*, p. 35.
30. Mircea Eliade, *Patterns in Comparative Religion*, trans. Rosemary Sheed (New York: Meridian Books, 1958), p. 286.
31. Ibid., p. 279.
32. Altman, *Sacred Trees*, p. 23.
33. Gupta, *Plant Myths and Traditions in India*, p. 35.
34. Malla, *Trees in Indian Art Mythology and Folklore*, p. 51.
35. For an English version of this account, see Deshpande, *The Padma Purana* 6.115.21-23, pp. 2713–14.
36. Shivadatta Mishra, *Kartik Mahatmya*, pp. 97–98. Suta proceeds to tell a story of how all the gods became trees from a curse of Parvati, and as a result, the two supreme gods Vishnu and Shiva became the pipal and the banyan. This story is available in English in Deshpande, *The Padma Purana* 6.115.24-29, p. 2714.
37. Skanda Purana 2.4.38 and 43. For an English translation, see Tagare, *The Skanda Purana*, pp. 62–63.
38. Narada Purana 55.23-31 (also confirmed in 56.25-27). See Tagare, *The Narada Purana*, p. 1879 (also 1891).
39. Crooke, *An Introduction to the Popular Religion and Folklore of Northern India*, p. 247.
40. This story is told in the Prabhasa Khanda of the Skanda Purana. See Tagare, *The Skanda Purana*, part 20, pp. 450–60. I translate the account here from the *Vata-Savitri Vrat Katha*, Sanskrit text with Hindi translation by Daivajnavachaspati Shri Vasudeva (Varanasi: Shri Thakur Prasad Pustak Bhandar, 1993). An account of the Savitri story is also found in Matsya Purana 208–14 (Joshi, *Matsya Mahapurana*, pp. 240–53), although here the type of the tree under which Savitri sits while holding Satyavan's head in her lap is not identified. A brief telling of the Savitri story is included in Madhur Jaffrey, *Seasons of Splendour: Tales, Myths and Legends of India* (New Delhi: Puffin Books, 1987), pp. 7–17.
41. Some Puranic accounts fix the date on the full moon of the month of Jyeshtha.
42. This ritual is performed in southern India on the full moon day of Jyeshtha. This is consistent with the ritual procedure outlined in Skanda Purana.
43. Skanda Purana 6.1.66.76-137 (Tagare, *The Skanda Purana*, pp. 456–60).
44. Diana L. Eck, *Banaras: City of Light* (Princeton: Princeton University Press, 1982), p. 229.
45. Singh and Rana, *Banaras Region: A Spiritual and Cultural Guide*, p. 158.
46. "Vata Savitri Vrat," in *Dainik Jagaran*, Varanari edition, May 16, 2007.
47. Bhagavatisharan Mishra, "Vata Savitri Vrat," in *Dainik Jagaran*, Varanari edition, May 16, 2007.
48. A priestess of a Kali temple located beneath a banyan tree in Haridvar told me that women perform the "Savitri puja" to the tree for a good marriage year round, and during my wanderings in Banaras I encountered several banyan trees wrapped with red string at other times of the year, including the Dharma Kup banyan.
49. Mishra, "Saubhagya ke lie Vata Savitri Vrat," p. 12.
50. There is textual support for this view in Skanda Purana 6.252.10. This verse says that Brahma resides in the banyan tree along with Savitri and grants life enhancing boons. See Tagare, *The Skanda Purana*, part 18, p. 1070.

Chapter 7

1. This occurred on November 20, 2006, and March 19, 2007, during my year of residence in Banaras to research the worship of sacred trees of India.
2. This happened on October 31, 2006, during my year of residence in Banaras.
3. This occurred on November 10, 2006, while I was living in Banaras; I also observed it on November 17, 2008.
4. The new moon of Jyeshtha fell on May 16, 2007, during my year of research.
5. Tangentially, my son Nathan, who had been exposed to the practice of wrapping trees with yarn by North American forest protection activists to deter chain saws (which would become clogged by the yarn were the trees to be cut), assumed when we first encountered the wrapping of trees in India that it was for the same purpose.

6. Cited by Malla, *Trees in Indian Art, Mythology and Folklore*, p. 77.
7. Email communication with Jagannath Poddar, February 26, 2012.
8. Ranchor Prime, *Hinduism and Ecology: Seeds of Truth* (Delhi: Motilal Banarsidass Publishers, 1994), p. 84.
9. Ellison Banks Findly, *Plant Lives: Borderline Beings in Indian Traditions* (Delhi: Motilal Banarsidass Publishers, 2008), p. 444.
10. Evolutionary biologists today maintain that trees commonly share over 50 percent of their DNA with humans, some reaching as high as 70 percent.
11. Even my Microsoft Word grammar program affirms and promotes this view.
12. See Thomas Friedman, *The World is Flat: A Brief History of the Globalized World in the 21st Century* (London: Allen Lane, 2005).
13. Descola and Palsson, *Nature and Society*, p. 7.
14. Robert Orsi, *Between Heaven and Earth: The Religious Worlds People Make and the Scholars Who Study Them* (Princeton, NJ: Princeton University Press, 2005), p. 2. Emphasis added.
15. See *Manu Dharma Shastra* 8.15.
16. Malla, *Trees in Indian Art, Mythology and Folklore*, p. 116.
17. Gupta, *Plant Myths and Traditions in India*, p. xxv.
18. Malla, *Trees in Indian Art Mythology and Folklore*, p. 20.
19. Ibid., pp. 82 and 116–17.
20. Poul Pedersen, "Nature, Religion and Cultural Identity: The Religious Environmental Paradigm," in *Asian Perspectives of Nature*, ed. Ole Bruun and Arne Kallard (Richmond, Great Britain: Cruzon Press, 1995), p. 266.
21. Emma Tomalin, "Bio-Divinity and Biodiversity: Perspectives on Religion and Environmental Conservation in India," *Numen* 51, no. 3 (2004): 267. Tomalin has also written a book expanding on this subject: *Biodivinity and Biodiversity: The Limits to Religious Environmentalism* (Aldershot, UK: Ashgate, 2009).
22. Ibid., p. 278.
23. Ibid., p. 268.
24. Sundara Rajan, "Ancient Indian Approaches Towards Plants," *Quarterly Journal of the Mythic Society* 82 (April-June 1994), p. 84.
25. Abbot, *The Keys of Power*, pp. 330–31. Abbot reports that this is also true for Indian Muslims.
26. Sunderlal Bahuguna, "The Message of Aranya Culture and Tradition: A Continual Renewal" (Publication of the Chipko Information Centre, n.d.), p. 1.
27. McGregor, *Oxford Hindi-English Dictionary*, p. 930.
28. This discussion occurs in the eleventh chapter of the Bhagavad Gita.
29. Federal Ethics Committee on Non-Human Biotechnology, *The Dignity of Living Beings with Regard to Plants* (Berne: Federal Ethics Committee on Non-Human Biotechnology, 2008).
30. "Open to Interpretation," *Nature* 453 (2008): 824.
31. Matthew Hall, "Plant Autonomy and Human-Plant Ethics," *Environmental Ethics* 31 (2009): 169–81.
32. Ibid., p. 170.
33. Ibid., p, 179.
34. Ibid., p. 172. This definition is based on the work of Thomas Heyd, *Autonomy of Nature*.
35. Ibid., p. 172.
36. Ibid., p. 173.
37. Anthony Trewavas, "Aspects of Plant Intelligence," *Annals of Botany* 92 (2003): 1–20.
38. Ibid., p. 2.
39. Hall, "Plant Autonomy and Human-Plant Ethics," pp. 170 and 177.
40. Ibid. p. 177.
41. Ibid., p. 179.
42. Ibid., p. 178.
43. Matthew Hall, *Plants as Persons: A Philosophical Botany* (Albany: State University of New York Press, 2011), p. 3.
44. Ibid., p. 155.
45. Ibid., p. 12. Emphasis added.
46. Ibid., p. 4.

47. Ibid., pp. 161–62.
48. Erazim Kohak, "Speaking to Trees," *Critical Review* 6, nos. 2–3 (1993): 371.
49. Ibid., pp. 371–72.
50. Ibid., p. 376.
51. Ibid., p. 377.
52. Ibid., p. 383.
53. Ibid., p. 386.
54. Ibid., p. 385.
55. One of the first to state this in a significant way was Lynn White, who wrote: "More science and more technology are not going to get us out of the present ecologic crisis until we find a new religion, or rethink our old one.... Since the roots of our trouble are so largely religious, the remedy must also be essentially religious, whether we call it that or not." ("Historic Roots of Our Ecologic Crisis," pp. 1206–7).
56. Descola and Palsson, *Nature and Society,* p. 2.
57. Ralph Metzner, *Green Psychology: Transforming Our Relationship to the Earth* (Rochester, VT: Park Street Press, 1999), p. 97.

BIBLIOGRAPHY

Abbot, J. *Indian Ritual and Belief: The Keys of Power*. New Delhi: Manohar Publishers, 2000, first published in 1932.
Adler, Margot. *Drawing Down the Moon: Witches, Druids, Goddess Worshippers and Other Pagans in America*. New York: Penguin Books, 1986.
Alldritt, Charles. *Tree Worship with Incidental Myths and Legends*. Auckland: Strong and Ready Ltd., 1965.
Altman, Nathaniel. *Sacred Trees*. New York: Sterling Publishing Co., 2000.
Amiotte, Arthur. "The Lakota Sun Dance: Historical and Contemporary Perspectives." In *Sioux Indian Religion*. Ed. Raymond J. DeMallie and Douglas R. Parks, 75–89. Norman: University of Oklahoma Press, 1987.
Bahuguna, Sunderlal. *The Message of Aranya Culture and Tradition: A Continual Renewal*. Terhi-Garhwal: Chipko Information Centre, n.d.
Barlow, Connie. *The Ghosts of Evolution*. New York: Basic Books, 2000.
Bekoff, Marc. *Emotional Lives of Animals*. Novato, CA: New World Library, 2007.
———. *Minding Animals: Awareness, Emotions, and Heart*. New York: Oxford University Press, 2002.
Berger, Peter, and Luckmann, Thomas. *The Social Construction of Reality*. New York: Doubleday & Co., 1966.
Berry, Thomas. *Dream of the Earth*. San Francisco: Sierra Club Books, 1990.
The Bhagavad-Gita. Trans. with commentary Ramananda Prasad. Delhi: Motilal Banarsidass Publishers, 1996.
Bird-David, Nurit. "'Animism' Revisited." *Current Anthropology* 40, Supplement (Feb. 1999): S67–91.
Brahma Purana. 4 vols. Trans. J. L. Shastri and G. P. Bhatt. Delhi: Motilal Banarsidass, 1985–86.
Brown, Peter. *The Cult of Saints*. Chicago: University of Chicago Press, 1981.
Bullard, Linda. *Freeing the Free Tree: A Briefing Paper on the First Legal Defeat of a Biopiracy Patent: The Neem Case*. New Delhi: Research Foundation for Science, Technology and Ecology, 2005.
Carrasco, David. *Religions of Mesoamerica*. San Francisco: Harper & Row, 1990.
Carter, Forrest. *The Education of Little Tree*. Albuquerque: University of New Mexico Press, 1976.
Chapple, Christopher Key, and Tucker, Mary Evelyn, eds. *Hinduism and Ecology*. Cambridge, MA: Harvard University Press, 2000.
Coburn, Thomas B. *Encountering the Goddess: A Translation of the Devi-Mahatmya and a Study of Its Interpretation*. Albany: State University of New York Press, 1991.
Comte, Auguste. *The Positive Philosophy*. Trans. by H. Martineau. Cambridge: Cambridge University Press, 2009; first published 1853.
Conrick, John. *Neem: The Ultimate Herb*. Twin Lakes, WI: Lotus Press, 2001; Indian reprint: Varanasi: Pilgrims Book House, 2001.
Cronen, William, ed. *Uncommon Ground: Toward Reinventing Nature*. New York: W. W. Norton & Co., 1995.

Crooke, W. *An Introduction to the Popular Religion and Folklore of Northern India*. New Delhi: Asian Educational Services, 1994; first published in 1894 by Government Press, North-Western Provinces and Oudh.

Cummings, Charles. *Eco-Spirituality*. New York: Paulist Press, 1991.

Dafni, Amots. "Why Are Rags Tied to the Sacred Trees of the Holy Land?" *Economic Botany* 56, no. 4 (2002): 315–27.

Davidson, H. D. Elis. *Scandinavian Mythology*. London: Hamlyn Publishing, 1975.

De Bernieres, Louis. *Birds Without Wings*. New York: Vintage International, 2005.

Descola, Phillippe. "Societies of Nature and the Nature of Society." In *Conceptualizing Society*. Ed. Adam Kuper, 107–26. London: Routledge, 1992.

Descola, Philippe, and Palsson, Gisli, eds. *Nature and Society: An Anthropological Perspective*. London: Routledge, 1996.

Dimock, Edward C. "A Theology of the Repulsive: The Myth of the Goddess Shitala." In *The Divine Consort: Radha and the Goddesses of India*. Ed. John S. Hawley and Donna M. Wulff, 184–203. Delhi: Motilal Banarsidass, 1984.

Dubois, Abbe J. A. *Hindu Manners, Customs and Ceremonies*. New Delhi: Book Faith India, 1999; first published in 1897.

Dvivedi, Ram Narayan. *Dainik Jagra*, October 31, 2006. Varanasi edition.

Eck, Diana L. *Banaras: City of Light*. Princeton, NJ: Princeton University Press, 1982.

———. *Darsan: Seeing the Divine Image in India*. New York: Columbia University Press, 1998.

Eliade, Mircea. *Patterns in Comparative Religion*. Trans. Rosemary Sheed. New York: Meridian Books, 1958.

———. *Rites and Symbols of Initiation: The Mysteries of Birth and Rebirth*. New York: Harper Torchbooks, 1975.

Evernden, Neil. *The Social Creation of Nature*. Baltimore: Johns Hopkins University Press, 1992.

Federal Ethics Committee on Non-Human Biotechnology. *The Dignity of Living Beings with Regard to Plants*. Berne: Federal Ethics Committee on Non-Human Biotechnology, 2008.

Fergusson, James. *Tree and Serpent Worship; or, Illustrations of Mythology and Art in India in the First and Fourth Centuries after Christ from the Sculptures of the Buddhist Topes at Sanchi and Amravati*. New Delhi: Asian Educational Services, 2004; first published in 1868.

Findly, Ellison Banks. *Plant Lives: Borderline Beings in Indian Traditions*. Delhi: Motilal Banarsidass Publishers, 2008.

Fox, Matthew. *Original Blessings*. Santa Fe, NM: Bear and Company, 1983.

Frazer, James George. *The Golden Bough: A History of Myth and Religion*. London: Chancellor Press, 1994; abridged volume first published in 1922.

———. *The Worship of Nature*. New York: MacMillan Company, 1926.

Friedman, Thomas. *The World is Flat: A Brief History of the Globalized World in the 21st Century*. London: Allen Lane, 2005.

Gadgil, Madhav, and Guha, Ramachandra. *This Fissured Land: An Ecological History of India*. New Delhi: Oxford University Press, 1992.

Gandhi, Maneka. *Brahma's Hair: The Mythology of Indian Plants*. New Delhi: Rupa & Co., 2007.

Gandhi, Mohandas K. *All Men Are Brothers*. Lausanne: United Nations Educational, Scientific, and Cultural Organization, 1958.

———. *The Bhagavad Gita, According to Gandhi*. Ed. John Strohmeier. Berkeley: Berkeley Hills Books, 2000.

Gell, Alfred. *Art and Agency: An Anthropological Theory*. Oxford: Clarendon Press, 1998.

Gifford, T., ed. *John Muir: His Life and Letters and Other Writings*. London: Baton Wicks, 1996.

Gokulnath. *Chaurasi Baithak Charitra*. Ed. Niranjandev Sharma. Mathura: Shri Govardhan Granthmala Karyalay, 1967.

Gold, Ann Grodzins. "If You Cut a Branch You Cut My Finger." In *Hinduism and Ecology: The Intersection of Earth, Sky, and Water*. Ed. Christopher Key Chapple and Mary Evelyn Tucker, 17–36. Cambridge, MA: Harvard University Press, 2000.

Goodall, Jane. *In the Shadow of Man*. New York: Houghton Mifflin Company, 1988.

———. "Primate Spirituality." In *Encyclopedia of Religion and Nature*. Ed. Bron Taylor. New York: Continuum International, 2005.

———. *Reason for Hope*. New York: Warren Books, 1999.

Gupta, Sankar Sen. "Introduction." In *Tree Symbol Worship in India: A New Survey of a Pattern of Folk-Religion*. Ed. Sankar Sen Gupta, xi–xxvii. Calcutta: Indian Publications, 1965.

———, ed. *Tree Symbol Worship in India: A New Survey of a Pattern of Folk-Religion*. Calcutta: Indian Publications, 1965.

Gupta, Shakti M. *Plant Myths and Traditions in India*. New Delhi: Munshriram Manoharlal Publishers, 2001.

Gupte, B. A. *Hindu Holidays and Ceremonials*. Calcutta: Thacker, Spink & Co., 1919.

Guthrie, Stewart. *Faces in the Clouds: A New Theory of Religion*. New York: Oxford University Press, 1993.

Haberman, David L. "Forty Verses in Praise of 'The King of Mountains.'" *Journal of Vishnava Studies* 12, no. 1 (Fall 2003): 9–14.

———. *Journey through the Twelve Forests: An Encounter with Krishna*. New York: Oxford University Press, 1994.

———. *River of Love in an Age of Pollution: The Yamuna River of Northern India*. Berkeley: University of California Press, 2006.

Hall, Matthew. "Plant Autonomy and Human-Plant Ethics." *Environmental Ethics* 31 (2009): 169–81.

———. *Plants as Persons: A Philosophical Botany*. Albany: State University of New York Press, 2011.

Hallowell, A. Irving. "Ojibwa Ontology, Behavior, and World View." In *Culture in History: Essays in Honor of Paul Radin*. Ed. Stanley Diamond, 21–52. New York: Octagon Books, 1960.

Harvey, Graham. *Listening People, Speaking Earth: Contemporary Paganism*. London: Hurst & Co., 1997.

Hill, Julia Butterfly. *The Legacy of Luna*. San Francisco: Harper Collins Publishers, 2000.

Hopkins, Edward Washburn. *Origin and Evolution of Religion*. New Haven, CT: Yale University Press, 1923.

Hosoi, Y. T. "The Sacred Tree in Japanese Prehistory." *History of Religions* 16, no. 2 (Nov. 1976): 95–119.

Hume, David. *The Natural History of Religion*. New York: Macmillan Publishing Company, 1992; first published in 1757.

The Hymns of the Rgveda. Trans. Ralph T. H. Griffith. Delhi: Motilal Banarsidass, 1973.

Jaffrey, Madhur. *Seasons of Splendour: Tales, Myths and Legends of India*. New Delhi: Puffin Books, 1987.

Jain, Pankaj. *Dharma and Ecology of Hindu Communities: Sustenance and Sustainability*. Farnham, England: Ashgate Publishing, 2011.

The Jataka or Stories of the Buddha's Former Births. Trans. by a group of scholars under the editorship of E. B. Cowell. Oxford: The Pali Text Society, 1990; first published in 1895 by Cambridge University Press.

Johnson, Douglas H. *Nuer Prophets: A History of Prophecy from the Upper Nile: The Nineteenth and Twentieth Centuries*. Oxford: Clarendon Press, 1991.

Karlsson, Klemens. *Face to Face with the Absent Buddha: The Formation of Buddhist Aniconic Art*. Uppsala: Uppsala University, 2000.

Kartik Mahatmya. Ed. Shivadatta Mishra. Varanasi: Shri Thakur Prasad Pustak Bhandar, 2001.

Kaza, Stephanie. *The Attentive Heart: Conversations with Trees*. Boston: Shambala Publications, 1993.

Kennedy, John. *The New Anthropomorphism*. Cambridge: Cambridge University Press, 1992.

Khaire, Avinash. "Neem: Spatio-Temporal Use in ITK and Contemporary Relevance." Paper presented at the XV Annual Conference of the Bombay Geographical Association, University of Mumbai, February 27, 2009.

Kinsley, David. *Hindu Goddesses: Visions of the Divine Feminine in Hindu Religious Traditions*. Berkeley: University of California Press, 1986.

Kohak, Erazim. "Speaking to Trees." *Critical Review* 6, nos. 2–3 (1993): 371–88.

Kumheriya, Devakinandana. *Shri Giriraj Chalisa*. Mathura: Giriraj Pustak Bhandar, n.d.

Leslie, Julie. "Shri and Jyeshtha: Ambivalent Role Models for Women." In *Roles and Rituals for Hindu Women*. Ed. Julie Leslie, 107–27. Delhi: Motilal Banasidass, 1992.

Lutgendorf, Philip. *Hanuman's Tale: The Messages of a Divine Monkey*. New York: Oxford University Press, 2007.

Macdonell, Arthur A. *Vedic Mythology*. Strassburg: Karl J. Trubner, 1897.
Mackay, E. J. H. *Further Excavations at Mohenjo-daro*, Vol. I. New Delhi: Government of India, 1938.
Mahabodhi Mahavihara: A World Heritage Site. Gaya, Bihar: Bodhgaya Temple Management Committee, 2005.
Malhotra, Kailash, Gokale, Yogesh, and Das, Ketaki. *Sacred Groves of India: An Annotated Bibliography*. New Delhi: Development Alliance, 2001.
Malla, Bansi Lal. *Trees in Indian Art Mythology and Folklore*. New Delhi: Aryan Books International, 2000.
Margulis, Lynn, and Sagan, Dorian. *What is Life?* New York: Simon & Schuster, 1995.
The Markandeya Mahapuranam. Sanskrit with English. Trans. Manmatha Nath Dutt. Ed. Pushpendra Kumar. Delhi: Eastern Books, 2005.
Markel, Stephen. *Origins of the Indian Planetary Deities*. Lewiston, NY: Edwin Mellen Press, 1995.
Marshall, John H. *Mohenjo-daro and the Indus Civilization*, Vol. I. London: Arthur Probsthain, 1931.
Masson, Jeffrey Moussaieff, and McCarthy, Susan. *When Elephants Weep: The Emotional Lives of Animals*. New York: Delacorte Press, 1995.
Matsya Mahapurana. 2 vols. Sanskrit with English translation. Ed. K. L. Joshi. Delhi: Parimal Publications, 2007.
Mauze, Marie. "Northwest Coast Trees: From Metaphors in Culture to Symbols for Culture." In *The Social Life of Trees: Anthropological Perspectives on Tree Symbolism*. Ed. Laura Rival, 233–51. Oxford: Berg, 1998.
McFague, Sallie. *The Body of God: An Ecological Theology*. Minneapolis: Fortress Press, 1993.
McGregor, R. S. *The Oxford Hindi-English Dictionary*. New Delhi: Oxford University Press, 1993/2004.
Metzner, Ralph. *Green Psychology: Transforming Our Relationship to the Earth*. Rochester, VT: Park Street Press, 1999.
Mishra, Bhagavatisharan. "Vata Savitri Vrat." In *Dainik Jagaran*, Varanari edition. May 16, 2007.
Mishra, Shivadatta. *Kartik Mahatmya*. Varanasi: Shri Thakur Prasad Pustak Bhandar, 2001.
———. *Shani Stotram*. Varanasi: Shri Thakur Prasad Pustak Bhandar, 1998.
———. *Shanivar Vrat Katha*. Varanasi: Shri Thakur Prasad Pustak Bhandar, 1999.
Misra, Babagrahi. "Shitala: The Small-Pox Goddess of India." *Asian Folklore Studies* 28, no. 2 (1969): 133–42.
Monier-Williams, Monier. *Religious Thought and Life in India*. Delhi: Great Publications, 1992; first published in 1883.
———. *A Sanskrit-English Dictionary*. Delhi: Motilal Banarsidass, 1981.
Mukherjee, Bharati. *Desirable Daughters*. New York: Hyperion, 2002.
———. *The Tree Bride*. New York: Hyperion, 2004.
Muller, Max. *Natural Religion*. London: Longman, Green, and Co., 1889.
Nagarajan, Vijaya. "Rituals of Embedded Ecologies: Drawing Kolams, Marrying Trees, and Generating Auspiciousness." In *Hinduism and Ecology*. Ed. Christopher Key Chapple and Mary Evelyn Tucker, 453–68. Cambridge, MA: Harvard University Press, 2000.
The Narada Purana. 4 vols. Trans. Ganesh Vasudeo Tagare. Delhi: Motilal Banarsidass, 1980–82.
Narayanan, Vasudha. "Arcavatara: On Earth as He is in Heaven." In *Gods of Flesh, Gods of Stone: The Embodiment of Divinity in India*. Ed. Joanne Punzo Waghorne and Norman Cutler, 53–67. Chambersburg, PA: Anima Publications, 1985.
———. "One Tree is Equal to Ten Sons: Hindu Reponses to the Problems of Ecology, Population, and Consumption." *Journal of the American Academy of Religion* 65, no. 2 (1997): 291–332.
Neihardt, John G. *Black Elk Speaks*. New York: Pocket Book, 1975.
Nelson, C. "The Development and Neural Bases of Face Recognition." *Infant and Child Development* 10, nos. 1–2 (2001): 3–18.
Nugteren, Albertina. *Belief, Bounty and Beauty: Rituals around Sacred Trees in India*. Leiden: Brill, 2005.
"Open to Interpretation." *Nature* 453 (2008): 824.
Orsi, Robert. *Between Heaven and Earth: The Religious Worlds People Make and the Scholars Who Study Them*. Princeton, NJ: Princeton University Press, 2005.

Otto, Rudolf. *The Idea of the Holy*. New York: Oxford University Press, 1968.
Padma Mahapuranam. 4 vols. Ed. Carudeva Shastri. Delhi: Nag Publishers, 1984.
The Padma Purana. 10 vols. Trans. N. A. Deshpande. Delhi: Motilal Banarsidass Publishers, 1988–92.
Pandey, Balaram. "Jyeshtha Devi (Daridra Devi) ka Avataran." *Kalyan* 81, no. 3 (March 2007): 582–84.
Parry, Jonathan P. *Death in Banaras*. Cambridge: Cambridge University Press, 1994.
Pascalis, Olivier, and Kelly, David. "The Origins of Face Processing in Humans: Phylogeny and Ontogeny." *Perspectives on Psychological Science* 4, no. 2 (2009): 200–209.
Patnaik, Naveen. *The Garden of Life: An Introduction to the Healing Plants of India*. New Delhi: Aquarian, 1993.
Pearson, Anne Mackenzie. *"Because it Gives Me Peace of Mind": Ritual Fasts in the Religious Lives of Hindu Women*. Albany: State University of New York Press, 1996.
Pedersen, Poul. "Nature, Religion and Cultural Identity: The Religious Environmental Paradigm." In *Asian Perspectives of Nature*. Ed. Ole Bruun and Arne Kallard, 258–76. Richmond, Great Britain: Cruzon Press, 1995.
Philpot, J. H. *The Sacred Tree; or, The Tree in Religion and Myth*. London: Macmillan and Co., 1897.
Pintchman, Tracy. *Guests at God's Wedding: Celebrating Kartik among the Women of Benares*. Albany: State University of New York Press, 2005.
———. *The Rise of the Goddess in the Hindu Tradition*. Albany: State University of New York Press, 1994.
Pipalayan, Madhukar. *Vandami Bodhi-Vriksham*. Delhi: Samyak Prakashan, 2006.
Preston, James. "Creation of the Sacred Image." In *Gods of Flesh, Gods of Stone*. Ed. Joanne Waghorne and Norman Cutler, 9–30. Chambersburg, PA: Anima Publications, 1985.
Prime, Ranchor. *Hinduism and Ecology: Seeds of Truth*. Delhi: Motilal Banarsidass Publishers, 1994.
Quinn, Paul, and Slater, Alan. "Face Perception at Birth and Beyond." In *The Development of Face Processing in Infancy and Early Childhood: Current Perspectives*. Ed. Oliver Pascalis and Alan Slater, 3–11. New York: Nova Science Publishers, 2003.
Rajan, Sundara. "Ancient Indian Approaches towards Plants." *Quarterly Journal of the Mythic Society* 82 (April-June 1994): 80–87.
Ramanayya, N. Venkata. *An Essay on the Origin of the South Indian Temple*. New Delhi: Asian Educational Services, 1985.
Randhawa, M. S. *The Cult of Trees and Tree-Worship in Buddhist-Hindu Sculpture*. New Delhi: All India Fine Arts & Crafts Society, 1964.
The Rig Veda. Trans. Wendy (O'Flaherty) Doniger. Middlesex, England: Penguin Books, 1981.
Rival, Laura. "Trees: From Symbols of Life and Regeneration to Political Artifacts." In *The Social Life of Trees: Anthropological Perspectives on Tree Symbolism*. Ed. Laura Rival, 1–36. Oxford: Berg, 1998.
Rocher, Ludo. *The Puranas, The History of Indian Literature*, no. 2. Ed. Jan Gonda. Weisbaden: Otto Harrassowitz, 1986.
Rowland, Benjamin. *The Pelican History of Art: The Art and Architecture of India*. New York: Penguin Books, 1981.
Ruether, Rosemary. *Gaia and God: An Ecofeminist Theology of Earth Healing*. San Francisco: Harper, 1992.
Sanders, Scott Russell. *Meeting Trees*. Washington, D.C.: National Geographic Society, 1997.
Santapau, H. *Common Trees*. New Delhi: National Book Trust, 2001.
Sastri, Kedar Nath. *New Light on the Indus Civilization*. Vol. I. Delhi: Atma Ram, 1957.
Shankara's Crest-Jewel of Discrimination. Trans. Swami Prabhavananda and Christopher Isherwood. Hollywood: Vedanta Press, 1947.
Sharma, Ramji. *Prayaraj Kumbha-Mahaparva Mahatmya*. Allahabad: Shri Durga Pustak Bhandar, n.d.
Shiva, Vandana, and Holla-Bhar, Radha. "Piracy by Patent: The Case of the Neem Tree." In *The Case against the Global Economy*. Ed. Jerry Mander and Edward Goldsmith, 146–59. San Francisco: Sierra Club Books, 1997.

Shultz, Eugene B., et al. *NEEM: A Tree for Solving Global Problems*. Washington, D.C.: National Academy Press, 1992.
Shyamdas. *Chaurasi Baithak: Eighty Four Seats of Shri Vallabhacharya*. Baroda: Shri Vallabha Publications, 1985.
Singh, Rana P. B., and Rana, Pravin S. *Banaras Region: A Spiritual and Cultural Guide*. New Delhi: Indica Books, 2006.
Singh, Vaidya Mahavir. *Pairh-Paudhon ke Tantrik Prakashan*. Hardwar: Randhir Prakashan, 2005.
Skanda Mahapuranam. Ed. Nag Sharan Singh. Delhi: Nag Publishers, 1984.
The Skanda Purana. 20 vols. Trans. G. V. Tagare. Delhi: Motilal Banarasidass Publishers, 1992–2003.
Smith, Jonathan Z. "When the Bough Breaks." *History of Religions* 12, no. 4 (May 1973): 342–71.
Smith, Laura, and Muir, Darwin. "Infant Perception of Dynamic Faces: Emotion, Inversion and Eye Direction Effects." In *The Development of Face Processing in Infancy and Early Childhood: Current Perspectives*. Ed. Oliver Pascalis and Alan Slater, 119–30. New York: Nova Science Publishers, 2003.
Smith, W. Robertson. *The Religion of the Semites: The Fundamental Institution*. New York: Schocken Books, 1972; first published 1889.
Snellgrove, David, et al. *The Image of the Buddha*. Kodansha: UNESCO, 1978.
Somvati Vrat Katha. Ed. with a Hindi trans. by Daulataram Gaur Vedacharya. Varanasi: Shri Thakur Prasad Pustak Bhandar, n.d.
Sri Sanivar Vrat Katha. Delhi: Haridarshan Prakashan Mandir, n.d.
Stankey, George H. "Beyond the Campfire's Light: Historical Roots of the Wilderness Concept." *Natural Resources Journal* 29 (Winter 1989): 9–24.
Starhawk. *The Spiral Dance*. San Francisco: Harper, 1999.
Svoboda, Robert. *The Greatness of Saturn*. New Delhi: Rupa & Co., 1998.
Tanaka, Kanoko. *Absence of the Buddha Image in Early Buddhist Art*. New Delhi: D. K. Printworld, 1998.
Tandan, Atul. "Sukarma aur Samyama ki Shiksha De Shani." In *Dainik Jagaran*, May 15, 2007.
Taylor, Bron. *Dark Green Religion: Nature Spirituality and the Planetary Future*. Berkeley: University of California Press, 2010.
———. "Earth and Nature-Based Spirituality: From Earth First! And Bioregionalism to Scientific Paganism and the New Age." *Religion* 31, no. 3 (2001): 225–45.
Tomalin, Emma. *Biodivinity and Biodiversity: The Limits to Religious Environmentalism*. Aldershot, UK: Ashgate, 2009.
———. "Bio-Divinity and Biodiversity: Perspectives on Religion and Environmental Conservation in India." *Numen* 51, no. 3 (2004): 265–95.
Trewavas, Anthony. "Aspects of Plant Intelligence." *Annals of Botany* 92 (2003): 1–20.
Tylor, Edward Burnett. *Primitive Culture*. New York: Harper and Brothers Publications, 1958; first published in 1871.
———. *Religion in Primitive Culture*. New York: Harper and Brothers Publications, 1958; first published in 1871.
Udomittipong, Pipob. "Thailand's Ecology Monks." In *Dharma Rain: Sources of Buddhist Environmentalism*. Ed. Stephanie Kaza and Kenneth Kraft, 191–97. Boston: Shambala, 2000.
Upadhyaya, K. D. "Indian Botanical Folklore." In *Tree Symbol Worship in India: A New Survey of a Pattern of Folk-Religion*. Ed. Sankar Sen Gupta, 1–18. Calcutta: Indian Publications, 1965.
Upanisads. Trans. Patrick Olivelle. New York: Oxford University Press, 1996.
Vahi, Tarun Kumar. *Pipal ka Per*. Delhi: Raja Pocket Books, 2006.
Varma, Ganapati Singh. *Pipal Guna-Vidhan*. New Delhi: Rasayan Pharmacy, 1980.
The Vayu Purana. 2 vols. Trans. G. P. Bhatt. Delhi: Motilal Banarsidass, 1987–88.
Vishnu Purana. 2 vols. Trans. H. H. Wilson. Delhi: Nag Publishers, 1980.
Wadley, Susan S. "Shitala: The Cool One." *Asian Folklore Studies* 39, no. 1 (1980): 33–62.
Wallace, Mark. *God in the Singing River: Christianity in an Ecological Age*. Minneapolis: Fortress Press, 2005.
Ward, William. 4 vols. *History, Literature, and Mythology of the Hindoos*. Delhi: Low Price Publications, 1990 (1820).

Warren, Henry Clarke. *Buddhism in Translations.* New York: Atheneum, 1974.
Weber, Thomas. *Hugging the Trees: The Story of the Chipko Movement.* New Delhi: Viking, Penguin Books, 1988.
"When a Neem Tree Married a Peepal Tree." *The Times of India,* New Delhi. June 12, 2007, p. 6.
White, Lynn. "The Historical Roots of Our Ecologic Crisis." *Science* 155, no. 3767 (March 1967): 1205–6.
Williams, Duncan. "Introduction" in *Buddhism and Ecology.* Ed. Mary Evelyn Tucker and Duncan Ryuken Williams. Cambridge, MA: Harvard University Press, 1997.

INDEX

Abbot, J., 106–7, 157, 158, 167, 196, 219 n.61
Agni, 72
Akshaya Vata (see banyan tree)
Alakshmi, 129–31
Allahabad, 161–62, 167
Altman, Nathaniel, 32, 37, 39–40, 168
amala tree, 53–54, 184, 185
animism, 2, 3, 4, 5, 7–9, 13–15, 17, 19–20, 23, 25, 27, 29–30, 35, 57, 64, 75, 87, 186, 188, 190–91
anthropomorphism, 4, 5, 6, 9, 12, 20–30, 57, 148–54, 158, 188, 190–92, 220 n.81
Assi Ghat (Banaras), 5, 55–56, 59–60, 64, 71, 76, 82, 93–94, 168, 170, 177, 178, 184, 185, 197
Ayurvedic use of trees, 54, 68, 135, 184

Bahuguna, Sunderlal, 45, 197
banana tree, 54–55
banyan (*vata*) tree
    Akshaya Vata (Immortal Banyan), 160–64, 166, 167, 224 n.2, n.3 and n.5
    general references, 5–6, 26, 57–58, 67, 155, 159–82, 183–85, 197–98, 220 n.81, 224 n.15
    identification with Savitri, 174, 180–81
    identification with Shiva, 168–69, 181, 184
    physical features, 164–67
    shrines, 162–64, 170–71, 174–79
    theological conceptions, 168–70, 180–81
Bekoff, Marc, 27–28
bel (*bilva*) tree, 50, 184
Berry, Thomas, 11, 210 n.9
Bhagavad Gita, 44, 59, 73, 78–80, 90–91, 197–98
Bird-David, Nurit, 19
Bishnois, 52
Black Elk, 33
Bodh Gaya, 4, 70, 92, 94–98, 101–5, 139
Bodhi Tree, 37, 41, 59, 67, 70, 94–98, 100–105, 220 n.69

Brahma, 64, 66, 72, 73, 77–78, 104, 225 n.50
Brihaspati (Jupiter), 55, 108, 110
Brown, Peter, 25

Chipko Movement, 45, 52, 89, 197
Christian destruction of sacred groves, 8–9, 34, 210 n.7, 213 n.19
Comte, Auguste, 3, 15–16, 21
Conrick, John, 134, 135–36
Cronen, William, 107
Crooke W., 107, 137, 170
cultural construction of nature, 2, 5, 10–20, 29, 183, 188–203

Dafni, Amots, 36
dead, care of, 33, 131
Descola, Philippe, 10–11, 18–20, 42–43, 202
Dharma Kup compound, 173–76, 180, 225 n.48
Dubois, Abbe, 26, 80
Durga, 76–77, 84, 132, 138–42, 156, 168–69, 170, 184

Eck, Diana, 46, 152, 173
ecological and ethical perspectives on trees, 194–203
Eliade, Mircea, 33, 159, 168, 213 n.15
embodiment, 16–18, 36, 38, 41
    Hindu conceptions of, 44–47, 50–51, 55, 57, 64, 67, 76, 78–81, 116, 119, 144, 146, 169, 174, 184, 193
Emerson, Ralph Waldo, 38
Evernden, Neil, 10–13, 24

Fergusson, James, 33–34
Feurbach, Ludwig, 21
Frazer, Sir James G., 3, 8, 16–17, 34–36, 37, 123

Gandhi, Mahatma, 45
Ganesha, 55, 76, 84, 87, 169

Gaya, 4, 104, 161–64
Gold, Ann Grodzins, 77
Goodall, Jane, 27–28, 212 n.112
Gupta, Shakti, 31, 41–42, 68, 71, 72, 78, 137, 156, 165–66, 168, 194, 218 n.16
Guthrie, Stewart, 21–25, 148, 192

Hall, Matthew, 199–201
Hallowell, Irving, 19
Hanuman, 75, 76, 82–85, 87, 94, 107–8, 110, 113, 116, 119–20, 150, 169–70
Hill, Julia Butterfly, 28–29
Hopkins, Edward, 31, 34
Hume, David, 3, 15, 20–21, 23, 25

idolatry, 5, 9, 14–15, 18, 22, 25–26, 29, 33
immortality and longevity, 6, 36–37, 41, 48, 51, 57, 62–63, 67, 73, 85, 112, 114, 130, 159–68, 169, 171, 176, 178–82, 185, 192
Indus River Valley civilization, 48–49, 71, 98–99, 134
interconnected and sacred nature of all life, 43–45, 49–50, 57

Jataka stories, 94, 99, 188, 218 n.7, 220 n.81

kadamba tree, 54–55, 185, 217 n.122
Kali, 55, 76, 140, 169–70
Karlsson, Klemens, 99
Kaza, Stephanie, 28, 214 n.47
Kennedy, John, 26–27
Kinsley, David, 141
Kohak, Erazim, 183, 201–2
Krishna, 47, 51, 55–56, 59, 73, 78–79, 160–62, 169, 184, 185, 198, 216 n.108

Lakshmi, 54, 64–65, 76, 130–31, 184

Mahabharata, 65, 73
Maha-Bodhi Temple, 92, 94–98, 101–5
Mahler, Andy, 40
Malla, Bansi Lal, 43, 68, 72, 168, 193, 194–95
Markel, Stephen, 221 n.13
Markendeya, 160–61
marriage with trees, 35, 36, 155–59, 187
Masson, Jeffrey (and Susan McCarthy), 27
Mauze, Marie, 28, 37–38
McFague, Sallie, 9
Metzner, Ralph, 202
Misra, Babagrahi, 138
Muir, John, 38–39
Mukherjee, Bharati, 157–58
Muller, Max, 3, 32

Nagarajan, Vijaya, 158–59
Nagendra Misra xi, 88, 107, 119, 125, 146, 154
Narayanan, Vasudha, 46

nature (see cultural construction of nature)
nava graha (nine astrological deities), 108–13, 115, 221 n.10
neem (*nima*) tree
  facemask, 133, 140, 143, 147–55, 191–92, 200
  general references, 5–6, 26, 48, 57–58, 67, 132–59, 168–69, 183–84, 197
  identification with Shitala, 137–46, 151–52, 154, 184
  physical features, 134–37
  shrines, 1, 85, 132–33, 140, 143–44, 146–55, 186
nonviolence towards trees, 79, 81, 98, 105, 183, 194, 196
Nugteren, Albertina, 48, 53

oak tree worship, 34–36, 38
Orsi, Robert, 192
Otto, Rudolf, 106

Palsson, Gisli, 18, 202
Panchavati (Five Sacred Trees), 53–54
Parry, Jonathan, 124–25
Patnaik, Naveen, 72, 73, 135, 218 n.16
Pearson, Anne Mackenzie, 217 n.1 and n.3
Pedersen, Poul, 195
personhood, 4–6, 19–20, 28, 34, 36, 40–41, 74–75, 99, 149–55, 159, 188, 190–91, 199, 201–2, 212 n.112, 212 n.114
personification of nature, 3, 12, 17, 20
Philpot, J. H., 2–3, 32, 34, 36, 37, 213 n.1
pipal (*ashvattha*) tree
  association with ghosts, 105–7, 123–28, 155
  association with Shani, 106–9, 113–23, 219 n.64
  Buddhist views of, 94–105
  dangers of harming, 74, 81, 128–29, 196
  general references, 4–6, 26, 48–49, 53, 57–58, 59–131, 133–34, 155–58, 168–69, 183–85, 189, 192, 194, 196–97
  history and texts, 71–74, 98
  identification with Buddha, 98–99, 101–3
  identification with Vishnu, 51, 57, 61, 63–67, 71, 73–74, 76–80, 87, 88–89, 91–92, 94, 98, 103–5, 106–8, 114, 116–20, 130, 139, 168–69, 184, 193, 196–97
  physical features, 67–70
  reasons for worship, 90–94
  shrines, 81–89, 156–57
  significance of Saturday worship, 92, 109, 113, 129–31
  theological conceptions, 74–81
  worshiped on Somvati Amavasya, 59–67, 79, 82, 185
Pipalayan, Madhukar, 98–99, 101–3
popular religion, 2, 5, 21, 25–26, 29, 107
Prime, Ranchor, 187

primitive religion, 2, 3, 7–8, 13–18, 20, 21, 25, 29, 189, 190–92, 201
Puranas, 44, 50–51, 52, 53, 57, 64, 73, 98, 108–9, 114, 123, 129, 134, 160–62, 169, 174, 179, 181, 184, 215 n.75
  Agni Purana, 77
  Bhagavata Purana, 44, 56, 217 n.122, 224 n.2
  Bhavishyottara Purana, 64
  Brahma Purana, 109, 162
  Devi-Bhagavata Purana, 44
  Markandeya Purana, 221 n.14
  Matsya Purana, 51, 123, 160, 169, 181, 224 n.3 and n.10, 225 n.40
  Narada Purana, 164, 169, 224 n.2, n.5 and, n.15
  Padma Purana, 51, 73–74, 78–79, 98, 169
  Skanda Purana, 31, 51, 74, 78, 88, 109, 119, 129, 169, 173, 181, 221 n.10, 225 n.42 and n.50
  Vayu Purana, 78, 163–64
  Vishnu Purana, 166–67

Randhawa, M. S., 99, 157, 213 n.1
reality, cultural construction of, 1, 9–10, 20, 188–89
redwood trees, 38, 39
relationship (*sambandha, nata, rishta*), 63, 75, 89, 91, 92–93, 144, 149–55, 157, 159, 182, 190–93, 198, 200–203
Religion and Ecology, 8, 201, 209–10 n.1.6
Rig Veda, 43, 49, 72, 123, 215 n.70
Rocher, Ludo, 50–51

Sanders, Scott Russell, 29
Santapau, H., 165, 224 n.17
Savitri, 168, 169, 171–82, 184, 225 n.40 and n.50
sentience of trees, 28–29, 31, 35, 37, 40–41, 53, 64, 74–75, 99–100, 105, 129, 155, 183, 186–87, 190, 199–202, 212 n.112, 215 n.69
Shani (Saturn), 105–9, 111–23, 131, 184, 193, 219 n.64
Shitala, 53, 137–52, 154–55, 184
Shiva
  association with Shani, 109, 116, 120–23, 150, 160
  connection with banyan trees, 168–70, 173–74, 181, 184
  connection with bilva (bel) trees, 50, 184
  connection with pipal trees, 64, 66, 72–73, 76–78, 84–85, 104, 116, 120
  temples and lingas, 47, 53, 88, 103, 116
shraddha, 104, 123–24, 163–64, 168, , 224 n.10
Singh, Rana P. B., 52, 77–78, 163, 174
Smith, W. Robertson, 3, 16–17, 36
Snellgrove, David, 98–99
Somvati Amavasya Vrat, 59–67, 79, 82, 88, 139, 185

svarupa, 46–47, 55, 79–80, 142, 144–46, 184, 193, 197–98
Svobhoda, Robert, 115

Thoreau, Henry David, 38
Tomalin, Emma, 195, 226 n.21
Trewavas, Anthony, 199–200
Tylor, Sir Edward B., 3, 7–9, 13–17, 20, 190, 211 n.56

Upadhyaya, K. D., 41–42, 71
Upanishads, 31, 49–50
  Aitareya Upanishad, 49, 215 n.75
  Bilva Upanishad, 50
  Brihadaranyaka Upanishad, 43–44, 49, 215 n.75
  Chandogya Upanishad, 31, 49, 167, 198
  Katha Upanishad, 72
  Maitri Upanishad, 72
  Shvetashvatara Upanishad, 49

Vata Savitri Vrat, 173–82, 184, 185, 197, 225 n.48
Vedic conceptions of trees, 49, 70, 71–72, 98, 123, 216 n.9
Vishnu (Vasudeva)
  association with Shani, 114, 116–17, 118–20, 193
  beheading of Rahu, 112
  connection with Akshaya Vata, 160–64, 180–81
  connection with pipal trees, 51, 57, 61, 63–67, 71, 73–74, 76–80, 87, 88–89, 91–92, 94, 98, 103–5, 106–8, 114, 116–17, 129, 130, 139, 168–69, 184, 193, 196, 197

Wadley, Susan, 138
Ward, William, 18, 25–26
White, Lynn, 8–9, 11, 210 n.8, 227 n.55
Williams, Monier, 69, 105, 165, 213 n.1, 215 n.69
Wishing-Tree (*kalpa*-vriksha), 52–53, 90, 162, 169, 224 n.5
worldwide tree worship, 31–41, 57, 123
  African, 37, 37
  Asia, 37
  European, 34–36
  European American, 38–41
  Native American, 32–33, 37–38
  Near Eastern, 33, 36
  sacred groves, 4, 34, 209 n.7
  Tree of Life (World Tree), 32–33, 49, 72, 90, 167
wrapping of trees, 52, 54, 55, 59–61, 65, 88–89, 96–97, 100, 118, 133, 147, 150, 155, 174–78, 182, 185–86, 214 n.47, 219 n.59, n.61 and n.68, 225 n.5

Yama (Lord of Death), 113, 114, 118, 123, 172–74, 181